The Reluctant Sailor

An Incredible Journey of a Lifetime

Enjoy the trip!

Janet Peters

Janet Peters

ISBN: 1537637304
ISBN 13: 9781537637303

*To my husband Al who started me
on this journey and got me safely home.
Our love lasted throughout.*

Contents

INTRODUCTION

Collingwood, 1995

"How would you like to sell our house, furniture, car, and belongings, and sail around the world?" my husband asked out of nowhere.

The sun glistened on the frozen vista of Georgian Bay, seen from our condo windows. My husband and I were comfortably settled on the sofa, reading, and very relaxed after a morning of skiing in the fresh crisp air of the Blue Mountain escarpment.

"What do you mean, sail around the world? Are you crazy? What gave you that idea?"

"I'm retiring in five years but I'm not ready for a quiet life of leisure. I've worked hard as a lawyer, and I love sailing on the bay."

"You could keep sailing on the bay," I said, hopefully. I had a good life in Toronto. Our friends and family lived there, and I was busy with many clubs and activities offered in the city. I wanted that life to continue.

"I can't give up the idea, and the more I think about it the more exciting it sounds."

The discussion continued into the afternoon. I knew the intensity of Al's thinking. He was a very determined man who liked to live on the edge. He was energetic for his age, trekking, mountain climbing, playing tennis, snowboarding, and cross-country skiing. I went with him on many of these adventures, so he probably thought "why wouldn't she want to do this?"

"We don't have enough experience for such an undertaking. It would take too much preparation and money."

I hoped these arguments would discourage any further discussion. The next day, we went back to Toronto and I soon forgot he had talked about sailing around the world.

Unfortunately, Al continued formulating his plans. He started taking courses to prepare. I wasn't ready to make up my mind. He often accused me of vacillating, and he was right. I thought of the pros and cons. We had another discussion at our condo as the glistening water rippled lazily under the hot sun beyond our windows.

"What's your problem?" he asked.

"I can't swim very well, and what if we are in a storm?"

"That's simple. We'll make sure the boat we buy is very sturdy and well-made for blue water sailing. It could handle a storm easily."

"But I'll miss our children. They need our help occasionally, and our grandchildren will grow up fast while we're away."

"We'll keep in touch, and you can go home and visit."

He seemed to have an answer for every question. While he still wasn't certain about my intentions, he started looking at "crew wanted" websites.

"Do you mean that you would sail alone if I didn't go, or worse, take one of these women from the internet?" He nodded. *Oh my God. He couldn't mean it.*

"OK, what are your other problems?" he asked pointedly.

"Since you ask, I don't want to be left alone for such a long time. And what if you like your 'crew' too much?"

"Yes, that would be a problem," he laughed.

Back and forth we went, from questions to practical answers. I could feel that he was convincing me more and more; his legal manipulative skills were amazing. I finally gave in. It was becoming important to me that we should share this experience. I would have to trust him to do his very best in preparing for the voyage.

Once Al was satisfied that I would be on this adventure, we began to take courses together. He had passed his advanced level Canadian Sailing Association course, basic diesel engine mechanics, advanced navigation, use of the sextant, and other important skills he felt that he needed. I joined him in the offshore sailing course given by Derek Lundy, a very competent person who wrote a book about the Vendee Globe round the world race in 1996-7, which had many disasters. Then we became qualified ham radio operators, which required hours of instruction, followed by a three-hour exam. Later, we took a two-day first aid course from an emergency nurse who had worked on an oil rig in the Atlantic. She filled two sturdy canvas cartons with all kinds of items for a severe accident, showed us how to give injections, how to bandage properly, and what to do for many injuries that could happen. As additional preparation, we chartered sailboats in Turkey and Desolation Sound on the BC coast. We also upgraded our French and Spanish skills in small classroom settings.

You can imagine how busy I was up to two years before Al's "big R" – retirement. It was fun doing these things together. Perhaps everything would work out and we could exist on a small boat without too much arguing and getting in each other's way.

Our friends in Collingwood would say to me, "How are you going to get along for all that time in such close quarters?" or "Al is such an active and headstrong person, won't he drive you mad?" I thought these remarks were made in jest, as Al was well liked and easy with others, but I had the feeling that no one would have taken my place.

I also heard, "Neither one of you has experience for such a voyage. It's really crazy." And I would agree, but the commitment had been made. Our three grown-up children didn't discourage this venture, but I know they had concerns for our safety. We planned to be in touch as often as possible.

While all these preparations were going on, we also sold our large home and moved into a condo in Toronto, but retained our Collingwood sanctuary. I didn't want to be without some place in case I needed to go home.

"If I really can't stay on a small boat for any length of time, I need to have our condo to get back to," I said when he asked why we should keep ties to Canada. "Also, in case something happens," I continued.

"What could happen?"

"Almost anything I can think of, such as the boat sinking." I hoped that would get him thinking, even though he was so caught up in the adventure.

I learned more about the cruising community, which spurred my interest. The World Cruising Club in Toronto met monthly. There were talks about boat mechanics, the recounting of sailing ventures taken by members, and important answers to many of my questions. I wanted to know how to store food, what to cook when the going was very rough, how to keep cockroaches off the boat, how to communicate with other cruisers, and so much more. I felt like a blotter soaking up all the information coming my way. The cruising community was very supportive. Most of the members planned to go no farther than the Caribbean, which was in itself a large undertaking, especially when leaving from Lake Ontario. I guessed that we overwhelmed them with our plans for circumnavigating the globe.

A year before Al's retirement, we went down to the Miami International Boat Show, a gigantic show with hundreds of boats, new and used. We had read many magazines and books beforehand about boats that might be suitable for our needs. There were sloops, ketches, yawls, and cutters. There were boats made of wood and fibreglass, boats with teak trim, and plain, small, and large boats. There were so many it was overwhelming. Al had researched blue water sailing boats diligently, and had more ideas about what we needed than I did. In the Miami harbour, we had a chance to sail on a Pacific Seacraft that had good recommendations, but was not exactly what we wanted. We looked at a Beneteau, Hans Christian, Tayana, and many more. Finally we checked out a Cabo Rico, a sailboat made in Costa Rica.

"How do you like this one?" Al asked.

"What's not to like? It's beautiful," I answered, looking down below at the comfortable salon, the roomy V-berth, the rear cabin, and the well-equipped galley with its gimballed stove, microwave, refrigerator, many cupboards, and deep sink, all surrounded by white Corian counters.

Everywhere I looked I saw warm teak, even in the head with its separate shower stall.

I was happy to buy this type of boat, but a new one would take a year to make. On the outside, it was a wonderful, sturdy sloop, 46 feet from tip to stern, and 13 feet wide at the beam. It had a large main sail attached to a 62-foot aluminum mast. This sail would give us good directional stability and control, and it could be raised by an electric power winch. There was also a large furling head sail, and a smaller furling stay sail just behind it to be used alone for stormy weather; the two combined could power us through heavy weather. Its modified full keel, weighing 10,000 pounds, would give the boat stability and sea kindliness. I hoped it would keep us upright. Of course, equipping the boat would cost twice the asking price, but I knew Al was thinking of my comfort and security when he suggested that boat despite the extra amount it would be.

So we ordered the Cabo Rico.

Later that year, we went to Costa Rica to see the boat in the process of coming together. The factory, a former car manufacturing plant, was in San Jose, the country's capital. As we entered, the dusty and hazy building was buzzing with busy workers, casting hulls, trimming wood, and placing teak on many boats under construction. Our sailboat, mounted on a stand, was half-finished. I stood in awe at the large unfinished shell of our boat; this was going to be our home for several years. Would I love or hate it? Time would tell.

Al was called over to answer many complicated questions about the mechanical gears and electronic devices. "How do you want the interior design? How do you want us to ground the radio antenna to protect the boat from lightning storms? Is this anchor storage big enough? How many through holes do you need?"

It was all overwhelming. I finally spoke up. "We will need the deck raised a little just behind the large steering wheel so that both of us, being short, can see ahead."

Once we left Costa Rica and the factory, we had to rely on the experienced building crew to finish the work before the end of the year.

The day we left Collingwood for Florida, the weather couldn't have been worse. Soft snowflakes filled the air around our condo, covering the area with a dense blanket. It was January 1, 2001.

"What a day to leave," I said. "We could just wait for better weather." I knew I wouldn't get the response I wanted, as my husband was focussed ahead, as usual; nothing was going to stop his progress. Our car was overloaded with all the necessities of a long journey to Florida. All the arrangements for leaving were on my mind, and my stomach was in knots, as this was the start of what would be a very long journey.

"OK," Al said, patiently ready to answer all my questions. He started to list off things to reassure me. "Our daughter will be checking our condo occasionally, will collect our mail, and drive your Nissan when she comes to Collingwood. We've had our shots, and have an impressive first aid kit and all the emergency medication that our doctor felt necessary. Our finances are in order, and important mail stopped. Shall I continue?"

"No." I had to trust my methodical husband who seemed to have thought of everything.

We spent the next six weeks in this cramped dock at the Cabo Rico boatyard in Fort Lauderdale. All the instruments and mechanics had to be installed after the basic boat arrived from Costa Rica. What had we got so far? A mechanical steering device, a wind generator, a water-maker, navigation instruments, anchors, a 56-horsepower Yanmar diesel motor, an electronic autopilot, an alternator, a rubber dinghy, communication equipment, radar, pumps, safety equipment such as a life raft, and many more items that were needed to complete the outfitting. Dave, the overseer, had a crew that worked on our boat from morning till evening. It was chaotic, and I often went to the beach just to get away, but Al had to be available. After all the lines (the rigging) were installed, we finally took the boat out into the harbour to try the mechanical steering monitor. By then, most of the commissioning had been done, but I could tell there was so much we had to learn about all that equipment. Our time in the Caribbean would be essential before the big passage across the Pacific Ocean.

From Fort Lauderdale to Key West, we learned how to handle this new yacht. Anchoring in high winds posed the greatest problem, especially when anchored boats around us complained loudly about our ineptitude. The skill of anchoring would take time to learn. Preparing the inflatable dinghy, when needed, was a slow process: inflating it, lifting it with its harness, and attaching the motor. This meant shore stops were few as we travelled down. Sailing our boat, with its large wheel and heavy main sail, took considerable practice. We were usually up at 05:30 and were on our way by 07:00. I was at the wheel trying to point into the wind, while Al stood by the mast to keep the huge sail between the lazy jacks (special lines to keep the sail straight). Then I would press the power winch and raise the sail. Once up, we would get the feel of the wind and get underway again. Then I would go down to the galley below and prepare our breakfast.

Eventually, we learned to work well together, and I began to feel I could handle the job of being the crew. We spent a few days in Miami, then briefly anchored in Rodriguez Key, Marathon, and Bahia Honda before

Key West where we could provision for our trip into the Caribbean. We were lucky to get temporary docking at a cement pier next to the Conch marina where we could hook up to power and have access to showers and toilets.

Old friends from our ski club were living in Key West and invited us for dinner. It was a great break to be off the boat for a while. The town of Key West was charming, and so unlike the parts of Florida that we had seen. Writers such as Hemingway and Tennessee Williams had lived there. The historic homes of the 1800s were meticulously restored with large, second-floor balconies, gingerbread mouldings, and surrounding porches hidden by palms and succulents.

The concentration of sailing and having so little rest suddenly hit me while we were there. Would we ever be able to handle this boat? The learning of all the instruments and mechanical equipment was a difficult task for both of us, and I was glad that we had a year in the Caribbean for that purpose.

We took a last-minute trip to a supermarket for provisions as we didn't know how much or what types of food would be available in Cuba. I stocked up for months with canned food, staples, and whatever I thought I would need (or even didn't need). It took the better part of three hours to load up and store it away. I kept a record of our supplies and directions to their location. We had normal cupboards and spaces under our floor, beneath bunks, and under seats to put supplies.

In order to leave the US, Al had to go to the authorities and fill out papers. When asked where we were going next, Al answered, "We're planning to sail overnight to Cuba." Everyone in the office looked up in surprise.

"We can't put that on the exit visa. No one can leave the US for Cuba," the official said, exasperated.

"OK, then we're going to Mexico."

With those words, we were able to leave.

PART 1

The Caribbean

CHAPTER 1

❦

Cuba

THE CARIBBEAN WAS my school, my paradise, my nemesis. How difficult it was that first year! Deciding to head to Cuba, sailing around its western tip and east toward the Windward Islands, was our first mistake. The prevailing winds from the Atlantic blew right on the bow, and we constantly fought them and the high waves. From the beginning, I couldn't contemplate how we would handle the sailing between us. Al portrayed the confidence I had yet to feel. Just to get the required knowledge and competence to sail that beautiful yacht was beyond me. The SSB (single sideband) radio was very important, and I took it upon myself to learn how to communicate using the ham radio and the computer for email and weather.

Our first overnight sail was from Key West to Havana. I had multiple questions for my husband as we left Florida: "What is it like sailing in the dark? Will we be seen by other vessels? What about the Gulf Stream, will it send us too far east?" I was such a novice!

We were lucky, though, as the night was beautiful and warm; millions of stars sparkled in the sky, and our hull quietly passed through the gentle waves. Sitting nervously by myself in the cockpit on first watch, I was aware of the sounds of the water hitting our boat. The sound was exaggerated in the dark because I couldn't see the water. I had to check for lights coming from other vessels and stay on course.

During my watch, I was interrupted by a call on our VHF (boat to boat) radio. A voice asked, "What are you sailing? I have a 45,000-pound boat, am using my motor, and I can only go 1 or 2 knots."

We were averaging 5 to 6 knots and I was feeling proud of our boat, *Solara*. I answered his questions and signed off as we sped ahead. Just before going to my bunk for a sleep, I saw a red crescent moon sink into the western sky and disappear. What a wonderful first night of sailing!

When we entered Cuba, the officials occupied our time with their procedures. All of them wore blue uniforms with official insignia stating their department. First came the medical man, wearing a white mask, who sprayed our sparkling new boat inside and out with a fungicide. When finished, and with no hesitation, he proceeded to ask us for money. We gave him US$5 hoping that was enough to satisfy him. We offered pop as the officials came on board, although warm pop didn't seem to please them.

Next came two portly women from agriculture who seemed to pop out of their tight-fitting uniforms, wanting to see all my fresh food. When I had shopped in Key West before crossing the 90 miles to Cuba, I wasn't thinking that I couldn't bring in fresh food. When they saw my fresh eggs, they said, "You have to cook these immediately or throw them out." I looked dumbfounded, and one of them kindly suggested, "Cooked eggs are good for you." I reluctantly proceeded to boil the eggs. Fortunately, our beef steaks passed the test.

The more official-looking customs people came next with more paperwork on top of all the others. They wanted our passports and gave us entry visas plus more forms to be filled out. One woman asked Al if he had any AA batteries. We carried batteries, but hesitated to part with such precious items. While this was going on, a big husky scuba diver jumped into the water beside our boat and checked its bottom. *Maybe he could clean off the barnacles that had accumulated there.*

But that was not the end! A young man appeared with a dog that sniffed around for drugs but found nothing. Immigration appeared with more papers. Then the *guardia* and coast guard with brown uniforms and serious faces opened and searched all the cupboards, cases, cracks, and crannies in our boat. I think they were looking for illegal cargo such as persons wanting to escape their country. All this checking was officialdom at its finest. Finally, after two hours, we were free to travel in Cuba.

We took a shuttle bus to Havana for a brief visit. I marvelled at the old '50s cars – Chevys, Fords, Buicks, and Plymouths – and the fact that the clever Cubans kept them in working order. Havana looked like a beautiful old woman, but tired and worn. Her attractive but broken-down buildings, once hotels and places for the rich and famous along the waterfront, had been made into apartments. Below the breakwater and running along the Caribbean, we saw many boys, men, and women sunbathing, swimming, or fishing off the exposed rocks. I could have stayed longer, but Al wanted to get back to our boat and check out for our next passage west.

.Our first stop from Marina Hemingway was Bahia Honda. The *guardia* actually came out to our boat in a military-looking tiny U-boat. He was more pleasant than the last *guardia*. He checked our papers and the next morning two men came on board to fill out more papers and snoop around our V-berth, perhaps looking for drugs or escaping Cubans. We then had to give them our next destination, Cayo Levisa. I was beginning to dislike all the bureaucracy of the country and was anxious to anchor somewhere apart from officialdom.

I was starting to feel comfortable in *Solara*, but not yet ready to brave the high winds. As we were sailing easily to Levisa in 10 knots of wind, a gentle breeze suddenly went up to 25 knots after my husband let out the genoa (the large forward sail) to its full size. *Solara* flew like the wind. Al stood behind the wheel, enjoying every minute, even though the water came over the toe rail as we heeled over at a dangerous degree. The waves were large and the cockpit filled with water.

"Please shorten the sail!" I cried. "I'm scared."

"This is fun," he replied enthusiastically, but agreed to furl the genoa, which was difficult to do. I think my husband had no idea how uncomfortable I was when we were sailing our boat in high winds. He was probably frustrated by not being able to use the full potential of the Cabo Rico, but I was thankful that he listened to my anxious cries.

A young woman from North Carolina, who was sailing with her husband, a small child of 8, and two cats, took our picture as we flew by their boat. We met them at our next stop.

"I videoed you flying by with all your sails up," she said. "It will look good on my website." *Well, good for her. If she only knew how scared I was.*

Levisa Island protected us from the northerlies, and we stayed there for a few days until the weather calmed down. There were several other boats anchored there as well, including two Canadian boats. We motored our dinghy to the long dock servicing a small hotel fronted by a lovely sandy beach. It was extremely windy on the beach. No tourists were in sight, but I saw beach furniture, windsurfers, and umbrellas scattered here and there. I went to the hotel to ask if I could buy some eggs and bread.

"We can't sell you eggs, but I'll give you a few," the man answered. I found out later that Cubans weren't allowed to sell produce to tourists.

While we were in Levisa Island, the woman who had taken our picture gave me information about our SSB marine radio and how to find a good weather fax program, which would be very helpful. Her help was our first encounter with the wonderful relationship cruisers had with each other. Reading material that we had brought about navigation and anchoring was good, but the cruising community was the best source when nothing else was available.

As we sailed across the northwest coast of Cuba, the land was desolate but beautiful. The high mountains in the background of our anchorages were silhouetted against the night sky. The mangrove trees edging the water were filled with frigate birds with pointed wings, sharp split tails, and bright red pouches under their beaks. Ducks swam nearby. Neither the frigate birds nor the ducks showed any fear of our presence. Dolphins chasing fish followed our boat in herds as we sailed into quiet anchorages. It seemed like paradise.

There were occasions when we had the chance to eat dinner with a family who had permission to serve a meal to tourists. In Esperanza, a small town of 6,000 people on the north coast, Dora – the town welcoming committee of one – greeted us at the town dock as we approached in our dinghy. She was a jolly, well-endowed woman with a wide open smile.

"Welcome to my town," she said in English. "You must come to my house and have a good Cuban dinner."

I was always glad to get away from our boat and not cook, so of course we had to go. I walked down the long main street of Esperanza to Dora's house, carrying a T-shirt and some hand cream as a gift. As we approached her small house, amongst many one-storied homes along the street, we saw a horse pulling a small cart, a few cars, and many bicycles. The people we met on the street were friendly, but curious. To them, it must have looked like we had everything; they were obviously lacking in material goods.

Dora's neat and tidy house was surrounded by beautiful blue, violet, and red flowering bushes. There was also a small garden at the back where she grew vegetables. As we entered, we saw that her walls were decorated with signatures of all the people from many countries who had come to have a meal. I wrote our names and our boat's amidst the others, proud that Canada was included. Dora asked us to sit down in her dining room and soon a meal was placed in front of us. She left us alone with a delicious dinner of fish, salad, black beans, rice, and fried bananas, washed down with a beer. The meal cost us only $6 each. I would have liked to talk with Dora, but she left us alone until we were finished.

When we were ready to leave, I asked if I could buy some vegetables, bread, or eggs.

"I won't be able to sell you anything, but insist you take what I have available," she said, as she gave me some tomatoes, carrots, and eggs. I was very grateful, as food was difficult to find in Cuba.

After leaving Esperanza and sailing by remote areas of northern Cuba, our plan was to round Los Cayas de la Lena to Maria La Gorda ("Fat Maria"). The strait between the Yucatan and Cuba was known to be a very difficult passage due to unpredictable winds and high waves. There was a channel before Lena which was part of a long peninsula that jotted out of the most westerly end of Cuba. The channel seemed to be a quiet place to anchor before proceeding. I saw a few fishermen waving at us.

"*Hola*," we yelled. It was always good to know that in an emergency, help was nearby.

While we were trying to anchor, the current in the channel kept dragging our anchor and wouldn't hold in the muddy bottom. Finally, Al took two ropes, swam out with them to the mangroves on shore, and tied our boat securely to the trees. That seemed to me a bold move, and I was proud that he could swim so well.

For two days we waited for calmer weather. I was running out of bread, but had time now for domestic duties. I started to bake, wash clothes, and clean the inside of the cabin. I saw more frigate birds. The immature frigate had a white head and breast. Those birds were our only company, except for the occasional fish jumping high out of the water.

On the morning of the second day, we woke up amongst the hungriest mosquitoes, as if we were in northern Ontario in May. While we were getting eaten alive, Al took the dinghy to the mangrove trees and untied the ropes holding our boat. Raising the dinghy and dinghy motor quickly, we motored away as soon as we could. The mosquito population was probably why we didn't see any cruisers in that channel.

We were told that rounding the west point of Cuba, one should wait for a calm northeast wind so as not to fight the Gulf Stream forcing its way north. It wasn't to be.

"We can't wait forever," Al said. "Who knows when the wind will die down?" I didn't say anything, but was fearful of trying to sail against the current and wind.

The passage was just as bad as I expected. Our motor did most of the work as the wind was right on our nose. The waves were very choppy, on top of 10- to 15-foot swells. The boat rocked back and forth, up and down. I tried to hang on in the galley with both feet planted firmly in front of the stove, the safety strap around my body. The waves tumbled over our cockpit constantly, but got flushed away in our drains. The noise was unrelenting, wild and furious. I was extremely glad when we reached Maria La Gorda just before dark.

"Let's keep going."

Did I hear right? Did my husband have other plans?

"No way. I can hardly wait to get a drink and go to bed," I replied, in no uncertain terms.

Although we had tied up on a mooring ball, the incessant wind rocked and rolled our boat, amidst the unrelenting white caps. I saw two other boats: *Guitar,* a Morris 44 pilothouse I recognized, and an American ketch I hadn't seen before. We were all waiting for better weather. While Al took the dinghy to shore to check in with the *guardia,* I stayed on board, sitting in the cockpit with a bowl of soup. Suddenly the wind picked up the soup from my spoon and blew it away. That did it. I wasn't going to leave that harbour, unpleasant as it was, until the storm passed.

Nevertheless, Maria La Gorda was an interesting stop once the winds died down. It was an international dive centre with a local resort, pretty beach, nice cabins, a restaurant, and a bar. The coral fish were nearby in the turquoise water, clear and beautiful. Al suggested that we do some snorkelling, which looked good. After tying our dinghy nearby, we swam out towards the coral until I found a problem with my new snorkel: it closed up when I tried to breathe. That was the end of my snorkelling, but Al swam further out towards the reefs, and later told me about the colourful fish of different shapes and shades he had seen swimming around the coral. I wasn't a strong swimmer, and didn't try to snorkel again.

Before leaving Maria La Gorda, I checked the resort to see if they would sell me some eggs and bread. I was always looking for these two items. I forgot to bring small dollar bills, and when I gave the manager a $20 bill he couldn't find the change. He finally found a $10 bill, which meant that the items cost me $10 instead of $6. It was still a bargain though.

On our last night, we invited the couple from *Guitar* for a light supper. They were English, but had lived in Toronto for a few years. We expected we might see them again on our travels.

Our next destination was Cayos de San Filipe, 60 miles away and an overnight sail, and then on to Nuevo Geruno on the Isla de Juventud. Al bought fuel first, from Filipe the attendant. When asked how much, Filipe said in broken English, "My gauge not working. You pay me $50." Another bargain, as our tanks had been empty.

Again we fought the winds and waves, which were 8 to 12 feet high. The boat rocked and rolled as before, with little rest for me when on duty. There was no end to the turbulence, and in the darkness of the night I could only imagine what was ahead. The narrow cockpit gave me some comfort, as it was possible to hang onto each side. I had an old Walkman to play tapes: Bob Dylan, Eric Clapton, Miles Davis, and Dave Brubeck. I loved jazz which would keep me awake on my watches.

After a brief overnight stay in Cayos de San Filipe, and another 15 hours of sailing, we motored into Nuevo Geruno's commercial port, passing a *guardia* tower at the entrance. I felt like we were entering a prison yard. We were allowed to tie up to the rough concrete wharf and connect to a power source attached to a large pole. The power source looked like spaghetti junction, with a multitude of cords going out in all directions. Al hoped that it wouldn't short our supply.

Isla de Juventud was famous for its prison, which was still being used. Fidel Castro had been incarcerated there when he started a revolution against Batista in the 1950s. We were allowed to visit the town, but not to anchor close to the island. As we walked around, the local people seemed very busy with their work. I saw no cars. The *guardia* were present everywhere, and appeared to have full control of all commercial enterprise. I saw a man selling shaved roasted pork on local bread. The smell drew me closer.

"Wait till later," Al said when he saw me looking like I was going to buy the sandwich. "We'll have dinner in town." I wasn't so happy with that suggestion, but tried to forget the delicious smell.

The buildings in Nuevo Geruno had been very neglected and looked to be plain and in need of repair. There were overhanging walkways that kept us from the hot sun, but I noticed a lack of flowers everywhere which added to the starkness of the streets.

As we were walking, a plainly dressed middle-aged man approached us in a friendly way and said, "You must come to my house for dinner. I'll meet you at the gate of the harbour and take you there. What time would you like to come?"

He said all this in one breath. Perhaps he was worried we wouldn't take him seriously, and wanted to ask us before we could change our minds. A time was arranged, and at 19:30 Juan met us at the gate.

We walked several blocks to his house in the quiet darkness of early evening as he made small talk. Once we arrived at the door, we were greeted by his wife, a friendly woman with a big smile. Their house was modest, but clean and comfortably furnished. We had a very interesting evening at their home once the formalities were over. She had the meal prepared before our arrival, and led us into her dining room. We sat down before delicious looking plates of lobster, crocodile, rice, plantain, soup, and salad. We were also offered juice or coffee. I'd never eaten crocodile before but it was very delicious, cooked in a sauce.

"You must have some Canadian music. I have a Celine Dion CD," Juan said enthusiastically. I hoped we didn't show that she wasn't a favourite of ours. He continued, "I was educated as an engineer but there is no job for me as I'm not a member of the Communist Party. I cannot buy fish at the market as it goes to the government's fishing stations, so I must catch it myself. Now that the Russians have stopped helping Cuba, the people are having a difficult time."

We could only sympathize, and say we hoped things would get better. Since this conversation was in Spanish, I was sure I missed many good points. Al had been able to retain his Spanish lessons better than I had.

The two dinners we had in private homes were highlights of our time cruising in Cuba, as was meeting the local people, who were friendly and approachable.

When it was time to leave Nuevo Geruno, our papers were processed with a stamp that allowed an extended time in Cuba, which cost us another US$25 each. On completion, the *guardia* spoke abruptly to us. "Leave right away." He appeared very authoritative in his crisp uniform and non-compromising manner.

"I have to unplug my electricity first," answered Al gruffly. I knew he was getting unsettled by the uniform and manner of the *guardia*, and unplugging the various wires would take some time.

Once that was done, we were off through the polluted river where we had tied up our boat, and past the guard in the tower who surveyed everyone passing through. Then we headed west where I saw no one, just quiet water pierced here and there by clumps of wild looking trees. Because it was getting dark, we anchored close to an island, hoping we wouldn't be discovered as it was illegal to anchor near Isla de Juventud. Our only company was several porpoises swimming around and a large pelican overhead: much better company than soldiers, raucous music, and smelly old boats in the river.

The next day brought very good sailing weather, good winds, and comfortable seas. Our speed of 6 to 7 knots was the fastest that *Solara* could go. *We should make our next destination in good time.* Suddenly, the boat came to an abrupt stop.

"I think we've hit sand. We're grounded." The small channel we had taken was marked in our guidebook as good, but the sand had silted in. Probably it had been meant for smaller fishing boats.

"What do we do now?" I asked with trepidation. "I don't want to stay here all night."

Al tried every manoeuvre he knew to free our boat, but we were left sitting at a 60-degree angle in that remote spot for the night. He planned to dinghy to the nearest resort and find help in the morning. Fortunately, before he left, a powerboat with two tourists out for a fishing trip motored by. I waved frantically to get their attention. Soon, the boat approached and the tour guide was able to help Al. In the meantime, I offered coffee to the two tourists and found out that they were Canadian.

"Can I take a picture?" asked one of them. "I'll send it to you by email." What could I say but yes, knowing that I'd never get the picture and probably didn't want it anyway.

When we were freed, I insisted that the tour guide get paid for his help, although he resisted at first. The experience of grounding with no one around had been very stressful.

Soon we were on our way again toward Cayo Largo. We sailed through the Archipelago de los Jardines de la Reina ("Gardens of the Queen") where we had managed to avoid the coral heads and shallow sandy areas with luck and fortitude as the sun in front of us made seeing very difficult. The water was a beautiful turquoise of various shades. The protected waters extended 93 miles along the south of Cuba, a favourite area of Castro who liked to fly-fish there. On the way, a lobster fishing boat stopped us for a trade, dollars or cigarettes. Since it was illegal for the fishermen to trade, we furtively put the six lobsters away from officials' eyes when arriving at Cayo Largo. Nevertheless, we had lobster for two meals, and gave the rest away to other cruisers.

There was a marina at Cayo Largo where we were fortunate to find a place for docking. The marina was an extension of a large resort area with several hotels, fronted by a beautiful sandy beach. It was heavenly, and I could get some domestic chores done, such as laundry and stocking up on supplies.

I found a hairdresser in one of the hotels. She was a small, wizened woman with dark brown eyes which stared up at me as I spoke.

"Se puede cortar pelo?"

I just wanted my hair cut to last for a while. She sat me down. I swear my hair looked like she had done it with a bowl over my head. I had no choice but to go back to our boat looking like a medieval monk.

One night, all the cruisers in the marina were invited to a buffet supper at the hotel as guests of the staff. For $10, and a $2 bus ride into town, we arrived at a banquet with a variety of food I hadn't seen for weeks. Al gorged so much he was sick on our return to the boat. Seeing all that food confirmed my thoughts about how the Cuban government enticed tourist dollars with their luxury hotels, while the rest of the population struggled to feed themselves. Government workers went to their own specific restaurants using free coupons. Hotel staff were usually searched when leaving work in case they smuggled food.

I left Cayo Largo reluctantly, as the weather seemed too strong from the east, our direction at the time. A brief stop at an anchorage, and meeting two cruising boats we had met before, left me feeling very low. They were sailing together, which meant they had each other for company and, if problems arose, there would be someone there to help. The women could chat about their problems and the men about theirs. Cruising always brought up questions about navigation, communication, boat parts, and weather, to name a few.

After a needed cry, and encouragement from my husband, he talked me into proceeding to the next anchorage not too far away. I acquiesced, and off we went in the rough and tumbling seas. After an hour or two, we came to a bleak and lonely island with a large lighthouse sitting on a rocky promontory. A wiry, dishevelled man came out of the building when he saw us approaching. He got into a leaky half-boat and rowed out through the choppy waves to a mooring ball when he saw us trying to fasten our line to its metal loop. I was trying, with little success, to manoeuvre our boat to allow Al to reach the mooring ball with a hook. The waves keep tossing the boat around, and I almost ran the old lighthouse keeper over several times. I felt really sorry for the guy, who seemed to have a pretty lonely and dismal life on this desolate island. The poor man struggled to help us while fighting the waves at the same time. *Oh, why didn't we stay where we were before in the quiet, sheltered anchorage!* Finally we were attached, and I offered him a beer, but all he wanted was cigarettes, which we didn't have at the time. He rowed back to his post while we spent the night rocking and swaying on the mooring ball, which fortunately kept us in place.

Cienfuegos was approached by a long 6-mile channel which opened up to a large bay. It was a beautiful sight. The small marina was surrounded by previously exclusive homes, shining white but in sad repair. One was a former palace called the Palacio de Valle, an elegant, eclectic mansion. Another was a former yacht club with crumbling plaster walls left standing, and a Moorish design building with wrought iron work that was open to the public. It had a flat roof where I saw people looking over at the ocean. But most of the locals were enjoying the water – swimming, surfing, waterskiing, and sailing.

There was a unique "taxi" to reach the city centre. It was dedicated to the local population, but Al and I persuaded the conductor to give us a ride. It was a cart holding about eight people pulled by a frisky little horse. The driver charged us a dollar and drove on side streets looking anxiously around to avoid the police. Once in town, I found a market and for US$1 bought a squash. With the pesos I was given for change, I was able to buy tomatoes, a mango, carrots, cabbage, and a pepper. Pesos went a long way in Cuba.

A local restaurant was going to charge us US$40 for one pizza, pasta, and two beers, but we paid 2 pesos since we had only pesos with us. The US charge was outlandish, and the food tasteless. We usually ate on our boat. Although the food was bland and uninviting, I enjoyed the Cubans' love for music. There were often groups playing on the street with a singer, guitar, percussion, bongo drums, and shakers. Their musical ability was professional.

I came to know other cruisers in the Cienfuegos marina. An Australian catamaran sidled in beside us. It was being returned to Florida for the owners. That was the first time I came across large expensive yachts being delivered. What luxury, to have one's boat to enjoy, but not to have to sail it through storms and long passages. I met people we had seen before. I remembered boat names such as *Guitar, Begin Again,* and others that would become important to us as we sailed in the Caribbean.

Manzanillo was our last stop before leaving Cuba. We would try to find provisions there. On our way, we anchored in a quiet, sheltered cove for the night. It was raining down in buckets, and the air was cold and damp. A small fishing boat pulled up to us with five men on board who wanted to sell us some lobsters. Their boat was a derelict remnant of a former craft that had seen better days. Only the wooden hull was left, with a small canvas strung over bamboo poles for protection from the wind and rain, although it wasn't doing much good. In the stern, they had set up a tin stove for warmth and cooking. The five men looked tired, cold, and bedraggled. They showed us their catch of several lobsters, which they sold to us for US$3, and threw in two more for good measure. The cost was so cheap, but that is all the money they wanted. The $3 would last a Cuban for weeks.

"Are you all sleeping in this boat tonight?" I asked in broken Spanish. They gave me a nod, and disappeared into the mosquito-infested mangroves nearby. Oh, how I wished them well.

In Manzanillo, we anchored right in front of the city dock. The officials soon came out in their large powerboat, all five with paperwork. They were soon finished though, and we promptly arranged to visit a ship chandler in town. Chandleries provisioned large ships, but they let us check their supplies of canned goods. I ordered cans of meat and vegetables, rice and flour, and Al arranged delivery of diesel.

Manzanillo had a tired old charm, with remnants of beautiful buildings, horse carts everywhere, but few cars. As we walked around town, the interior of the buildings looked cool with their tiled floors, shuttered windows and wrought iron gates. A man bicycling on the way to the market had a squealing pig tied up on the back. The young people looked like any young Westerners, with makeup and blue jeans. When I looked through the low windows in some houses, I saw people watching TV, just like at home. The sidewalks were crumbling and the roads full of potholes, but the central park was attractive with flowering trees surrounded by colourful buildings and covered sidewalks.

We checked out the market but could find only a few pickings. The dollar store (with imported goods for US dollars) had drinks and water available. I got excited seeing pasta, as the last time I'd had it was in Florida. I bought items that I hadn't had for some time, but they were fairly expensive. In town, there were line-ups for bread and ice cream when available.

I was looking for bread again and saw a bakery. It was afternoon and the bakery was closed, so I went to the back door to see if I could buy any leftover bread since the baker was still there. He saw my hopeful face from his window, opened his door, and gave me eight rolls, but he wouldn't take any money. Selling to tourists was illegal, I remembered.

Everyone in town wanted to be helpful, it seemed. They were friendly and always returned our smiles.

I was also looking for eggs. Unfortunately, there were no eggs that day at the dollar store, but a man noticed my frustration and approached me outside on the street. He was middle-aged, cleanly dressed in pale crisp pants and a tucked white shirt.

"I can get you eggs," he said. "Meet me at that corner in an hour." He pointed to a far corner down the same street. He appeared to be an educated man who spoke English very well, so I agreed to meet him.

An hour later, Al and I arrived at the corner, and there was the same man with a dozen eggs carefully placed in a brown paper bag. He asked for a dollar. I tried to pay more, but he quickly disappeared from view. It was obvious that he got the eggs illegally, probably from a friend who worked in a government restaurant or a hotel where food was more available.

In our two months in Cuba, my sailing skills improved dramatically. At times, Al was a harsh teacher. He would say, "We're not using the electronic steering. It takes too much power." He was adamant that we save on fuel. I found the mechanical steering device difficult to learn, as our boat would move to and fro because of its connection to the wind direction. I had to be at the helm (wheel) all the time I was on watch just to check that the mechanism was working properly. It took more time for us to reach our destination as we couldn't sail a straight line. That was very frustrating. I noticed that other cruisers didn't have a monitor steering device on their stern. I bet they were having more fun. Many of them, of course, weren't planning to sail across the Pacific. My husband was of the old school. Probably there was a bit of Joshua Slocum, the 19th century round the world sailor, in his brain. On the positive side, we learned to tack as a team, making a change of direction as quickly as possible, but probably not to the satisfaction of a racing captain.

I learned the SSB marine radio quickly, checking the weather and emailing our family. Luckily, I had help from other cruisers, as otherwise

I was in the dark about the right frequencies to use. The man in Florida who had set up our radio had it all wrong. I kept a book with all the SSB frequencies, which allowed me to listen to important calls about security, those coming from cruisers who wanted to keep in touch, and the Mississauga Net which gave us weather reports. Weather also came in from a special frequency which showed up on our computer. The weather report was most important for planning the next day's passage. My head was filling up with bundles of information, while Al's priority was reaching the Panama Canal.

On top of sailing, communication, navigation, and handling all mechanical devices, meals had to be prepared, clothes washed, and the boat kept clean, with its hardware working to perfection. I learned the 24-hour clock, where 02:00 meant two in the morning and 14:00 meant two in the afternoon. Al and I learned to change the oil in the diesel engine after a required number of miles. This was usually done at an anchorage, as it took at least two hours and a steady boat. The diesel engine course which he had taken beforehand was beneficial for servicing and coping with the 62-horsepower machine. I also began learning about the engine as we went about keeping it in good order.

Exchanging boat cards and information from other cruisers on our sail through Cuba was very important to me. I needed that social exchange and the company of other women. I needed to talk about my fears and apprehensions, which I felt my husband didn't understand. I missed my family, especially our daughter who was about to have a baby. She needed my help. There was no way I could go home until later in the year, but in my mind I was beginning to make arrangements.

Was I going to be able to complete the year in the Caribbean? Cuba was only the beginning of our trip. The worst parts of sailing in Cuba were the difficult times we had heading into the 8- to 12-foot waves and strong gusty prevailing winds from the east. The boat would pitch and roll; water would fill up our cockpit, coming in from the sides, but fortunately drained out again. Balancing myself at the stove was difficult. The only place that was comfortable was lying on a bunk in the salon, protected from falling off by a lee-cloth that could be tied up like a wall from the bunk to the ceiling of the cabin. We had many places below that we could grab to stop us from falling over. In the cockpit, when I was on duty, I was clipped in with a safety harness to a special hook which would stop me from being tossed overboard. The cockpit was narrow and I could hang onto each side for support. The noise of the wind and the turbulence of the water never seemed to stop. It was a relief when a storm passed and we could rest.

In spite of storms, I was beginning to feel comfortable with *Solara*, but physically unable to manage the times when strength was needed, such as pulling up the last 8 feet of anchor chain, or quickly winching the genoa. Al did all the work on deck outside the cockpit, as he was concerned that I might fall off. He was right. I felt more at ease in the cosy cockpit. The electronic instruments would take months of practice, but the radio and I became attuned. We were a pair. How I liked to listen or talk to other cruisers, or wait for the security net to come on every morning, letting us know who got robbed that day and how to be careful out there. "Lock it or lose it," I heard.

We literally left Cuba without proper papers. We should have gone to Santiago de Cuba to check out, but it would have meant a difficult passage between Cuba and Hispaniola. Our sail out of Cuba was a mixture of highs and lows. The seas were so calm while I was on watch during the first night in open water that I was unaware we were being pushed backward toward Cuba. We had to start the motor just to get going again.

I was also thinking of our daughter who was having a C-section that day, and wanted to get word from my contacts on the Mississauga Net. This wonderful ham radio net was run by retired and keen ham radio operators near Toronto. They helped communication between cruisers and were a source of useful information, including weather. Ernie, on the net, knew I was waiting to get word from him about the new baby. At the SSB radio, I turned to the correct channel and called.

"VE3 JCP," I said (my ham call sign), "calling VE3 EMG" (Ernie's ham call sign).

"You have a new grandson," Ernie said, having contacted St. Michael's Hospital for the news. "His name is Tichaonana and he weighs 7 pounds."

My God, I thought, Carolyn had named him an African name for his African father. Ernie was having a hard time trying to say the name.

"How wonderful. Are Mom and baby OK?"

"They were fine when I called."

"Thanks Ernie. That is great news. I'll be in touch another day."

How exciting that the Mississauga Net was able to do that for me. The old guys were great. I would get in touch with our daughter as soon as possible. A mother should be by her daughter's side at such an important moment. That was the most difficult part of being away.

"We're near Jamaica," I said to Al. "Instead of going on toward the east, we need food and I'm sure we'll be able to find a market." That became our next destination.

CHAPTER 2

❧

Jamaica

OUR CLOSEST PORT of entry to Jamaica was Port Antonio, once famous as a port for the Hollywood rich. It was the home of Errol Flynn, a swashbuckling movie pirate and adventurer from the '40s. The marina seemed to stay in that decade, with little new money being spent for improvements. It had a few rundown docks where we could tie up, and an old, tired-looking building with a bar that played loud music into the night. But it had a shower, for which I was grateful. Our boat shower was filled with diesel tanks, and saltwater bathing couldn't beat a marina shower no matter how rundown the marina.

Port Antonio showed its colours well. From one end of town to the other, we saw graceful old buildings with Jamaican gingerbread verandas and elaborate fretwork transoms, reminding us of the wealth from the banana trade years ago. Our main reason to go into town was to explore the market. I was excited about getting food I hadn't seen for almost two months while in Cuba. I wasn't disappointed, as the market gave me all I needed and more. The costs were considerably higher, but now we were in an area of private enterprise. The elderly women sitting by their stalls in the market advertised their goods in raucous voices in competition with their neighbours. The market was a fun place to explore. We never felt threatened in town, and went out in the evening to our favourite restaurant Anna Banana which, like all the restaurants in town, served chicken and rice.

There were a number of cruisers in the marina. We met an American couple named Ken and Nancy on their boat *To the Moon*. There was also Oak, a captain who came in to repair a broken engine on his powerboat, and had drifted for two days in calm seas – like we had, but with no engine. He reminded me of an old-fashioned swashbuckling pirate with a long beard, a face wrinkled and well-worn, and clothes that had seen better days. He was waiting for a new crew as his son, who had sailed with him, had to leave. Despite his appearance, he knew 100 percent more about the Caribbean than I did.

On Saturday, a large 55-foot yacht slowly motored into Port Antonio with 12 English soldiers on board. They had come up from Panama in very stormy conditions. Apparently, the boat had left England a year before to round Cape Horn and participate in a climbing expedition in South America. The crew changed hands in Panama for the trip home. The "volunteer" soldiers who had left Panama were recovering from sea sickness. They looked like a sorry lot. I couldn't imagine 12 sick men on a boat only 55 feet long.

There was fish fry one night thanks to a large dolphin fish caught by Oak, who marinated it in lemon juice during the day. Nancy and I brought salads, and all of us except the 12 soldiers ate on the dock until the rains came. The downpour lasted all weekend.

I came close to losing my life in Jamaica, an experience I'll never forget. Ken and Nancy suggested going on a popular excursion. *Rafting on the Rio Grande is the ultimate vacation treat*, said one brochure. Many years ago, the river was used to carry bananas on bamboo rafts from the interior highlands to Port Antonio. The brochure went on to say: *it is one of the most magical experiences of a slow idyllic meander through tropical rain forest, steered expertly by a local captain* and *there's always a pleasant surprise along the way* ….

Our ride to the river was on a small dirt road overhung with dark green, sweet-smelling foliage left over from the perpetual rain which had fallen for the last two days. A number of guides were lazily sitting around their bamboo rafts on the bank of the Rio Grande. They looked at us with suspicion, surprised to see anyone there that day. The swollen river flowed along wildly, bringing with it tons of debris: yellow banana leaves, brittle tree branches, and other unknown garbage.

"This looks like it's going to be a lot of fun," said my ever adventure-some husband. I felt otherwise. Why would we go rafting in this?

The fragile raft, made of bamboo poles and tied together with what looked like thin rope, seemed to me to be very "unseaworthy." We had no life vests, and all our personal baggage such as backpacks, cameras, and money came with us. But, we were persuaded that there would be no problem. Ken and Nancy sat on one raft with Keith, and Al and I took the other raft with Jimmy for a guide.

As we started, it was inevitable that our old guide Jimmy, poling at the back, couldn't handle our fragile raft due to the swift current and debris. After a few minutes, he fell off into the river. Al pulled him back on, but soon a large branch came barrelling into us and the raft tipped over. Into the river we went. Caught under the raft, I saw only dark murky water, brown and smelling like rotten leaves.

"Janet," screamed Al desperately, as he looked for me.

With no life vest, the backpack and the clothes I was wearing weren't helping. Fortunately, I eventually popped up, and was ready to leave the river and forget the trip. Jimmy was told by Keith, in no uncertain terms, that his job was finished, and he would have to find his way back to the beginning alone. So away he went, and our raft sat by itself on the bank for someone to pick up.

Reluctantly, we started off again, all four of us on one raft poled by Keith, who showed us how brave and strong he could be. He had convinced us that nothing more could happen. Our friends said not a word. They also seemed helpless to do anything. I was soaking wet and scared.

"I hope this is over soon," I shivered. Unfortunately, trouble wasn't over yet. Our bamboo raft was heading at breakneck speed straight for a large fallen tree hanging over the raging water. Its sharp branches spread out dangerously, ready to impale whatever was coming its way. When we hit the tree, the bamboo poles of the raft broke apart, and all of us were left to save ourselves. Nancy was clinging to the tree; my husband – after almost losing his eye on a branch – was trying to swim toward me; our impetuous guide, not seeming to bother with us, was just looking for his shoes; and I was following the debris down the river and heading for disaster. This is the end, I thought. The water flowed so fast I couldn't possibly swim over to the riverbank. Soon, but not soon enough, I saw my husband and Ken swimming fast towards me. I was grabbed on each side and helped to the shore. My heart beat fast, thinking of what could have happened if they hadn't caught up to me.

Our wet, shivering group climbed the steep bank many hundreds of feet above the river and, in a vehicle sent to meet us, we eventually managed to return to our marina. It wasn't until I was in our cabin that night that I finally broke down from the fright of the day, and it was a long time before I felt secure in our small dinghy, which we used constantly riding from our boat to shore.

Our new Jamaican "friends" apologized profusely for the mishap as we recuperated. But we got no compensation from the tourist office who had arranged the trip. I had lost my camera and rain jacket, while Al had lost his glasses and almost his eye. It was with unpleasant memories that we left Jamaica, but agreed to keep in touch with our new friends Ken and Nancy.

CHAPTER 3

❦

Hispaniola

THE STORM LASTED a week as we sailed toward Hispaniola and the Dominican Republic. The prevailing easterly winds hit us with 25 to 30 knots and 10-foot waves, right on our bow. Everywhere, *Solara* took in water no matter how tightly we fastened the portholes and dorades (openings on the deck to let in a breeze). On top of the saltwater, the rain never stopped coming down. I had lost my good rain jacket in the river, and spent more time down below than Al, who excitedly enjoyed the experience of fighting the wind and waves. The cockpit would fill with water, which fortunately drained out again but left a wet puddle for our feet. It didn't matter that we had a bimini (canvas roof) over the cockpit, as the waves just came over the sides.

When my turn came to take over, I would reluctantly get up from my sodden bunk and put on damp clothes that never dried. Then I would put on my safety harness and climb up the companionway to the shrieking and moaning wind that tossed *Solara* back and forth, holding on for dear life so as not to be knocked over.

"Any directions for me?" I would shout over the noise as I tried to see ahead. The whitecaps of the waves were all that were visible a few feet in front of and to the sides of the boat. Our sails had been shortened when the storm started, and I would handle my turn at the wheel as best I could.

"Keep to the same tack and carry on," Al replied. *Gosh, he was sounding more nautical every day.* "Watch out for lights and other vessels." And his usual sign off, "Call me if you need me." Then he would make his way into the cabin for a needed rest.

At night, we would change watch every three hours, and during the day Al would handle the boat most of the time, while I tried to keep us fed and occasionally took over so he could rest. The trip was making me really tired. If I could only be as strong as our boat!

"I don't know how much more I can take," I cried. I was also scared, but didn't want Al to know how much. I had to remember how dependable and seaworthy our boat was supposed to be, and how it could deal with weather like this. The waves weren't super high but constant, along with the heavy rain, which never let up. If only the sky would show some light, but I only saw heavy clouds of grey and black. How much longer would we have to go before we saw land?

On top of that, since the boat was lurching constantly, Al fell on his safety harness which had a hard disc-like attachment to blow it up if needed. I heard a sudden cry from above that woke up in my bunk.

"What happened?" I called.

"I hurt something in my chest when I fell," he said feebly. We both thought he had broken a rib. How painful it was for him, but he soldiered on in spite of that.

Finally, at the southwest tip of the Dominican Republic, we saw a formation in the mist which we determined was Isla Beata. The land, stretching north from the island for almost 200 miles, marked the border between Haiti and the DR. Between this island and the mainland was a treacherous channel, too difficult to navigate. The frothy waves through the channel were propelled by the constant wind, which we would have to fight. On the other hand, trying to sail around the island and up the other side became a struggle. I had the helm for two hours and never made any headway because of the currents working against our boat and pushing us into the channel. Finally, using the motor, Al managed to make more distance toward the nearest town.

"We've got to stop soon, dry out, and get some sleep. I can't take anymore." I needed some sympathetic reply.

"The next port is Barahona, but our guidebook doesn't recommend it. It's just a commercial port," Al answered.

"I really don't care at this point."

So that was how we ended up in the dreariest place in the Caribbean.

CHAPTER 4

❧

Dominican Replublic

AFTER ANCHORING IN the busy, commercial harbour of Barahona, we were greeted by Bill, a self-appointed interpreter and all-round guide. Although I didn't trust him too much since he insisted on calling me "Mama," we needed someone who could help us check in and find fuel for our boat. He rowed us to the harbour office on his dilapidated rowboat with our papers, which were checked over very casually by the police and harbour-master, who then asked us where we planned to stop on our way through the Dominican Republic. Al gave them a list of ports we thought should get us across the south coast of the country.

It was a harrowing experience for Al to buy fuel. He was directed to a couple of young men who took him to a gas station on their scooters. Since he had four tanks to fill with diesel, the ride back on the scooters was a nightmare, so he told me later. The first driver held one, Al held one in each hand, and the second driver held the fourth tank.

"Never again," said my husband later that day; each tank weighed at least 40 pounds. We realized that Barahona was a place not easily forgotten.

The next day, after we cleaned up all the salty water caked on our boat from the storm, I wanted to go into town for some provisions. Unfortunately, it was a holiday and the stores were closed, but Bill showed us a place to have lunch. There were scooters rushing here and there in town, the only means of transportation I could see. The gated storefronts were guarded by police. Everywhere I looked I saw only dark and dismal buildings, poorly dressed pedestrians, and suspicious glances towards us. I didn't feel welcome, and the sooner we got out of there the better.

The only thing I liked about that country was its Presidente beer, wonderfully cold on a hot day.

The next morning, after preparing our boat for departure, Al started to pull up our anchor but found it was caught on a chain lying at the bottom of the harbour. After a struggle, two men appeared in their old boat and came to our help. *Maybe I will change my opinion of Barahona.*

It was beautiful weather and a good sailing day as we headed west following the south coast of the Dominican Republic for Las Salinas, and later to Boca Chica. It was late afternoon when we arrived and prepared to anchor in the Salinas harbour. It was a lovely protected harbour, with beautiful homes of white stucco on the hillside overlooking the water, and large yachts sitting majestically in the marina. There was also a large yacht club. After anchoring, we got a visit from an official who, after looking at our papers, said that Salinas wasn't on our *despacho* from Barahona so we had to leave. I thought afterward that any foreign yacht wouldn't be welcome as the place reeked of mafia or locals making illegal "arrangements." What a disappointment; it was such a lovely spot. Leaving there meant an overnight sail to Boca Chica since there was no place to stop.

Using the harbour guide, we sailed into Boca Chica. Since the first marina was full of large powerboats, we continued to the second marina. Luckily – or not, as we soon discovered – there was a space at the end of one pier to tie up *Solara*. The man who was helping us into our berth broke the light on the stern of our boat. Al thought that the broken light would be an easy fix, so we left it and explored the marina amenities. Although the clubhouse at the marina was grandiose, it was empty of people during the week. There was a bar, restaurant, swimming pool, and showers; the showers were our first priority.

A trip into town was most disappointing for me. It seemed to cater to the sleazy crowd of tourists who liked bars, skimpily-clad and loose women, and sunning on the crowded beach. Maybe I was getting too old to understand their priorities. Luckily, we found a cybercafé in order to send important emails to our family. Ken and Nancy on *To The Moon* arrived, but they had to anchor nearby, close to a wrecked sailboat tipped halfway over after hitting something in the harbour. I hoped that our friends wouldn't end up the same way. The four of us made another trip to town for lunch, but the chilly winds were high on the beach and few tourists were around.

The few days at the marina were busy as we prepared to head west again to Puerto Rico. We were experiencing a lot of rain, which helped with the cleaning of the boat. Another employee of the marina told us he would fix our stern light. That was when the trouble began. He used a soldering iron incorrectly, and suddenly started a fire which burned out our aerial. Unfortunately, that meant no radio or communication until it was fixed. I was truly getting fed up with the DR. After bidding goodbye to Ken and Nancy, promising to keep in touch, Al checked out at the office, which took two hours after being held up by immigration for no discernable reason.

As might be guessed, I had no soft spot for this island: poor sanitation and constant pushiness to buy souvenirs. The beaches were very nice, and I was sure tourists were well looked after at the resorts. There was a feeling of depravity, and an immense need for tourist dollars. I was glad to leave.

CHAPTER 5

Puerto Rico

"WHAT'S A TROPICAL wave?" I asked after we left the Dominican Republic. The computer map showed one heading our way south of Puerto Rico.

"It's a precursor to a hurricane," Al read, after checking our library. "Don't worry about it. Right now, all we have are the winds that come beforehand."

Our passage to Puerto Rico and our time there built up a battle with my husband that convinced me that a break from sailing and a trip home would be inevitable.

"I want to go back to a port. I have had enough of storms," I said in frustration.

Al had become difficult to live with over the past two days of struggling to fight the strong current and winds coming out of the Mona Passage that separated the Dominican Republic and Puerto Rico.

The Mona Passage took up a whole section in the book *The Gentleman's Guide to Passages South* by Bruce Van Sant, who had mastered the area many times. The seas in the area were formidable, unpredictable, and nasty if the winds were high. Van Sant had written a "go/no-go" decision table for sailors planning to cross the passage. Out of eight predictable scenarios involving wind direction, wind speed, and sea conditions, only two were a "go." I wasn't sure which scenario we had around us, but I felt it was a "no-go" one. Not only did the Mona Passage have unpredictable currents everywhere, but also shoals scattered here and there. We were supposed to take two nights and a day, as the best conditions were at night. We didn't seem to be making any headway for some time, and Al didn't want to put on the motor.

"I'll go in any direction that the wind will take me so I won't have to turn on the engine," he complained. At the time, we were only 30 miles to Puerto Rico, and I didn't want to float around the Caribbean like a turtle.

"Please calm down and get us to land," I pleaded. I knew Al didn't like losing control and was fighting his frustration all the way. *How could you sail as much as we were and have everything just right?*

Finally, after many agonizing hours, we reached Ponce which became our first stop. There was a large marina connected to a private club, and we were given a temporary berth. Checking into an American territory was done by a serious official who looked over our papers carefully and proceeded to take all the canned goods that I had bought in Cuba, especially canned meat. Apparently, there was a full-blown epidemic of hoof and mouth disease in the world and he wasn't taking any chances with our meat.

Apart from Al and me, I saw no other cruisers in the berths nearby, only powerboats up for sale or being repaired. We were allowed to use their washrooms and showers but not their other facilities. The place seemed very unfriendly, but we didn't plan to stay very long. Across the way from our berth and the marina, Ponce had built a large public boardwalk with lots of pubs and fast food. That brightened my mood tremendously until the weekend, when the noise and loud music went on into the wee hours of the morning.

During our stay, Al rented a car to take an inland trip to Farjardo where there was a West Marine, my husband's toy store. There, he bought up half the store to fill our boat with many spare parts needed over the months ahead. On the way back to the marina, through the interior of Puerto Rico, I saw beautiful mountains blanketed with green low-lying foliage, a sharp contrast to the rugged coast which was my usual view of the island.

In the few days we had left, there was much running around in our rental car looking for more boat parts and making a last-minute provisioning trip. I found a Sam's Club which was like a Costco with large stores of canned goods and easily cooked packaged meals that would keep in hot weather. Al picked out cans of chilli, thinking he would be alone if I took a trip home, as I was anxious to do once we got to Grenada. In my grocery cart were a few cans of peanuts, which later would cause a perplexing problem.

We checked out, turned back the car, and paid our dock fees. It would be a four-day sail to the Leeward Islands to our east. As we got on our way, the BG compass wasn't working, and neither was the auto-helm. We continued nevertheless, using our mechanical monitor and other instruments. Then, at 18:00, I heard on the weather report that a tropical wave was approaching our way – another precursor to a hurricane.

"Please turn back," I pleaded with my husband. "We're still close to Puerto Rico and the Salinas harbour." Al heaved to (positioning the sails so that the boat remained steady) near the shore until dawn, when it would be light enough to find our way among the reefs and into a quiet bay near Salinas. Since we were having trouble with our electronics, Al contacted an electrician in Boqueron who would come the next day.

"Well, we aren't getting very far on our passages these last few days. We might as well make use of our time and enjoy Salinas," I said eagerly to my husband. He was still looking tense and anxious as we were stuck in Puerto Rico much longer than he had planned. *Planning was just a word in my sailing experience.*

It was a long, hot walk along a dirt road to the town of Salinas, where we looked for a cybercafé. We found one, but they were using the computer as a teaching tool and only allowed us a few minutes to send a message home – very disappointing.

I decided to have my hair cut while in town. The lady in charge said to me, "You must get that white out of your hair. Here in Puerto Rico, no one lets their hair go white. Let me put a wash in your hair." Since these words were all said in Spanish, much of the meaning was lost to me and I let her go ahead. Well, the look on Al's face when he saw me caused me to wash out my hair immediately. No more fooling around with my hair, I decided.

Back to the harbour and our boat for supper and relaxing in the cockpit. An Australian couple whose boat was next to ours came over in the dinghy to say hello. They had been travelling for eight years and had many tales to tell, including one about being attacked and robbed in New Guinea. They now kept a dog on board. We found out that many cruisers carried weapons, especially Americans. It made me think that we should have something to warn us during the night when we're anchored in a quiet bay.

While waiting for Tuesday, the day for the electrician's visit, Al decided that we should clean the algae off *Solara,* the speed indicator at the bottom of the boat, and the water line. Well, I became more frustrated with my husband that afternoon. While he went around the boat in the dinghy, I was to tie the dinghy with a bowline to our boat each time he moved.

"You're not doing that right," he would yell at my effort to tie the knot. I found it hard doing it in an upside down position. I had learned the knot right side up. I later proved I could do one with my eyes closed.

My husband was getting more and more difficult, probably from being stuck in Puerto Rico. When the Tuesday for the electrician's visit came, we quickly motored to the dock in Salinas. A nice young Canadian couple helped us into the difficult berth between two pillars.

From Tuesday until Friday, we remained in the marina at Salinas; more frustration for Al. Who would have guessed that my canned peanuts, purchased at Sam's Club, were the cause of our problem with the electronics! We had stored them close to the internal compass. It was fastened to one of our storage compartments and we were unaware of its importance. The metal in the cans interfered with the electronics. The autopilot then had to be recommissioned and checked out. Benjamin, the electrician, was very competent and proceeded to repair the aerial that had been burned in the Dominican Republic. He also connected our GPS to the chart plotter. I could have used Benjamin as a second crew.

Finally, we could leave Puerto Rico. Two manatees cavorting around our boat kept us waiting until they left. They were so docile and huge, but vulnerable to injury. I loved seeing them. Now we were on our way to the Spanish Virgin Islands.

CHAPTER 6

❦

Leeward and Windward Islands

ISLA DE VIEQUES, in the Spanish Virgin Islands belonging to the US, was our first stop after Puerto Rico. There was a lovely anchorage at Green Beach, surrounded by palm trees and a sandy beach protected from the east wind. I could see Puerto Rico from our boat with its lush green rolling hills, but I was glad we weren't going back there again.

The next day, we sailed to Culebra and anchored in a quiet spot off Cayo de Luis Pena. At least we thought it would be quiet, but unbeknownst to us, it was Memorial Day weekend in the US, and all the quiet anchorages began to fill with boats. In spite of the crowd, jack fish surrounded our boat, herding smaller fish which shimmered in the sunlight. Culebra was an ideal holiday weekend playground for boats.

The British Virgin Islands had been our playground and sailing school a few years ago, and we had many wonderful memories of the various islands and their incredible beauty. Norman Island's pirate ship bar had been replaced by a Nova Scotia barge, which was also being used as a drinking spot. This time, we had to pay for an expensive mooring ball since there was no place to anchor as we had been able to do years before. The next day, we sailed through the Drake Channel to the Virgin Gorda Yacht Harbour and took a slip for the night. Virgin Gorda was always my favourite place, especially The Rock restaurant where we sat outside among beautiful large boulders and cascades of water, surrounded by colourful bushes. Would I ever get back to the BVIs?

We had an overnight sail to St. Martin. The seas were choppy and uncomfortable, but we reefed our main sail and used only the stay sail, which would be best for sleeping when off watch. This would be the beginning of our passage down the chain of the Leeward and Windward islands. Leeward meant the northern islands away from the wind, such as St. Martin, St. Kitts, Nevis, Antigua, Guadeloupe, Montserrat, and Dominica.

On the way, we seemed to be surrounded by boats going here and there. One powerboat almost collided with ours, and later in the night I received a call on the VHF from another sailing craft asking if the large cruise ship on our starboard side was coming towards us. I felt slightly more experienced and assured the voice that we weren't going to be rammed by a cruise ship.

To anchor in Simpson Bay in St. Martin, it was necessary to enter through a channel that was closed by a bridge and only opened twice a day. Since we missed the 11:00 opening, we had to wait until 17:00. I thought to myself, why did we hurry during the night only to anchor outside the bay for hours? *I thought better than to say it out loud.* Once inside, I saw hundreds of boats anchored here and there. Circling Simpson Bay were all kinds of boat services, marinas, bars, restaurants, and stores. There were also a few wrecked boats, the result of a devastating hurricane in 1999 called Lenny.

We met another couple from Canada, Reg and Maureen, who were also sailing south after St. Martin. Through them we also met Cheryl and Dave, who had taken the offshore course in Toronto with us. They had been caught in the St. Martin hurricane and lost their boat. Now they were repairing another one. It was fun talking to cruisers again. We had so much to share, and talked over common problems and future plans.

Al had fun again checking out the nautical stores, and I was able to provision well, with lots of Dutch and French choices. We were then ready to leave St. Martin for our next stop, the Federation of St. Kitts and Nevis. It was a great sail, good winds, and waves only 3 to 5 feet. Since it was too late to check in to the country, we anchored offshore by the sleepy village of Sandy Town in St. Kitts, sheltered from the prevailing easterly winds.

Our next passage wasn't as gentle: stronger winds, accompanied by high seas and squalls from unsettled weather. Nevertheless, in Nevis we saw beautiful Pinney's Beach, with a famous bar sitting among large, swaying palm trees. Two windjammer vessels had dropped off their load of tourists, who were enjoying the beach and bar. Of course, we had to join them. A short trip into Charlestown the next day gave me a glimpse of its British colonial history. The Georgian-style buildings were made of wooden upper floors over a stone ground floor, providing security from any earthquakes like those that had destroyed the stone buildings many years ago. The few stores didn't provide much, but I was able to buy something for our daughter's birthday in June.

My husband asked about the large wooden dock in Charlestown which appeared fairly new, and much larger than we had seen anywhere. The answer was most disturbing. Japanese had built the dock in return for permission to fish for whales in the neighbouring waters. Thus far, we had seen no whales, and hopefully they were hiding somewhere else.

It was a tough slog of 70 miles to the archipelago of Guadeloupe, which included Basse-Terre, Grande-Terre, Marie-Galante, and La Desirade. It was a stormy night, and dark clouds hung menacingly in the horizon, but a full moon brightened my spirits somewhat. We passed Montserrat, or at least what was left of it after a volcanic eruption – this after a hurricane that had already destroyed 90 percent of the island. In the morning, we reached a sheltered bay in Guadeloupe called Deshaies where we rested from the passage, having had little sleep during the night. I was hoping the weather would improve on our way to Les Saintes, islands like idyllic tropical jewels sitting between the larger islands of Guadeloupe and Dominica. High winds and waves hit the boat from the east once we left the shelter of Guadeloupe, causing Al to be in a foul mood since we were using our motor too much, trying to beat the waves at our bow – another struggle through high seas.

After anchoring among many boats in the harbour at Les Saintes, we explored Terre-de-Haut, the main town, which was ideal for tourists: no cars, beautiful shops, and tasty restaurants. The old clapboard buildings, with elegant ironwork balconies surrounded by colourful flowers, gave off a very French flavour. High concrete sidewalks lined the street, perhaps protecting people from future floods. I could smell fresh croissants and hurried to find them in a nearby bakery. One can't beat French croissants in taste and texture. I indulged myself by buying a dress and shorts dyed beautiful Caribbean colours of azure blue and turquoise. While I was having fun in the shops, my husband, oh so historically minded, walked up to the French fort used during the fighting between the British and the French in the 18th century. We finished our tour of Terre-de-Haut with pastries called *tourment d'amour*, filled with guava, coconut, and banana.

Dominica, also known as the "Nature Island," was our next stop down the Leeward chain of islands. Christopher Columbus named it Sunday for the day he spotted it on his travels. Our sail from Les Saintes went so fast due to high winds that we passed our planned destination of Rupert's Bay and went on to Roseau, the capital of Dominica. Because of the island's reputation for its beauty and lush tropical forest, I was sorry we couldn't spend time there and explore. After we anchored *Solara* in front of the town's main street, a boatman called James approached us in his rowboat.

"Captain, let me take your stern line and I'll tie it to shore," he said. "You won't have any trouble in a storm." We had been warned on our VHF about boat boys in Dominica, but wanting to please the locals we paid US$8 for James to row our line to a place on the shore where he tied it to a spot on a building backing on to the water. Because the weather was unsettled, we stayed on our boat that night. The backs of the buildings that lined the shore looked so dilapidated and depressing we felt like leaving there as soon as possible. It was obvious that we were in the wrong place to visit Dominica. The next day, we couldn't find James, who had tied our line very high up on a building. Poor Al. First he had to take down our dinghy, then motor into shore, and, since it was low tide, climb up part of the building to untie the line.

We were beginning to experience the best of our Cabo Rico on our sail to Martinique. The yacht handled the 25- to 30-knot winds with ease, and the 8- to 9-foot seas with our shortened sails. We anchored at Saint-Pierre, but in order to reach the town we had to climb over barriers across the damaged dock, which hadn't been repaired from Hurricane Lenny in 1999. Saint-Pierre had also been devastated by a volcano in 1903, killing 29,000 people. The story went that although the volcano was forecast, the town council was having an election and needed all the inhabitants there to vote them in again. The only building still standing from that time was the jail on the main street, and the only survivor a prisoner protected from the disaster by the stone structure of the jail.

My captain husband had quite a time trying to check into Martinique with the elusive customs man. After three tries, Al finally found him about to leave his office, although the hours stated at the door were 09:00 to 16:00. He quickly hurried Al up the stairs to his office where there was a pretty girl hanging about and wearing his official customs hat at a rakish angle. Official business was done in a hurry, and we were finally checked in. Oh, those French!

We made two more inconsequential stops while in Martinique, and a third stop in Le Marin, where there was a large yachting center and facilities for boat repairs and boat parts. The place was filled with French cruisers who seemed to be settled for the season. They socialized among themselves and had little to do with us, perhaps because I couldn't understand their fast French or make myself understood.

It took us only six hours to reach St. Lucia and Rodney Bay the next day. But finding that the winds were good and there was time to go further, we finally ended up in Marigot Bay in St. Lucia. It was a good choice for anchoring, well-protected and beautiful, surrounded by flowering trees. Settled at the end of the bay was a restaurant called JJ's which stayed opened most nights with loud music until 03:00. In spite of that, we stayed two nights. While we sat in our anchored boat – reading, eating a meal, or just resting – large tourist barges would motor by while their passengers took pictures of our boat. I felt like a specimen in a zoo. During the night, we slept easily under the stars, fresh breezes, and to the sound of the tree frogs chirping among the dense green forest of tropical trees.

South of us, and now part of the Windward Islands, were St. Vincent and the Grenadines. For a week, we explored these beautiful islands, a favourite playground for cruising yachts. On our way to St. Vincent, Al saw a huge body near our boat, which just happened to be a pilot whale. That was the first whale he had observed in the Caribbean. Unfortunately, I was making breakfast down below and missed it. How sad!

At St. Vincent, we anchored in a small inlet called Petit Byahaut. The place had mooring balls owned by a restaurant high up on a hill at the tip of the bay. We could pay for the mooring ball or use their restaurant, so we paid, not wanting to climb up from the beach. The snorkelling was good, according to my husband – angelfish, butterfly fish, gurnards, flounder, snapper, bluefin tuna, and parrot fish. How amazing, I thought; my snorkel was broken, and I only could see from our boat.

The next morning, *Solara* was surrounded by 10 fishermen who had thrown their large net in front of our moored boat. We couldn't move out of their way so enjoyed watching how they fished. Would they find all the various fish that Al had seen? First, two snorkelers would swim around looking for schools of fish. When they found fish, they would wave to the boat, and the fishermen would throw a very large net in the spot indicated by the snorkelers. The net was held upright by floats which the men pulled down to catch the fish underneath. When the men thought they had a net full of fish, they would haul it up to their boat. After an hour, all I could see in their net were a few silvery fish, which didn't look that great to me. All that work for a few fish!

We made a few more stops before Grenada – Bequia and Carriacou, where Al could check in at Hillsborough, the nearby town. Since the bay at Hillsborough seemed unfriendly and unappealing, we motored to Tyrrel Bay next door. There were many yachts there, more shops and restaurants, but again I noticed an unfriendly atmosphere, not something that I could describe, just a feeling. Perhaps it was the fact that they had also been hit by Hurricane Lenny. Carriacou had not yet recovered and was in the process of rebuilding their waterfront and shoreline. When Al took out our dinghy and drove around the bay, he ran over a covered broken object which made a small hole in the cover of the dinghy, causing a slow leak.

We finally reached Grenada, often called the Spice Island, and a very British one, but independent since 1974. Many cruisers stayed there during hurricane season since it was noted that the worst storms in the Caribbean wouldn't come that way.

St. George's was the main harbour, situated in a beautiful bay. The streets above the harbour climbed up and down, with winding alleyways lined with many shops and services. It was a colourful spectacle with houses painted blue, pink, and yellow, layered with red roofs of tile. The British flavour was everywhere, noticeably from the St. George's Church which played Westminster chimes on the hour, policemen that looked like British bobbies, and old colonial buildings. The yacht club in the harbour welcomed cruisers to their bar, and we were invited to a party celebrating a just-finished regatta.

But we needed to move to another location where it was quieter with cleaner water. Then the rains came, long and hard, day after day. We collected rainwater in our primitive fashion for washing clothes and my hair. Nothing like rainwater for hair! Prickly Bay was where we met all the permanent cruisers, whose activity was in full force. Parties, potlucks, celebrations of July 1 and July 4, and games like Mexican Train. It was the spot to be, and many boats appeared to have been anchored there forever. We were planning to stay at a marina called Secret Harbour that wouldn't be as much fun, but good for a daughter's visit with its beautiful pool high on a hill overlooking the dark blue waters of the Caribbean.

After six months of slogging through storms, trying to learn everything that needed to be learned about the boat, putting up with the occasional bad-tempered "captain," and making too many adjustments in my life, it was time for a visit home to see my new grandson. I made my arrangements in Grenada to fly home via Trinidad then onto Toronto. Al would sail our boat to Trinidad by himself, but first he would have a visit from our older daughter, Vicky, who worked in the film industry and was able to be with us on occasion. I felt better knowing she would be with him for two weeks and that she was a good cook and could maybe teach him how to prepare a few meals while he was alone. Before leaving, I made the mistake of saying to my husband that I wouldn't sail across the Pacific, but meet him in Tahiti. The consequences of that mistake lasted for months, and subsequently led to some disastrous decisions.

Going home brought my life in balance. Cruising took me away from family and our daughter, who was struggling with work and motherhood and needed more help than I could give her. I was actually glad to get back to the boat after three weeks, but happy to have seen our new grandson, a healthy and happy boy, and to visit with old friends and catch up on doctor's appointments. Al picked me up at the airport in Trinidad to take me to the Crews Inn marina.

"How was your sail to Trinidad?" I asked my husband on our way from the airport to the marina.

"Terrible," he said. "It was an overnight of 90 miles, so I wasn't able to sleep. The weather was bad, and when I arrived in the harbour the rain was so heavy I wasn't able to see where to go with the boat." I was beginning to regret the question.

"Well, you're here, thank goodness."

"If it wasn't for some very nice cruisers who helped me find our berth, it would have been much worse." His solo trip to Trinidad was mentioned numerous times, and he told our friends at home that Janet "jumped ship on me."

Crews Inn was a beautiful and well-run marina in Chaguaramas. It had a large pool, exercise room, laundry, and showers. I was always thankful that we had enough resources to frequently pick marinas that were comfortable and a pleasant diversion from the boat.

The cruising boat next to us in the marina was *Sojourner,* with Pete and Julie from Texas. Pete helped Al into our slip when it was raining so hard he couldn't see, and helped me with our ham radio connection to Winlink, which would give me access to proper email and weather, both vitally important. Pete was also well-versed in finding a cheap beer bar wherever he went. If Pete was around, word went out and the most popular drinking spot was where Pete established himself. He gathered people together and made friends wherever he went. We also met with *Guitar* again. We hadn't seen them since Jamaica. The Canadian boat *Heart of Oak* was also in Trinidad.

The cruising community there was a busy one, and I suspected that many cruisers stayed for the winter. The bay had boat services that handled just about all problems. Bridge and domino games were popular, shopping was good, and the pool fabulous for cooling off in the hot, humid climate. I could have stayed there forever. On the other hand, we were isolated from the Trinidadians, except for a wonderful and friendly taxi driver, Jesse, who took us to town for shopping and excursions. Outside the gate of the protected marina, robberies could happen. There was also an incident of a woman molested by a local just outside the gate. Poverty and crime lurked around every corner in Trinidad.

Jesse took a group of us to a western beach in Trinidad to see the leatherback turtles laying eggs, and to see other eggs ready to hatch. We had to go late at night as the baby turtles didn't go into the sea during the day. We were there to help these tiny creatures reach the water before shorebirds had them for supper. I could touch the huge female leatherback as she laid her eggs in a state of rapture. She was enormous with a soft, black, leather-like body weighing between 800 to

2,000 pounds. She laid about 100 eggs at a time! Only a very small percentage of the newly hatched babies would reach adulthood, and the ones who did would return to the same beach 25 years later, after exploring the ocean for thousands of miles. I could have stayed there all night picking up those tiny creatures, waddling on the dark sand to my white tennis shoes instead of the water because they shone so brightly in the full moon. We took another excursion on a boat tour through the Caroni Swamp where we saw the scarlet ibises and various other birds. The colourful ibises were beautiful against the deep blue sky as they flew back to their nests before nightfall.

Tragedy happened while we were in Trinidad. On September 11, a date remembered by all, we saw the planes destroying the twin towers in New York on TV and the terrible scene stayed in our minds no matter what we were doing. There were many Americans in Chaguaramas who were trying to come to grips with this, and a get-together later in the week was an attempt to comfort each other. Jesse had tears running down his usually happy face, but agreed to take a few of us on an excursion to visit a pottery factory and a Hindu temple. He kept the radio on and gave us the latest news. The security of the US took a decided turn after that tragedy, especially with border crossings and airport travel. The world would never be the same, but we went on our way determinedly, with the Panama Canal beckoning.

Before leaving Trinidad, Al had some needed boat service done, and we made an arrangement with a couple on a Canadian boat, *Stormy Petrel*, to join us on our next passage to Margarita Island, Venezuela, since the area between Trinidad and Venezuela was known to be subject to boardings and robberies. Crossing along the coasts of Venezuela, Colombia, and Panama had many problems which we had read about and heard on our radio. We chose that route in spite of its dangers in order to get to the Panama Canal.

PART 2

Across South America

CHAPTER 7

❧

Venezuela

Venezuela: the country of diverse cruising experiences, attempted robberies, and breathtaking inland excursions. It had it all. The Spaniards in the late 15th century called the land Venezuela, meaning "Little Venice," when they saw the local indigenous people living in *palafitos* (thatched huts on stilts).

After leaving the shelter of Chaguaramas in Trinidad, we stopped at Scotland Bay for fuel and met our companions on *Stormy Petrel*, Ken and Bonnie. They would sail with us to Los Testigos, beautiful islands off the coast of Venezuela. The evening sail went well, with peaceful seas and a bright shining half-moon as we sailed past the multitude of offshore oil rigs, and by early morning we had reached the little village at Isla Iguana. The anchorage sat in front of a lovely beach on a spit, which protected us from the waves on the other side. It was a peaceful spot with only us, boobies, and frigate birds, accompanied by the sound of the waves.

Margarita is known to tourists for its large hotels and isolated resorts. We got to know Margarita by its series of robberies. After sailing 50 miles to Porlamar Bay, we found an anchorage among many other boats. It didn't protect us from the constant waves entering the bay, although a second anchor at the stern helped. Vemasca and Marina Juan were services that competed for the cruisers' business. Juan took in laundry, provided showers for a price, and offered a visit to the supermarket three times a week. Juan also had a restaurant called Jaks which was a meeting place for boaters. Most of us came to Margarita to stock up on tax-free booze and supplies.

A disaster on our first visit to the supermarket put a stop to using Juan's free service. Having us wear special name plates and use ID gave Juan a commission from our total purchases, which were labelled and stamped by a security guard. Neither of us liked bureaucracy to that extent, but to top it all off I bumped into a display of whiskey and broke two bottles.

"You have to pay for those," yelled the grim woman who had brought us there.

A group of friendly cruisers had surrounded me and were definitely on my side in the matter.

"Don't listen to her," said one. "That display was ready to be knocked over." He was right. The store had made a pyramid of bottles which would have challenged the ancient Egyptian builders of Giza. The lady guide was running up and down frantically. Finally I ignored her and continued with my shopping.

"You won't come on my bus again," the grim lady said. I was glad to follow her orders.

Our own trip into town proved much better, as we could explore galleries and shop where and when we liked. We saw the Modern Art Gallery, displaying the famous Venezuelan artist Francisco Narvaez, who painted in the '20s and '30s in Paris. In Pompatar, we found an historic fort dating from the 18th century. We also sailed up the east coast of Margarita to Juan Griego on the north of the island and anchored in a bay just before the town. It was a lovely spot filled with pelicans diving for fish and with colourful fishing boats on shore after their early morning work. It was picturesque.

In the morning, we discovered that the beach was a popular spot for locals who rented Ski-Doos and proceeded to skim their craft around our boat just to take a look.

While in the anchorage, I managed to slip on the companionway and hit my chest on the hard teak galley cabinet. I cried out, "I can't move and it hurts to breathe." I was curled up on the floor, holding my chest.

"I think you've cracked a rib or two," Al replied anxiously after scurrying down to help. It seemed that way as the discomfort and pain lasted a long time. Sailing and living on a boat wasn't an easy life.

We scouted the town of Juan Griego a few times, but our dinghy motor was giving us a hard time. It wouldn't idle, and to leave a spot meant a quick rush away hoping nothing was in our path. Another job to be done in a proper marina!

When we got back to Porlamar, other cruisers said that we should pull up our dingy at night and lock it. Many cruisers had lost their dinghy motors while asleep. Apparently, the robbers were so clever that they would quietly swim out to a dinghy, break the lock, and let the dinghy quietly drop to the water, take the motor, and leave the dinghy to float away. There were at least eight motors that disappeared while we were in Margarita. They could have had our stubborn motor. The police nearby were no help, and usually slept through the night.

After a nice dinner on Dave and Di's boat, *Amoenitas*, we left the next morning, having had enough of Margarita.

The first settlement of Europeans was in Cubagua, in 1500, due to the pearl farming. The Spaniards had worked the native population like slaves. An earthquake and tidal wave destroyed Cubagua in 1541, but there were still remnants of the old village. After a perfectly glorious sail from Margarita, we found a peaceful anchorage in front of the dry desolate island, sheltered from the waves beyond. We took a walk along the sandy beach and over a salt flat in the desert-like atmosphere, thinking that no one could possibly live in the conditions we were experiencing. Suddenly, a mother with four small children met us on our way back to our boat. She was holding a sick child in her arms and asked if I had some medication for her child. The family went barefoot and wore very little clothing, and I could only guess what type of shelter she had. After hurrying to our boat with our dinghy, I was glad to bring back some aspirin for the child, some milk, and a large can of chicken meat that I thought she might like. We learned later that the families there lived very frugally, with no electricity, water, or supplies, except what the husband brought back from Margarita after selling his fish. It was evident that only a small percentage of Venezuelans lived the "good life," and most lived in poverty such as we encountered. Nevertheless, Al enjoyed the place, as anchored nearby was a French cruising boat with a young nude couple calmly doing their boat work.

We found a deep, quiet bay in Mochima National Park, our next anchorage, in a large sound of many small bays. It was peaceful and beautiful with its high hills and grazing goats, which called to us constantly. We were nervous, nevertheless, after hearing stories about muggings and robberies in the area. We anchored near one other boat from the US called *Jette*; the woman on board had been a dancer in New York some time ago. I felt more comfortable having them near. We stayed for three nights, and celebrated Canadian Thanksgiving with them. I found another can of chicken which could be fixed up with onions and other spices to make a reasonable dinner. It was like heaven: peaceful nights, quiet surroundings, and time to read my many books.

Leaving there, we passed many more small islands with rocky sides made of soft grey limestone, and dolphins playing and jumping around us as we sailed. It was a scene to remember, but it was time to go to a port to have *Solara's* hull cleaned of all the barnacles and other strange creatures that liked to live there.

Along the main coast of Venezuela was Puerto La Cruz, an upscale marina called Bahia Redonda with boat services. Our purpose in coming there was to have our boat taken out of the water for a paint job on the hull. Nearby was the lagoon development called El Morro, where the rich and famous had large white stucco homes flanked by pools and terraces overlooking the water. Although started in 1972, the development was still not finished. We had time to take a trip to a mountain town called Merida, a university town up in the Andes Mountains. It was important for us to get away while our boat was out of the water, sitting on a high cradle with no plumbing, water, or toilet, and air filled with dust and dirt in the 90-degree heat.

We took a flight from Barcelona, near our marina, to Merida on a small Beechcraft. Looking out the plane window, there was a wonderful view of the high peaks of the Andes through the clouds. Our plane landed on a tiny airstrip at 10,000 feet. I was glad the pilot was capable of making a landing which seemed very difficult.

Merida had a very important university called the University of the Andes. Many young students from the US came there to study Spanish. Consequently, there were many places to stay. The *posada* we chose was called Montana Azul, run by a friendly middle-aged woman who spoke only Spanish, which suited our purposes of practicing the language. It was clean and neat, with Spanish-tiled floors, and reasonably cheap. She filled her small house with brightly coloured flowers. Sunbeams slipped through the many windows enhancing the ambience, and all around colourful parrots sat in cages. I wondered if they spoke Spanish.

One day, we travelled up the mountain away from Merida with a guide, Gioia. The scenery was beautiful. Crops of many shades, growing in two directions up the mountainside, belonged to the native population, a mixture of Indian and Spanish. The ruddy complexion and high cheekbones reminded me of the Tibetan people I had seen in Lhasa, with their ability to live in high altitudes. I saw a farmer riding his small horse ascending the mountain with almost unbelievable control and speed.

There was a captive breeding program of Andean condors in the area. Most of the wild condors had disappeared, and we were told that only seven remained in the region. We saw a very large vulture with a wing span of 10 feet or more. The condor in the wild could fly up to 30,000 feet, an amazing height. This specimen was huge, with black feathers covering its body, a ruff of white feathers around the base of the neck, and a large red comb on the crown of its head. Andean vultures liked to scavenge for large carcasses such as cattle and sheep. They were a threat to farmers and had almost been eliminated in Venezuela

I loved Merida. We walked around town with its young and enthusiastic university crowd, savoured the spicy food, and took in a noon-hour symphony concert with a Spanish theme, playing music by Manuel de Falla and Caprezio Espanol by Shostakovich. On one of our last excursions in Merida, we took the highest cable car in the world. It rose for four stations up to 16,000 feet. The view from the cable car was spectacular. We could see far across the high snow-capped Andes and down to the town of Merida, which became smaller and smaller as we rose. Merida spread out in the valley surrounded by high mountains like a patchwork quilt topped by the high steeple of the cathedral. It was difficult to leave that heavenly environment, but go we must. Our boat was calling.

Cruisers will tell you that the worst part of sailing is having the boat out of the water on a stand, and climbing a steep ladder if you want to be on your boat while work is being done, either by the captain and crew or hired labour. We tried this type of living for a few days, but one night I had to visit the bathroom, at least 10 minutes away from our boat. I didn't wake Al, and quietly slipped down the iron ladder and proceeded to walk quickly across the dirty yard. Suddenly, I was alarmed by growling, and then loud angry barking. Oh, no, I thought, the security dogs were loose and ready to attack. After standing quietly, and listening close-ly, I finally determined they were in their enclosure, and proceeded on. Nevertheless, I was scared, and next time would pee in a bucket during the night if needed.

Because of that experience in the yard, we decided to take a short trip to Gran Sabana in the southeast corner of the country, bordering Brazil and Guyana. Gran Sabana covered an area of 35,000 square miles and was only inhabited by Pemon Indians. It was also dominated by gigantic, flat-topped mountains called *tepuis*, which could be seen for miles. I was anxious to see this very beautiful, mystic, and empty savannah filled with thundering waterfalls.

We had to take an overnight bus from our marina to St. Helena, with one stop to change buses. Fortunately, we took a sleeping bag as we were told that the bus would be freezing from the AC. It was 05:00 when we arrived in St. Helena, and Roberto, our guide, soon met us with his 1980s Toyota four-wheeled vehicle. Although the car was temperamental, we were glad that it could take us on otherwise impossible roads. Roberto's English was good, and while driving he began extolling the virtues of Chavez, who had come to power in 1998. There was no doubt that he leaned toward the communist doctrine and its social benefits. He also believed in UFOs, and constantly told us to watch for them.

Our first excursion on a terribly dusty road was to see Salto Jaspe, small falls running down through beautiful, flat rock of red, orange, and yellow jasper. We were able to go under the falls for a refreshing swim. We had planned to have lunch in a small town called San Francisco, but the restaurant owner had been killed with her two children in a car accident the night before, and the whole town was closed in mourning. Roberto drove further along to a place situated by other beautiful falls to have lunch. We could walk up the nearby hill and view the full spectacle around us. I saw those wonderful and interesting leaf ants which carried their leaves to the nest in marching order.

"Stop guys!" I called. "I want to watch these marvellous ants." They were carrying large pieces of leaves much bigger than their own bodies. "I'm going to put down a piece of leaf and see what they do."

You could tell that the ants came in different sizes: larger ones were carrying leaves, and smaller ones appeared to be protecting the carriers from a pesky fly trying to lay its eggs on the ants' heads.

"Look," I said, pointing. "This ant has just picked up my leaf."

My husband and Roberto finally came to look since I wasn't going anywhere. I could have stayed much longer to find out where my leaf was going, but the men wanted to move on. There was so much to see and do in that park.

The night was spent in one of the "camps" run by an Indian family with comfortable beds and adjoining bathrooms. After breakfast, Roberto took us to spectacular falls called Salto Chinak Meru, which required a boat trip to the top and a full three-hour walk to the bottom, continuing along the river's edge to a private pool where we could dip under the falls. After walking back up to the top, we had lunch at the next village.

Our next night was spent at Chivaton, the highest point of land (4855 feet) on the savannah. It was a beautiful spot, with many flowers planted by the owners. We shared breakfast with their pet parrots and macaws, which flew around in the wild, landing on our shoulders and trying to eat our breakfast.

After breakfast, Roberto drove us to a remote town called Kavanayen, established by Franciscan monks and built in stone by the Indians. After the village was developed, the monks built a large monastery and church. It was in a beautiful setting but very remote, and serviced by a large generator, a small airstrip, and communal road transportation. An oil company building had been set up for conferences and retreats. The Venezuelan president also had his retreat there, overlooking the wide valley. One of the monks, who had visited a small Franciscan monastery in British Columbia, was interested in talking to us, not having visitors very often.

The next day, Roberto drove us to our last hotel called Ya Koo, luxurious in comparison to the other places we had been. After a wonderful breakfast of many fresh local fruits and breads, Roberto drove us out of the park on a road that would take us to the beginning of a trail up a local mountain. It was a breathtaking 90 minutes to reach the top, but the view was spectacular, looking over the expanse of the Brazilian Amazon valley. The local guide hurried us along, directing us up and down, and seemed to be glad to be finished with the job. After the hike, we headed back to Ya Koo for a delicious dinner of stuffed chicken breast, tomatoes and cucumbers, rice, fried eggplant, and fruit custard. A wonderful ending to a most fantastic trip before heading back to our boat on the overnight bus.

It was another uncomfortable, cold ride. At a designated checkpoint, everyone was told to get off and show their ID. As we were comfortably settled under our sleeping bag, we stayed on under the assumption that all the passengers were local and that the checkpoint was to look for Colombian people sneaking over the border or others bringing back contraband. The police didn't bother us, but when the passengers returned to the bus there had been many left behind.

Another bus trip in the morning brought us back to our marina at 13:00. The heat of the boatyard after our wonderful trip was oppressive, but the CMO Yard Company was finished with the job on our boat, which now could be put in the water. With our provisioning finished, water and diesel tanks filled, we were ready to leave. Even the dinghy motor was working for now. We left the boatyard and set sail for Tortuga.

Isla La Borracha was the place to stop on the way to Tortuga, a further 50 miles to the west. It was quiet and peaceful, with no dust or dirt. We shared the anchorage with a catamaran filled with six Swiss cruisers, who proceeded to stare intensely at our boat. Did they want us to leave? No way. We were determined to have a restful night.

The island and cays across the northern coast of Venezuela were a beautiful mixture of tropical breezes, clean, white, sandy beaches, turquoise waters, and anchorages sheltered from the harsh reality of the stormy Caribbean to the north. Wealthier Venezuelans used this area as their playground as they could powerboat across from the mainland in no time. Tortuga was named for the numerous turtles discovered by Amerigo Vespucci in 1499, but apparently they had been a good food source as they had all disappeared.

Our water-maker was on the fritz, as usual, which was unfortunate as our next few stops would be in very dry areas. Our next stop, Los Roques, was 90 nautical miles away from Tortuga. That meant an overnighter, but we expected to make good time, until later, when the waves rose to 8 feet.

We usually shortened our sails before dark for an overnight passage, but when it got rougher, I said anxiously, "Couldn't we put in another reef?" Al got out of his warm bed to help as it was hard to do in the dark. He always was good that way, making me feel secure.

Our trip took 17 hours, and our watches of only two and a half hours each made us very tired by the time we reached the anchorage.

We decided to stay in Gran Roque for a couple of days to rest. Unfortunately, our quiet lagoon became filled with tourists from the mainland. We had windsurfers, kitesurfers (the first we had seen), an ultralite, and a DC-3 airplane from the 1940s. It couldn't have been any worse. We decided to move.

The second anchorage, Sarqui, was a better choice and closer to our next destination. We faced a long, sandy beach anchored on the edge of a coral reef. There were many birds, such as frigate and boobies, which I could identify, plus others. The warm breezes kept us free from insects, but we were also protected from the turbulent seas beyond. For two days, we could enjoy snorkelling and swimming in the warm water around us. It was like paradise. There were four French boats there, which told us it was a good place to stay, as the French seemed to know where to go.

Just 35 miles west of Los Roques was Los Aves ("The Birds"), a low archipelago north of the Venezuela coast. It was a haven for boobies, frigates, and pelicans. They flew all around our boat and darkened the sky with their antics, swooping and swirling in all directions. Once at anchor, I watched the frigate birds ganging up on the smaller boobies; I couldn't tell why.

Later in the afternoon, a Norwegian boat arrived and had difficulty anchoring as the light was fading and the shoals were hard to see. It helped them to see our boat safely anchored. Later, in Bonaire, we talked to the captain who told us that his dinghy had been stolen in Tortuga, and therefore he couldn't do any snorkelling or diving through those wonderful islands. We also heard a boat called *Hallelujah* on our radio calling a fellow boater who hadn't arrived for a meeting. It was a Canadian boat from Ottawa. Not long after, *Hallelujah* had a terrible disaster in a storm off Colombia.

I was starting to open our stored cans, used our last four slices of bread, and opened boxed milk. I couldn't make bread in the oven due to the propane problem, but since the microwave worked I could make a meal. We were saving power and usually used the microwave as a storage cupboard. We didn't stay in Los Aves any longer, as we were having trouble with our stove, propane tank, and water-maker and felt that there would be service in Bonaire or Curacao. Given the fact that we had a new boat, new equipment, and new everything, you had to wonder why so many repairs were needed.

CHAPTER 8

❧

The Dutch Antilles
(ARUBA, CURACAO, AND BONAIRE)

The ABC ISLANDS are in the southwest part of the Caribbean. Many cruisers sailed to these protected Dutch islands from the north or from Trinidad and skipped the passage across the unknown and often precarious coastline of Venezuela and Colombia. But we would continue to follow the coastline to avoid the constant stormy conditions in that part of the Caribbean after stopping at Bonaire, Aruba, and Curacao.

I loved the neat and orderly ambience of Curacao, the tourist diving attraction of Bonaire, and the sparkling look of Aruba, the "Las Vegas of the Caribbean." Supplies were easy to obtain and internet service and ATM machines available.

We passed the southeast point of Bonaire and for two hours sailed along the leeside of the island, noting a large salt production plant and the long sandy beach where scuba diving was available. After getting work done on our propane tank, a leaky boat shaft, and finding someone to look at our water-maker, we left the Harbour Village Marina and anchored out on a mooring ball for the rest of our stay.

Leaving the marina, Al had a problem with our dinghy motor as he tried to motor 2 miles to the town of Kralendijk to check in with our boat papers. Suddenly, the motor conked out and he began drifting out to sea. Desperately, he grabbed an anchored boat, which happened to be the last one he could catch, and managed to fix the motor and get it started again. After he'd checked in and got back to our boat, I got the whole story. It had been a very scary incident, and he was relieved and thankful that he could fix the temperamental motor. I was relieved that he hadn't drifted out to sea.

It was American Thanksgiving while we were in Bonaire, and the American cruisers had planned a wonderful dinner at a local restaurant called Richard's. For $2, we had a delicious meal of turkey, vegetables, potatoes, and pumpkin pie. The Americans were always very generous, helpful, and welcoming to cruisers, no matter where they were from. On many occasions we were the beneficial recipients of this generosity. I enjoyed meeting cruisers from places such as South Africa and Europe. It was good to talk to other people again. We had been alone across the barren islands of Venezuela for a few weeks, and I needed the camaraderie and exchange of ideas, especially from women. My husband didn't seem to understand this need, or at least that was my observation.

After a 35-mile rocky sail, due to wind and sail direction, we entered Curacao and the anchorage at Spanish Water. It was a bus ride into Willemstad, the capital of the Netherlands Antilles, to check in to customs and immigration.

The town of Willemstad showed its marvellous historical architecture of colourful houses and buildings. We read in a tourist brochure that *by royal decree, you (and your neighbours) are commanded to repaint your houses immediately – any colour at all but white.* The hues of the various buildings went from *a lemony yellow with mango accents, cerulean blue accented with kiwi trim or an orange-poppy colour of the Dutch countryside.* A living architectural palette was created in the capital city. The pot-shaped pediments, gabled windows, intricate rococo detailing, and one-of-a-kind front doors became proprietary ancestral legacies.

Our trip to the immigration office was most unique. Instead of the cursory attitude of most officers, we were welcomed to have tea and a chat before the papers were filled out. Apparently, the man had spent time in Canada many years ago.

"I have a brother/sister/cousin who lives in Toronto (Mississauga usually). Would you know him/her?" We would be asked this question in almost every country we visited.

Work on our water-maker took time, and so did my shopping at the supermarket. Filling our boat with new purchases took at least two hours. Everything had to be inventoried, sterilized, and stored in the many areas of the boat; it was a most important part of cruising. Out went the old milk and mayonnaise from Cuba.

We saw old friends Ken and Nancy from *To the Moon,* and an American couple Lynn and Ron on *Zephyr,* going straight to the San Blas Islands from there. Lynn told me that she and Ron took six-hour shifts while sailing, and that she made bread while on watch. I couldn't do that, but I was impressed. Four of us decided to anchor further north on Curacao to give us a good run to Aruba the next day. We would catch up later in Cartagena before Christmas. Following the coast of Colombia instead of going straight, we hoped that the weather would treat us right and that we wouldn't be boarded by pirates.

"The sky is getting really dark," I said as we were sailing toward Aruba. *To the Moon* was within sight of our boat, but didn't seem to be aware of the ominous colour of the sky.

"I think the storm is following us," Al replied.

All of a sudden, the worst squall we had yet to encounter hit us from behind. The winds went up to 38 knots and the rain filled our cockpit like buckets of water pouring into a basin. The water ran down the companionway before we could close the hatch. I looked frantically around to see what could be done, but in a few minutes the squall was over. Unfortunately, the water disabled all our instruments in front of the steering wheel. This meant we had no depth finder, no auto-helm, no compass, and no chart plotter. The depth finder was the most important for our next stop in order to anchor off the Aruba beach.

"I can navigate with our maps in the meantime," Al said. "We'll be just like the sailors of long ago." He had taken several courses in navigation and I trusted his expertise. "I'll call the B&G Company in Florida once we're anchored in Aruba, and see what help they can give us."

In the meantime, we self-steered *Solara* into the night and arrived mid-afternoon in front of the beach of Aruba. Ken, who had been contacted, was there to help us find the proper depth to anchor our boat. I still couldn't get over the speed of the squall and how quickly it disabled our instruments. The B&G man talked Al through a temporary fix. If Al disconnected the depth sounder, which was completely disabled, the other instruments would work, the man said over the phone. When that was done, we would have to be very careful when anchoring until we could order a new depth sounder in Cartagena.

Los Monjes was a pile of rocks no bigger than a New York City block. We decided to break our passage to Colombia and stop at that very barren and desolate outpost diligently manned by a few Venezuelan coast guards protecting its territory. We started to get calls on our radio when we were many miles away.

"What is the name of your vessel?" We were asked in Spanish. "Where are you going? Give us your coordinates. What country are you registered under?"

These questions were repeated off and on, and we tried to answer them in Spanish until we were suddenly looking at the gap where our boat would enter. It was a difficult manoeuvre between two monstrous rocks with a thick cable fastened across the water to the other side. The bay was about 150 feet across and 65 feet deep, and we had to tie up to a rope attached to the cable and pray that the rope was strong enough to keep us secure from the wind and high waves coming in. As we attached ourselves, our spinnaker pole nearly knocked over the young men sitting beside the tire-edged pier who had come down to board our boat.

"Watch out," shouted Al. They scampered out of the way just in time.

Despite our neglectful entrance, the coast guards were very friendly and welcoming, and checked us into Venezuela. We declined their invitation to visit the lighthouse, as we were planning to leave very early in the morning. I noticed one man jogging with his dog from one large rock to the top of the other rocky elevation. What would a man have to do to be sent to that faraway place in the middle of nowhere? Insubordination? Neglect of duty?

Midnight, and my husband wanted to leave in the dark. Setting the sails, avoiding the large rocks at Los Monjes, and navigating in the correct direction was hard enough, but in the dark it was doubly difficult, especially with the 20- to 30-knot winds and 8-foot seas we were having. Fortunately, we were going downwind, and arrived at Cabo de la Vela, Colombia, at noon the next day.

CHAPTER 9

Colombia

CRUISERS READ A small magazine called *Seven Seas Cruising*. In the monthly booklet, cruisers write about their experiences and offer suggested routes or places to stop. This was where we had read about sailing along the coast of Colombia. This interested me as we could stop each night yet work our way to Cartagena. The only problem with using someone else's suggestion and waypoints (places where we could stop) was that they were given by an unknown person who could have made mistakes. The other problem with the route was that we were going into unsafe territory and unsettled seas. Nevertheless, I wanted to go this way to avoid the long route and unknown waters from the ABC islands. I still didn't like the overnight passages.

We began to hop from place to place along the Colombian coast, starting with Cabo de la Vela, a very windy, wide bay, as suggested by its name. We eyeballed our way among the fishing nets which were strung between their handmade buoys. Not having a depth sounder then, we had to guess where we could anchor. We were not disturbed except for one fisherman who asked if he could fill his water jug. In the early morning, three boats arrived that appeared to be travelling together: one German and two Dutch. I felt that they were smart to be in a group, while we were sitting ducks for any robbers.

The next night, among many bolts of lightning which brightened up the sky above us, we sailed 120 miles west to a place called Five Bays. It was a lovely night and with our sails out full – main on one side and the stay sail on the spinnaker pole – we had a comfortable all-night sail, although we had to avoid a large oil platform and oil rig. Just above these bays hovered high mountains, causing tricky winds that came whirling down to the water below.

We chose the third bay, which we had read was the most popular. It was a very desolate area with few signs of habitation. For safety's sake, since we were the only boat in the bay, we put out our flare guns, pepper spray, and a horn in case we had "visitors." None of those things would do us any good, as robbers usually carried guns, but we felt a little safer. We then anchored our boat securely while the winds twirled around our rigging, causing our boat to circle all night.

It was getting close to Christmas and I wanted to send a message to my family in Toronto who were having their annual gathering. It was always a fun party, with lots of delicious food, good discussions, and the chance to see how much the younger members of my extended family had grown. I tried to call on our satellite phone just to say a quick hello. Unfortunately, so many wanted to talk that confusion reigned. Al kept saying, "That's another $1.50 each minute you talk." I was finally forced to say goodbye. Oh, how I missed them. It would be two years before I was home again.

We had a good rest the next day and I checked in with Mississauga Net to inform them of our whereabouts since we were alone. As we twirled around in our anchorage all day, I could see a number of small houses at the far end, perhaps a village. The odd small boat motored past but didn't bother us. That didn't mean I wasn't tense and nervous being in Colombia after hearing stories of cruiser robberies. The three boats that we had seen before in Cabo de la Vela passed the opening of our bay but didn't come in.

It was a wild ride to our next stop, Rodadero. The winds, fortunately on our stern, were up to 30 to 40 knots, but using only our small stay sail we could handle the weather. Rodadero Beach was our only stop in front of a town. It was full of local Colombians on their two-week vacation. There were fancy hotels on shore surrounded by shops selling tourist "junk," and restaurants that looked good enough to suit my appetite for off-boat eating.

Robert, an American cruiser from California wearing dirty, dingy shorts topped by a crumpled T-shirt, came by on his dinghy to say hello. He invited us to come on his boat nearby, but we declined, perhaps thinking that it might be as unkempt as his hair – long, sun-bleached tendrils falling down his back, but very few wisps at the top. He had a Colombian girlfriend and a wife in the US, a typical single-hander sailor. Nevertheless, he very nicely took us to shore to do some errands. We walked around among many staring Colombians; I imagine very few North Americans took their vacation in Rodadero. Some of the locals tried to practice their English on us with little success.

There was a boat taxi service that we could use since we didn't want to take down our dinghy. It was a dilapidated, tin-roofed, motorized contraption like an Indian tuk tuk on the water. We hailed one from our boat and manoeuvred ourselves onto the seats. It was necessary to crunch down onto the hard wooden seats and for $2 we got a ride almost to the beach, but then had to wade in from there.

It was an interesting experience being in Rodadero, but we felt that our stay was not very welcome as the officials came around soon after we returned from dinner in town and told us we had to leave as soon as possible, since we hadn't checked in.

"We're leaving tonight, but could we stay a few more hours?" Al asked the port captain politely in broken Spanish. He didn't look as imposing as the customs official.

"OK," said the captain indignantly. "But we don't want to see you in the morning."

Although they had every right to send us away after a day, we felt like we had committed a grave error. Apparently, the three foreign boats we saw off and on along the coast had been sent away immediately by these two officials before they approached our boat.

"It was either my good manners or our grey hairs that did the trick," laughed Al.

At 02:00, we left Rodadero for the last part of our Colombian journey.

On our way to Cartagena, we had to cross the mouth of the infamous Rio Magdalena where we would encounter strong turbulence and rough seas accompanied by logs and debris that came down with the current of this very large river. I anticipated this part nervously. We had winds of 30 to 40 knots and rolling seas on a downwind sail as we looked carefully for logs and ships nearby. The muddy waters from the river tossed *Solara* around, and the wild spray coming off the waves flew into the cockpit continually for two hours.

"I can't take much more of this," I shouted impatiently over the noise of the wind and waves. "It looks like you're enjoying this experience, so I'm going below."

It was true. There was my husband with a wide grin on his face as he controlled the boat through the water as he would in a storm. I spent the rest of the time curled on the sofa below and wondered how long it would be before we got to Cartagena.

I was grateful to Dave on *Amoenitas,* whom we had met off and on the last few months, or we might have hit the cement pier which had been erected at our last anchorage. It had not been recorded in the *Seven Seas* article we were following. Dave and Di, from England, had helped us many times with their extensive boat knowledge, and were a wonderful example of experienced British sailors. Dave, who travelled this way just before us, had sent us the proper waypoints to enter behind the pier and away from the heavy seas, which beat constantly against the breakwater.

"Oh my God," yelled Al after we had anchored. "One of those three boats that we saw is heading right for the cement pier. I must get them on the VHS and tell them to turn back." Just in time, the boat quickly veered away, and with the new waypoints was able to join us behind the breakwater. We never heard about any more mishaps, except that the anchorage became known to the locals and robberies began to take place.

I was glad that the trip across the Colombia coast was almost over. Thank goodness the winds were much lighter closer to Cartagena. Ken on *To the Moon* called us on our VHS to let us know that he would be at the opening of the submerged wall of Bocagrande, where we would enter the bay into the city. Since we had no depth gauge we needed his guidance, as there was only one place for a boat our size, with a 6-foot hull, to go through. As well, he had made reservations at the marina Club de Pesca for the month, which was lucky for us as the marina was completely full when we arrived. I would never forget how our cruising friends helped us through those tangles on our passage to Cartagena. We were very lucky.

I loved Cartagena. It was friendly, safe, and beautifully decorated for the Christmas season. Local tourists were enjoying themselves, riding horse carriages in groups and touring the city. The restaurants served delicious meals for a modest price, and we could explore this dazzling place, full of history and old architecture. One night we had Argentinean beef tenderloin for only $10 each. As we overlooked the city square, I saw roving musicians and entertainers, and to complete the picture there was a newly married couple just coming out of a church while tourists clapped spontaneously.

Cartagena still retained much of its sturdy stone walls surrounding the old town. One couldn't visit here without learning about Don Blas de Lezo. As a young soldier in several battles for Spain, he lost a leg, an eye, and his right arm. In spite of that, he remained a tenacious and courageous commander, and was sent in 1740 to Cartagena to help defend the city from the British. There were fewer than 2,500 Spaniards against the British, who were in 186 ships with about 2,400 men waiting beyond the walls to get orders to go ashore. The numerous forts guarding the city with their strong firepower, as well as widespread sickness among the troops, kept the British at bay. After several weeks with many losses, it was the British, under Admiral Vernon, who had to retreat back to England.

I left Cartagena with a brass engraved plaque which came from a Collingwood ship broken up somewhere in the Caribbean for its parts. A museum-type store with a naval twist had it sitting on a shelf.

"Look Al," I almost shouted. "There's a piece of an old Collingwood ship!"

"Shh," my husband quietly replied. "You can't negotiate a price now that the owner sees that you really want it." That was a lawyer for you, even a retired one.

Of course, he was right. I paid the full price, but gladly. On my next return home to Collingwood I gave it to the museum, and found that it had come from a 1952 cargo ship that had worked in Canadian waters.

Unfortunately, our stay in Cartagena finally came to an end. We had a new depth sounder, which was delivered by courier, went to a few parties held by cruisers, and celebrated Christmas and New Year's. My birthday came and went without any fanfare. On New Year's Eve, the city had a wonderful display of fireworks just beyond our marina, lighting up the exquisite old buildings, while behind them was a full silvery moon. It was a beautiful impression that remained with me for a long time.

It was now 2002. We had been sailing for one year and soon we would be leaving the Caribbean much stronger, wiser, and more confident that we could go beyond the comfort of North America.

CHAPTER 10

San Blas Islands

LEAVING CARTAGENA MEANT motoring out of the large harbour where we had been staying to a southwest exit called Bocachica. The winds were light, and we could sail comfortably in the 10- to 15-knot winds. It always took a while for me to feel my sea legs again after being on land for a week. Basically, I was a "landlubber" at heart.

Just off Colombia were the Rosario Islands where we spent our first night. The Rosario Islands and San Blas Islands of Panama were interesting places to visit before our final stop in the Caribbean, the Panama Canal.

While in the Rosario Islands, a fisherman motored over to our boat and offered a fresh crab for me to cook, but I declined, not being very adept at handling the huge claws. For US$15, he took it away and soon presented it to us well cooked and cracked, on a fancy plate surrounded by fresh limes. We had a lunch fit for royalty, with a brisk, cold white wine, garlic butter, and the delicious crab. Hey, how often could one eat a fresh crab in such a wonderful Caribbean atmosphere?

Our anchorage was apparently very close to a hotel, and powerboats with Colombian tourists whizzed by us constantly, waving friendly greetings, as we sat relaxing in *Solara's* cockpit after lunch.

It was supposed to be a two-day sail to the San Blas Islands where the Kuna Indians maintained an independent living, but under the protection of Panama. They lived a very primitive life as far as we could see, using the rivers and waterways for fishing and transportation, and the mainland for hunting and gathering. We sailed so quickly that Al had to shorten our sails in order not to approach the islands in the dark. The light of day was needed to see the various hues of the water which marked the different depths, and to distinguish between shoals and coral. I stood at the bow where the visibility was best, and told Al what to avoid and which way to turn the boat. Dark and murky colour marked the shoals, and the emerald green and brilliant blue of the clear and deeper water contrasted significantly. We motored behind the reefs, which sheltered us from the turbulence of the open water, and anchored.

The Kuna women, dressed in colourful embroidered tops and wrap-around skirts, quickly approached our boat in their primitive dugout canoes. There was no doubt that they saw us coming and were ready to sell their *mulas* – colourful, handmade materials that were popular with tourists. The chief of the district arrived soon after the women in his own dugout with a young boy beside him.

"You must pay $5 to stay here," he said with authority. We gladly gave him the money, but he continued. "I need some sugar and rice."

I'm not sure he said "please," but we gave him what we could. It was obvious that the Kuna men had complete command of the village and among the cruisers there.

Throughout our stay, we were never without women and children surrounding our boat. The women had gold rings in their noses and ears, breastplates made of some sort of metal, and intricate beadwork on their arms and legs. I also saw some with painted faces. The children were numerous, friendly, and constantly asking my name in broken English. One woman insisted on wrapping a colourful band of beads on my arm, which took a very long time to complete, although it didn't make me look at all like a Kuna. We were also offered bread made from coconut flour and baked in a primitive oven. The bread had a very agreeable, smoky flavour.

The various palm-treed islands were beautiful and peaceful as we anchored at one and another. We finally caught up to Dave and Di, our English friends. Dave had heard about our dinghy motor problems, which had frustrated us for months. He came over to our boat the next day, took the carburetor apart, cleaned the float, and got the engine working again. We watched carefully as he worked, like interns in an operating theatre, and made sure we would never forget the procedure. From then on, the engine worked beautifully. I was grateful to Dave forever.

We made two more anchoring stops before leaving the San Blas Islands. Outside these sheltered bays, the waves continued to beat against the reefs, forming high, foaming spouts. It was obvious that the Caribbean Sea was in turmoil and that it would be best for us to stay until it calmed down for our passage to Panama. Some of the other cruisers had gathered in a popular place called East Holandes where there was a sandy beach, a shore fireplace, and an old upside down boat used as a table for potluck parties. We were encouraged to anchor there but found no room amongst the other boats. It would have been fun for a few days, as I always liked to party. Oh well!

We were alone again, but had a few more quiet days, reading, swimming, and sleeping. We were as one. Each day, I realized that our dependence on each other was growing. Neither one of us would want to handle the work of sailing *Solara* alone, or for that matter living on the boat by ourselves. We each had separate jobs, yet together we blended. But it was the next incident that convinced me of my vulnerability.

When it was time to leave that beautiful place for good, Al went forward to work the windlass motor that pulled up the large anchor. The windlass also had a problem, and the last 20 feet or more of chain had to be pulled up by hand. As he pulled up the last few feet of the heavy chain, I motored out carefully to avoid the reefs. He then came back to the cockpit to take over, but before he got there he fainted, collapsing on the narrow deck and almost falling into the water.

"Al," I cried. "Can you hear me?"

I got no reply and he was like a dead weight at my feet. I tried to pull him into the cockpit. I put the motor in neutral, and at the same time had to watch where we were heading – we were surrounded by reefs and shallow sandy spits. He was unconscious and scaring me. His eyes rolled back and all I saw were the whites.

"Wake up!" I implored, with no success. Thank goodness I was now familiar with our boat, and proceeded to continue out of the bay with some trepidation, having had no responsibility of running the boat by myself. Whether he was suffering from low blood pressure I couldn't tell, but I knew that he had a tendency to faint once in a while. *Why did he have to do it right now?* Of course, I didn't ask him that question. Eventually, he recovered enough to help me unfurl a reduced sail, and I could then make it to the last island while he rested.

I was feeling really depressed after that fainting incident, which happened again the next morning in the anchorage. Everything had been going so well, and now that I had decided to make the journey across I was looking forward to reaching the Pacific. The prediction for the weather over the next few days called for higher winds and seas, which meant we should leave the San Blas Islands as soon as possible. It was near the end of January, and we had been there for nearly a month.

The next day, everything went well for our departure. Al seemed his buoyant self again, and reassured me that it was time to go. It was a long sail in brisk winds toward Portobelo, which sat in a deep bay just before Colon, Panama. There was a large historic fort across from the town for defence from the English. Sir Francis Drake attacked the fort for the treasures he believed were stored there before they could be shipped back to Spain. After a long career in piracy, buccaneering, and exploration, Drake was laid in a metal coffin and dropped in the ocean just outside Portobelo. At least, that was the story.

We were invited for a drink on an Italian boat owned by a young couple hoping to find work in Australia. She served homemade focaccia bread.

"This is delicious," I said, after taking a good-sized bite. "Perhaps I can have the recipe." She was happy to do that, but I never could duplicate the wonderful bread she made as long as my oven was on the fritz.

"We're looking forward to doing some duty-free shopping in Colon," Al ventured. "What about yourselves?"

"We loaded up on wine in Margarita," her husband said. "We have found places for 100 bottles of Italian wine to take us across the Pacific."

Gosh! It was hard to respond to that, but we wished them luck in Australia.

CHAPTER 11

❀

Panama

WE APPROACHED THE Panama Canal and a large anchorage called the "flats," where we encountered at least 50 boats anchored on the muddy bottom. We heard the jingle of their rigging, and saw their masts waving to and fro from the windblown waves which crossed the open dirty water of the anchorage. We were all preparing to cross the canal, and didn't want to be in that windswept place for long. Just beyond the tangle of boats, I could see the beginning of the Panama Canal, the first chamber, and the railroad track on either side for the special cars that followed each boat as it went through.

In 1902, Theodore Roosevelt convinced Congress to take over the unfinished attempt by the French to build a canal across the isthmus. By siding with Panama to separate from Colombia, and helping in their independence, the US was able to take control of the Canal Zone, building the canal between 1904 and 1914. According to a treaty, the US turned over the Panama Canal to the Panamanian authorities at the end of 1999.

Bouncing over the waves, a long dinghy ride away we could reach the Panama Yacht Club's showers, restaurant, and facilities. From there, we could take transportation to the shopping in Colon, and the duty-free store selling wines and liquor for a very cheap price. I bought 12 bottles of Tanqueray gin for only $70, 12 German wines for $30, and 12 Chilean wines for $20-plus. Al made his own choices. This supply would last us for many months and across the Pacific, although we didn't plan to drink our way to French Polynesia.

As we sat on the "flats" for a few days, we saw a wreck of a boat approaching. It was *Hallelujah*, the Canadian boat from Ottawa that we heard on the VHF back in Los Aves, calling for their friends. Everything on top of their boat was gone: the mast, the rigging, the sails, and the stanchions (poles around the deck that supported the wires and protected anyone from falling overboard). Everything was gone! When Al talked to Mike, the husband, he heard a terrible story. On their way there, they encountered the bad weather we noticed off the coast of Colombia. On a sea with waves of more than 10 feet, their boat had suddenly turtled, end to end. The bow went down a high wave and the boat went upside down, tearing everything from the deck. Fortunately the family – father, mother, and two children – were in the cabin with all openings shut tightly. Mike was absolutely shaken when he spoke to Al, but his wife, Kim, was determined to cross the Pacific. She was a strong woman, and began the task of ordering all the necessary parts and equipment that needed to be replaced. At the Pedro Miguel Yacht Club in the canal, Mike learned to put the boat together again.

It took two weeks to prepare our passage through the canal. First, we had to arrange a pilot who would be available. The cost would depend on the length, width, and weight of our boat, which was measured very carefully by an ad measurer who would approve our transit. Next, we had to line the outside of our boat with large tires wrapped in garbage bags to protect the outside from damage. These were rented, as were the very long lines (ropes) that would be used. We needed extra crew who would mind the lines coming down from the sides of the canal. When we rose, the lines had to be shortened, and then lengthened when our boat went down. The up and down was caused by water coming in and out of the chambers as we went through the rise and fall of the water. It was important that the lines were kept tight, or we would be in danger of tipping over with the turbulence from any large freighter that would be in the same chamber with us.

Al had crewed on one boat to get the experience through the canal, and found a crew for *Solara* when it was our turn. We had Dave from New Zealand, Philippe from France, Sechuk from Turkey, plus the son of a Panamanian taxi driver. My job was to feed and water seven of us for the day.

It was exciting to know that we would soon be on the Pacific Ocean. It was now February and more than one year since we had left Canada. I could just guess how Vasco Nunez de Balboa felt in 1513 when he crossed the isthmus and became the first European to see the Pacific. "*Dios mio, otro oceano!*" he could have said. At least he must have been just as thrilled as I was.

On the chosen day, we were up at 04:30 to welcome the pilot on board. We were at first scheduled to tie up with a large American power-boat which had three levels and a railing that came out beyond its deck, and would likely destroy our stanchions and rigging. The day before departure, we met with the loud-mouthed American "captain" of this large fishing boat, who looked at our yacht in disgust and said in a sarcastic voice, "I refuse to tie up with this boat and its black tires. They will mark up the white sides of my boat." He said this to the authorities in charge, dangling a large cigar in his mouth, while my husband looked on.

"Great," answered Al. "I'll be glad to go alone." He looked so relieved that I hoped it didn't show or that we would be told in no uncertain terms that we had no choice but to go with the American fishing boat.

Going alone proved to be a blessing in disguise. We could have been ordered to tie up with two other sailboats, but fortunately we ended up in the centre of the chamber with our lines completely under our own control. Mishaps could easily happen.

The day of our transit in the canal, our pilot arrived at 03:00 and quickly climbed on board *Solara*. He was an egotistical, self-centered man who made sure we knew he was in charge. I couldn't relate to him, but had to acquiesce to his authoritative personality. Although I had a good variety of food available, he wanted only bottled water, Pepto-Bismol, and extra pizza. He spent most of the morning in our "head" nursing himself from partying the night before. Although he was supposed to pilot the boat, Al had the job of making sure we stayed in the centre of the canal. Once in a while, the pilot would come up to our deck and give out orders after talking on his radio and taking the opportunity to show his authority.

As we entered the first lock, the workmen on top threw down the "monkey paws" (large heavy ropes with a large roped ball at the end), which had to be tied to our lines, and which anchored our boat at four corners. The large fishing vessel that didn't want to be with us was tied up against the canal wall just in front of us. In front of that, and centred in the chamber, was a huge freighter. As the large metal chamber doors opened for all of us to move forward, the turbulence of the freighter produced piles of waves and foam as it pulled out. All of a sudden, the fishing vessel almost lost its hold against the wall, which would have been a disaster if it hit the freighter. We were very glad that we weren't fastened to it as first planned. It turned out that the "captain" was partying at the top with his friends, leaving all the work to one poor soul he had hired to work the lines. And so our transit went, from chamber to chamber, until mid-afternoon when we stopped at the boat club near the Pedro Miguel

Locks, built by the Americans many years ago when they were in charge of the canal.

The Pedro Miguel Boat Club was a rundown, tacky old place with a large community building and various workshops where boaters could repair their boats if needed. (This was great for *Hallelujah*.) Even so, it was charming and comfortable with a community kitchen and a number of stoves and refrigerators for everyone to use. Each night, the "cooks" would gather in the bright, large kitchen/dining room to prepare the meals for their crew. I was always curious about the various international meals that were prepared. The men were just as adept at cooking as the women. I learned how to cut garlic more precisely, and to make a delicious pasta sauce. We saw cruisers from all parts of the world who were planning to cross the Pacific. It was also where temporary crew arranged to meet their captains who had hired them for the Pacific crossing. There was also a volleyball court available for use when time permitted, but mostly everyone was busy getting ready for the long push westward. Supplies had to be purchased, boat parts itemized, sails made ready, and a multitude of tasks done by the captain and crew of each boat. I filled our boat with staples such as potatoes, cabbage, carrots, onions, rice, flour, juices, fruit, cans of this and that, and much more that had to last for three months for four people. I squeezed as much as I could into the various storage places of our boat.

When I agreed to go on this venture and sail for weeks across the Pacific, I asked Al to find a crew to help us with the boat. But while in Grenada, when he thought I was going to desert him for this passage, he found two young men to sail with him on a "crew wanted" website. After speaking to cruising friends and reading about the Pacific islands, I told my husband when I came back from my visit home that I'd decided to cross with him.

"I've been told that, not going, I would miss the adventure of a lifetime."

"Well, I guess you can change your mind. I'm glad you have made a decision. Just make sure you don't change your mind again." I was sure my husband was annoyed with me for vacillating, but the sailing in the Caribbean hadn't been easy.

Al contacted the crew and they were willing to stay on even though there would be four of us. Al had been in touch with them a few times and was satisfied with their qualifications and personalities, at least as much as he could learn from emails.

Philippe helped with our transit to the Pedro Miguel Boat Club, and I learned more about him while there. I was pleased that he was so accommodating, friendly to all the cruisers, and especially that he liked to cook. He had raced on the Bay of Biscay, a formidable body of water, and so was very suitable crew. He was like a lovable teddy bear, charming everyone at the marina and willing to do all kinds of jobs preparing the boat.

Philip, on the other hand, came from the US with a Dutch background. He arrived at the Pedro Miguel Yacht Club ready to be in charge, and loaded down with many pounds of extras from the REI camping store in Washington State. He brought powdered eggs, three dozen cans of anchovies, and leaves of seaweed, to name but a few of the items. He was willing to help, but was also prepared to let us know how things should be. Both men wanted to get to the French Society Islands: Philippe to meet a girl he had met while travelling in South America, and Philip to teach in Asia.

How was I going to deal with these two? Did they have to have almost the same name? Did Al pick them because their names started with a *P*? That was crazy thinking, but my mind was already in turmoil about the crossing. How was I going to manage feeding us and finding somewhere to be alone? OK, my husband was in charge, and I would let him solve the problems facing us. I knew that was a cop out, but it was his idea to circumnavigate in the first place. The act must continue!

On March 3, we arranged the ad measurer again, checked out at immigration and customs, bought last-minute meat and produce, and set out through the Miraflores Locks. We tried to let our family and Mississauga Net know when we would be transiting as TV cameras took pictures for the Panama Canal website. Our pilot was much nicer this time, but he brought a clumsy trainee with him who seemed to always be in the way. I fed everyone again, and our passage went well. We were centre-chambered with a huge freighter just behind us, which took up the entire width of the chamber. As we went under the Bridge of the Americas, which joined North America to South America, we toasted the Pacific Ocean by pouring a few drops of wine from our glasses into the water. "*Dios mio, otro oceano!*" as Balboa might say.

PART 3

The Pacific

CHAPTER 12

❧

A New Ocean

WHAT A VAST ocean lay ahead! Would the four of us make a team? Al had scheduled our watches and it seemed to be fair with time for rests. Watches were set up for the three men and I had the job of feeding the crew and doing my usual radio communications. I would also help anywhere I was needed. Did I have enough food? Baskets of potatoes, onions, and carrots filled any spaces on the floor, and cabbages hung in cotton hammocks swinging from the handhold above the galley. Our fresh food was stored in the small refrigerator, but meat wouldn't stay fresh for long in the tropical heat.

Las Perlas were beautiful islands just off Panama, and a good starting point to head out towards the Galapagos 1,000 miles away. We anchored near an island called Contadora and had our first swim in the Pacific. The sea was much colder there than in the Caribbean. We had our first cocktail hour as a group and our first full meal a la Philippe. On exploring Contadora, we found it was obviously a tourist destination, with two exclusive looking hotels and a few expensive holiday homes. Philip even found ice at a small store for our cocktails, a last-minute luxury.

Of course, in paradise something had to go wrong.

Beyond the shelter of the Panamanian coast, we began to lose power. Two hours of motoring wasn't charging the batteries. I noticed with concern that we were slowly losing our voltage.

"We have to check our alternator and engine."

Now, you might wonder why I was the one to notice, or even have the temerity to suggest a mechanical failure. Mechanical me always kept an eye on things. Out came Nigel Calder's well-used book on boat mechanics while the "boys" checked out the Yanmar motor, alternator, fan belt, etc. After studying the book, Philip suggested we check the fuse, which was somewhere in the spaghetti junction of wheels, gauges, belts, filters, pipes, and tubes. Lo and behold, once found, the fuse turned out to be corroded, but could be replaced from our supply of parts. Philip could do no wrong in Al's mind, and I admit he was a saviour at the time. Luckily we avoided having to return to Panama for repairs.

We caught our first fish once outside Panamanian waters. It looked like a 3-pound tuna.

"Oh! Look how beautiful it is," I cried. It had rainbow scales glistening in the sun. "We have to put it back." I was prepared to wait until we hooked an ugly monster like grouper.

"We have to have sushi," answered Philip. "I know exactly how to make it."

Of course he did, I thought, he knows how to do everything. *Why was I being sarcastic?* I didn't know why Philip annoyed me so much.

When you're in the "doldrums," a few degrees north and south of the equator, the winds are fickle and unpredictable, and often not there at all. Al worked hard to choose the right sail combination to give us some needed speed.

"Let's put up the spinnaker," he would say to our crew, and up it would go, giving us an extra mile or two of speed. The sail was huge, light and beautiful blue with a large sun embossed in the centre, and picked up any breeze it could catch to move our boat.

Or he would say, "The winds are behind us, so let's sail wing on wing." Then the large main sail would be let out to one side, and the large genoa let out to the other side. We would rock back and forth in the very unsteady breeze. Some days we went only 20 miles, and others somewhat further. We wanted to reach the Galapagos within 10 days, if possible. The goal was to head at least a few miles south of the equator to find the prevailing trade winds from the east, which would take us to our destination. Captain James Cook, especially, was aware of the easterly trades which had also helped the many native populations in the Pacific go from island to island. For cruisers, it was called the Coconut Milk Run, the easiest way to cross this vast ocean.

In spite of the winds, our passage was running smoothly. Food kept us from boredom and I tried hard to make the meals interesting. We had our routines, and I got on the radio each morning and evening for the Pacific Crossing Net for cruisers.

"*Solara* checking in, we're at x degrees west and x degrees south." I usually gave the coordinates from our GPS. "How's the weather ahead?"

It was good to know what we might encounter the next day. The net was somewhat of a security net, but in case of a problem no one was actually nearby. At least everyone on the Coconut Milk Run knew we were part of a group of cruisers crossing the Pacific.

"Weather is forecast to be x knots tomorrow with rain squalls." When I heard that I would warn Captain Al of the possibility of poor weather, but sometimes it was very local.

Amazingly, I didn't feel afraid of this immense ocean around us since the water at the equator was flat with quiet rollers which rocked our boat like a baby's cradle. It was also very eerie. The horizon blended into the grey tone of the sky. It was all one hue. I tried not to think of the deep ocean below, and thought of *Solara* as a small island of safety and repose. I would cozy up in the cockpit, read, and chat with the crew. At the moment all was well, but we had thousands of miles ahead, and the calm was temporary. Beyond us, there was no sound except the quiet movement of the waves. When the clouds were gone, we could see millions of stars at night, sparkling like Christmas lights. The sky at home was never like that.

It was a historic moment when we crossed the equator for the first time. We were getting very close to the Galapagos.

"We must have a ceremony," Philip said. "I'll make a Neptune crown and sceptre for Al, and he will sprinkle all of us with saltwater."

That was an exciting suggestion, and we took to it with eager anticipation. Out came a bottle of champagne with drinks all around for the celebration, and pictures for posterity.

Even though Philip often annoyed me, there were times like that when he entertained us delightfully. As the days went by, I felt like I was losing my position on our boat, and Philip was taking over. He made me feel like I couldn't do anything right, although I knew *Solara* well after a year's sailing in the Caribbean.

"I see a bird!" shouted Philippe. "We must be getting closer to the Galapagos."

It was early morning on the 10th day, and Al's calculations were dead on. How was that for navigating, I thought. It looked like we would be able to make it to the Marquesas Islands 3,000 miles away, our next destination.

"It looks like a petrel," I said, looking carefully to spot the pointed tip of its wing. "We saw them in the Caribbean."

Soon after seeing the bird, there was a freighter in the distance going north, and the tip of a sailboat going the same way. But we were heading for Academy Bay at Santa Cruz Island, where cruisers were allowed to go.

CHAPTER 13

— ❦ —

The Galapagos

ACADEMY BAY WAS full of anchored boats, many of them cruisers we knew from the Caribbean. It was like old home week.

"There are *Amoenitas, Zephyr, Tara,* and *Free Radical,*" I said with anticipation. "It'll be great to get together with them."

We set up two anchors, one at the bow and one at the stern so as to bob rather than rock from the constant waves coming in to the bay, and then we were free to scout the small town of Puerto Ayora, a taxi boat ride away. It met all our needs for food, internet, restaurants, and laundry.

Our two crew members had their own agenda once in town. Philippe immediately found an internet café to contact his girlfriend, and Philip made plans to bike and camp.

"We'll have some time alone," I said to Al.

Although having crew was helpful when we were sailing, I wanted to put them in a cupboard for safekeeping while the boat was anchored. Unfortunately, they came back the same day, not finding a place to sleep.

Dave and Di on *Amoenitas* asked us to join them on a scuba diving excursion. As a private yacht, we weren't allowed to explore the other islands, probably in order to protect the environment and boost the local economy. I readily accepted their invitation, but Al was reluctant to be away when he felt he needed to prepare the boat for our next passage. *For goodness sake! How often do people have this opportunity to visit the Galapagos?*

It was a wonderful trip to see the local fauna and ocean mammals, even though the boat was old and dilapidated, with cockroaches running around. But the meals were very substantial and tasty. There were six scuba divers aboard, and Di and I snorkelled. While on the diving boat, we saw tortoises, sea lions, blue-footed boobies, sea iguanas, red crabs, seals, sharks, frigate birds, and sea turtles, to name a good number of the varied and most interesting examples of life there. The scuba divers swam with the sharks, dove with seals, and saw much more under the water than Di and I could see snorkelling. Al said he was in heaven. I was sure he was glad to have come. On land, we saw volcanic rock formations, and walked on rivulets of hardened black basalt from a recent volcanic eruption, sprinkled here and there with crabs in their bright red shells dotted with yellow. Everywhere we went was a picture moment.

It was easy to get comfortable on the anchored boat, but soon we had to leave that quiet haven. Preparations were made and finished: provisioning, laundry, last-minute emails.

As I was putting food away and cleaning up the galley, I heard Philip say, "I insist on a discussion."

"Could you wait until I finish up?"

"No," he answered. "I have been unhappy for some time, and we need to talk."

"You're right," I said. "We're just not getting along, and you want everything your way."

I could have been wrong, but that was what I felt at the moment and he did have many complaints.

"It would be best if you found another boat," I had to say.

My husband had joined us but did nothing to back me up. I knew that for him Philip could do no wrong, but he was a man and couldn't understand that Philip was a male chauvinist, or at least I felt he was. If one of us had to go it certainly wouldn't be me. I looked at Philippe's face nearby, and felt disheartened by his look. He and Philip had been having a good time together, and he would lose his new friend. *Was I being fair? Was my age showing that I couldn't handle the stress?* No, if I was going to be on our boat with Philip for several more weeks, I wanted to enjoy the passage. This was a personality clash at its worst.

Looking back later, I came to the conclusion that Philip was an egotistical, self-centred, and self-indulgent individual. It was too bad those qualities outshone his other good points. I felt like a heel leaving him in the remote Galapagos Islands, but he soon found passage on a French single-hander yacht. The captain, unfortunately, drank steadily, which meant Philip had to do most of the work on board. He emailed Al sometime after he arrived in Tahiti. He had decided to fly back to the US. I guess sailing the Pacific "took the wind out of his sails."

"Did you know," I said to Al, "that Philip had a pink bunny with him when he was on watches during the night?" I got a look from my husband that was inconclusive.

Our special supply of pills purchased by our goddaughter in London to prevent sea sickness was missing after he left. They had all disappeared.

CHAPTER 14

To the Marquesas

IT WAS NOW the middle of March, and I said my final goodbyes to the Galapagos as we headed out to the vast ocean ahead. With all our preparations, surely we were ready. Again, we became a small floating self-sufficient island, ready to tackle what was ahead. Al set our course to reach the Marquesas Islands. Due to variable winds, it was difficult to determine how long our trip would take. Every 15 degrees latitude west, we would move our watches one hour behind. That gave us an extra hour of daylight and relaxation, which we used for our cocktail time. It was amazing how the distance flew by. Two weeks from the Galapagos, we had gone 1,500 miles and were halfway to Hiva Oa, our first stop in the Marquesas Islands.

I checked with the Pacific Crossing Net each morning to give our position to cruisers before and behind us. This contact made me feel more secure, although I saw no boat nearby. Looking out in all directions, I could only see the constant waves around us. Often it was hard to tell from which direction they came but the current of the ocean drove us westward.

Was there life beneath us? When we tried to fish, our line invariably broke. We used stronger line, but again had no success. There must have been huge bodies of fish below our boat, or we were very inept fishermen. Each morning there were a few flying fish and squid lying on the deck, which had managed to jump in. They were dead when discovered, so Al had to throw them overboard. One night, a flying fish hit him in the face as he was on watch. That must have startled him. Flying fish had very sharp, wing-like pectoral fins that helped them escape from predators in the warm tropical waters. We would see schools of these fish flying out of the ocean in dark cloudy waves, sometimes going for hundreds of feet. During the night, other creatures were heard from time to time, such as dolphins swimming by, and one time a huge whale – bigger than our boat – was seen by Al and Philippe while I was sleeping, unfortunately.

How was my food supply? I had no more bread but could make biscuits for breakfast along with cereal and pancakes. I was using canned fruit and vegetables, but the fresh meat was gone. The potatoes were still edible, as well as the onions and squash. Each day, I discarded the outside of the cabbages which were wrapped in paper towels in the hammock. The large supply of bananas that had been hanging on the stern had quickly turned brown, and we had to eat them every day until I finally threw them overboard. Unfortunately bananas ripen all at the same time, but I had plenty of juice, milk, and eggs. Philippe happily cooked a few meals, which was a good break for me, and he wouldn't accept my offer to take his watch in return.

However I got tired of the constant rocking and rolling of the boat in the endless sea, and trying to move myself on the slanted floor of the cabin. It was well known that every seventh wave on the ocean was bigger and stronger than those before, and if there was a breaking wave on top it was a time for concern. I had to spread my feet far apart to steady myself while cooking, although there was a special belt that fastened around my waist to keep me from being hurled into the hot stove. Can you imagine how tiring it was to stand with your knees bent and legs wide apart for balance? It was like a daily exercise routine. One day, my dish of scrambled eggs got thrown in the nearby sink by an extra strong wave. Often I would lie down on the couch in the centre cabin just to rest my body. My solace was the fact that each day we were that much closer to the Marquesas.

On quiet nights, the sky was beautiful. We now saw the Southern Cross along with the Big Dipper. When the moon was full, our cockpit filled with the silvery glow. Some nights would be very black with threatening clouds. On a few days we had squalls, and winds up to 35 knots.

That was when I felt most vulnerable, and glad we had another crew on board. You could calculate the moon's phases. The waning moon in the southeast had a red tinge from the setting sun, and then rose later and later each night. I loved the monthly transformation the moon took on its pass through the sky.

We were very careful about using too much power, which put a crimp on my use of the radio. Our mechanical steering device saved needed fuel as the auto-helm was a power-hungry mechanism. As it was, we used only 30 gallons of fuel for the whole trip to the Marquesas. The fuel fed the motor to charge our large group of batteries used for lights, radio, refrigerator, water-maker, radar, and chart plotter. There was lots of time to read, clean the boat, bathe, cook, and of course, sail. Sleep fitted in between watches. The bow where privacy was possible was used for bathing.

"I'm going to bathe," I would call to the cockpit. "Keep your eyes elsewhere." Of course I needn't worry, for Al had seen me many times and Philippe probably wouldn't care to look, as I wasn't a beauty queen. I would take a bucket with a long line attached to the bow and bring up saltwater. Then I would pour it over myself, wash down with soap, and rinse with the precious freshwater from our boat, which was put in a large container with a spray attachment. That was Al's invention, and worked very well. We were now in very hot temperatures, and needed the freshness of bathing. Leaving saltwater on one's skin caused a sticky feeling, and we couldn't bring salt into the cabin from our bodies or into the bedding since it couldn't be washed while we were at sea. Life on the ocean brought many complications, but we learned about saving power and fuel, not wasting water, and eating a healthy diet. The environmental powers that be in Canada would have been proud of us.

After Philip left, I was on a two-hour watch during the night. When I took my turn, I would ask for one reef in the main in case the winds came up. Philippe, on the other hand, liked a full sail, and was happiest when we were skimming across the 6- to 8-foot waves with winds up to 25 knots. At those times, I found it hard to sleep from the motion and the sound of the water as it swished past our hull. I contacted two ships while on night watch, and lo and behold got good responses. Usually large vessels, being on autopilot and hurrying to make their destination, ignored small yachts. I gave one ship our GPS coordinates and our heading since it was very close and I thought we were on a collision course from looking at the radar.

"Not to worry," said the captain from the freighter in a soothing voice. "We will pass you on your stern and there won't be a collision."

Maybe he noticed my quiet female voice and was being reassuring, not the usual type of captain of those large vessels. Sometimes it was difficult the read the lights on those ships, and their direction. I was often teased about this by Al, as he seemed to read the lights much better than I did.

Then came a frightening occurrence one day in 10-foot waves. Of course, these things tended to happen in the worst weather. While Philippe and Al were bringing in the genoa to make it smaller, the spliced halyard (the line that holds the main sail in its tracks) snapped, causing the large sail to fall, and the small bit left of the halyard that hadn't fallen was left dangling. Al had to go up the mast in those turbulent seas in order to bring down the line. Out came the Bosun's chair, which could be hauled up the mast by the winch at the bottom and attached to a spare line. Thank goodness we had Philippe, as it would have been too difficult for me to work the winch. I took the helm and tightly grasped the wheel, trying to keep the boat steady, which unfortunately was almost impossible as the waves were coming in all directions.

Poor Al hung on for dear life as he was slowly cranked up the 62-foot mast. At the two spreaders (horizontal metal beams that held the standing rigging and mast in place), he had to manoeuvre around each while trying to cling to the slippery aluminum mast. My heart went out to him. It was a nightmare. If he lost his grip, the fall would finish him or send him into the sea, where we might lose him for good. To make things worse, the mast swung like a pendulum back and forth, back and forth, 20 feet one way and 20 feet the other. He had no choice but to retrieve the end of the halyard as soon as possible, or it would have slid down the inside of the mast. Once he had the end and was starting down, the line slipped from his fingers and he had to go up to the top again. I felt terrible for him. The colour had left his face, and his eyes were often shut to avoid looking down. Philippe and I were shouting encouragement over the sound of the storm around us. Finally, after what seemed like forever, his feet touched the deck, and we all collapsed with relief. He immediately tied a proper knot in the halyard, having learned the hard way that a splice was not necessarily reliable. A double scotch was in order that day. That night I had trouble sleeping, thinking about my husband's climb up the mast and the fact that I almost lost him.

"The pain is getting worse," I said quietly to my husband after leaving the head. I had been having sharp cramps since Colombia, and they weren't diminishing.

"What do you think is causing your pain?"

"It could be a kidney stone, but hopefully not. It's most likely a bladder infection."

"Our doctor gave you antibiotics for that. You should take the pills and hope for the best."

I knew it wasn't my appendix, as I'd had it out a few years ago.

"OK, you're right. I'll take them immediately and see what happens. Many women have this problem."

About three days later, the pain went away. The miracle of medicine! The problem of having to diagnose any illness or pain would always be with us.

CHAPTER 15

✤

The Marquesas

WE'D BEEN AT sea for 23 days and it was now nearing the end of April. How anxious I was becoming to reach solid land. The winds were steady as they had been for countless sailors across the Pacific. I admired the men who had challenged their crew with a strong desire to see beyond their horizons of knowledge. I thought mostly of Magellan, Drake, Cavendish, and Cook, the first Western explorers to cross the Pacific.   At least we had our waypoints and GPS.

"I see land!" shouted Philippe. "We've made it."

Al and I popped up from our seats and, with eyes squinting, saw a dark image far away. There it was in the mist, a pointed peak of land jutting out into the darkened sky. How excited we were that all our instruments worked, and we were approaching Hiva Oa. The new and waxing moon appeared as we got closer and gave us a bright clear sky to help see at night. Although anxious to get off the boat, we waited for the morning and reefed our sails outside the harbour.

A few days before, we had heard of an Australian boat whose captain decided to enter the protected harbour of Taa Huku Bay on Hiva Oa at night. There was a fairly large breakwater in front of the harbour for protection from the waves. As he got close to land, a squall – very similar to the squall we had near Aruba – suddenly came and knocked out all his radar and electronics. The boat ended up on the rocks and sank. Fortunately the family survived with help from many of the locals and cruisers who also rescued most of the gear.

The next day arrived beautifully, with high mountains silhouetted against the pink sky beyond. We now had a clear view into the protected harbour of Taa Huku Bay, 9 degrees south of the equator. We anchored behind a break wall deep into the bay near the town of Atuona, once the home of Paul Gauguin, the famous French painter. Gauguin lived in Tahiti in the early 1890s, but when his sexual proclivities became public knowledge he returned to France for a short time. Not welcomed back to Tahiti, he boarded a steamer and arrived in Atuona in 1901. He behaved himself long enough to gain the approval of the Catholic Church, who owned most of the land around Atuona, and built a house which has long disappeared. He then reverted to his old ways, and sought out 12- and 13-year-old girls to take to his studio. The Church soon retaliated, and kept the young girls away by sending them to a church-run boarding school. Gauguin retaliated against the clergy by publicly humiliating them at every opportunity. But all things must come to an end, and Gauguin was found dead two years later, overcome by drugs, alcohol, and his own lifestyle.

On one of our many walking tours of the island, we visited Gauguin's grave. Although he was perverted in life, he became renowned in death because of his artistic talents. In Papeete, Tahiti, there was the Paul Gauguin Museum, visited by many tourists. The grave was marked by a statue called Oviri, meaning "savage" in Tahitian, which he sculpted in France between trips to Polynesia. Also in the cemetery was the grave of Jacques Brel, a famous Belgian singer and songwriter. It was interesting to note that the beauty of the island provided a final resting place for these "visitors."

I loved the Marquesas with its luscious vegetation, friendly natives, and French flavour. On our sail throughout the islands, we also visited Ua Pou and Nuku Hiva. In every case, the beautiful flowers were in full bloom, surrounded by spectacular volcanic mountains. When we first arrived and anchored at Hiva Oa, a group of young boys waved and hollered to us as though we were the most important guests to their island.

It was a cruisers' paradise. At the time of our visit, cruising boats were the most likely visitors. The official port of entry into French territory was in Papeete, an expensive flight away. For Pacific-crossing sailors, the Marquesas was usually the first landfall. One could stay for months and still find special anchorages and gunkholes. Because we weren't European, there was a time limit the French government put on our stay. We were given three months in the French Society Islands, which included Tahiti, Bora Bora, and the Tuamotus, to name a few. To extend our stay, we would have had to fly to Easter Island, which would have given us another three months. There was no time. We had to reach Fiji, another 6,000 miles, before the cyclone season. How jealous I was of the European cruisers who had no time limits! .

Over the centuries, the islands were visited by the Spanish, Americans, British, and the French, resulting in exploitation and disease, until the French claimed the islands through military influence, missionaries, and forced authority. It was obvious on our travels that the islands were more modern than we expected, with decent roads, well-stocked – albeit expensive – supplies, and beautiful homes, often lived in by French retirees from overseas.

Our stay in Taa Huku Bay was enhanced by the nearby shower and sinks for doing laundry and filling jugs with the excellent water available. After 23 days offshore, these were the most important parts of the bay. We tied up our dinghy to a precarious ramp, and I carefully made my way to the rocky shore. The first time on dry land after such a long time at sea played with my balance and I rocked back and forth while trying to move my feet.

"Where are you going?" asked my husband, following me out.

"I'm going to have a shower," I explained, holding my towel and soap. Although the seawater kept us cool enough when sailing, the salt seemed to stick to my skin even when I had rinsed with our supply of freshwater. The concrete enclosure just came up to my chest, and I looked around for onlookers just in case. How refreshing it was! The water was cool and abundant. Al soon joined me when he heard the joy in my voice.

Soon after, we made our way into town – 2 miles by road, good exercise for our weakened legs. It was very neat and clean, with a bakery, bank, post office, and a snack hut called Snack Make Make where we could get a cold Hinano beer and a hamburger. What luxury! Also in town was a light blue two-story market called Magasin Shan Pierre, where Paul Gauguin still owed money for wine when he died. Al was able to check in easily to the country at the *gendarmerie*, though we had to check in again at each island we visited.

Another day, we walked along a dirt road and came across a farm that grew the most delicious grapefruit-like fruit. The huge melons, called pomelos, were ready to pick from the trees. The farmer came over and told us to pick what we would like and offered to help. I'd seen this fruit in our supermarkets at home. There was no comparison to the freshly picked and sweet tangy flesh of those grapefruits.

Philippe was in his glory now that we were in French territory. He bought some baguettes immediately, and then went to the post office where there was internet in order to contact his girlfriend. We visited other islands while there, taking time in Tahuata to clean off the hull which had become covered in all kinds of plants and animal life since it had last been cleaned six months earlier in Venezuela.

The largest island, Nuku Hiva, had a large wide bay called Taiohae Bay where many boats were anchored. The rolling swells entered the bay as the entrance lacked a breakwater. Coral reefs, which were found in other parts of the Society Islands and formed natural breakwaters, did not exist on the Marquesas. There was also a village there with various stores and services, including a small museum owned by an American woman, Rose Corser, who had settled and built a hotel many years before. She showed us a number of stone *tikas*, carvings made by the Marquesans a few hundred years ago. On our travels throughout the Society Islands, we would come across various sites used in the past for ceremonies and, sometimes, sacrifices. During my stay in Taiohae Bay, I bought a painting on cobra paper (outer coconut shell covering), and a beautifully carved wooden bowl with engravings.

I could never travel far without having some kind of an accident. This time, on the old stone dock in Taiohae Bay, I slipped off backward into our dinghy, which lay about 6 to 8 feet below. The dock was very slippery and I fell down hard, but fortunately the bottom of our dinghy was soft except for the seats. My one elbow hit the seat and damaged the nerve; no more funny bones on that elbow for a while.

"Are you OK?" Al cried. The scared look on his face showed concern, but it had happened so fast I didn't have time to react and tighten up which probably saved me from further damage.

"I'm fine, but a little shaky. It looks like we won't get to the market today after all." The local market had crazy hours, and we were too late. Apparently, one had to get up in the dark before 05:00 and dinghy over to the town to see what was for sale. It was so dark, some cruisers brought their flashlights.

A tooth was giving me a hard time as well. Taiohae Bay seemed to be the best place to go to the dentist. There were a reasonable number of people with healthy smiles. Did they go to this dentist, or was it their good diet? There was a good chunk of my tooth gone somewhere, and who knew how long it would take to reach Tahiti, which would certainly be a better choice for a dentist. Nevertheless, I found a small, quiet building with a dentist sign in French attached to the front. I hated going to the dentist, and I guess so did most of the population in that town. He was alone, waiting patiently for patients.

"People are afraid of the dentist," he explained, as I looked around for some assurance. "I can take you right now."

I reluctantly got in his chair surrounded by primitive looking apparatus that reminded me of the dentist office I had gone to as a child. As he worked on my tooth, I began to realize why the locals were afraid. I had been spoiled by a gentle dentist at home, but this one had the touch of a gorilla, and did only an adequate job, which would cause me to need a root canal much later, in Australia. I guess a partial job was better than having only part of a tooth.

Our favourite anchorage was Anaho, on the same island of Nuku Hiva. It meant sailing to the opposite side from where we had been, but the conditions were just right, and dolphins cavorted around us as we sailed. This bay had everything one would want: a beautiful beach with a freshwater tap, great snorkelling in clear water, and a tropical paradise on shore. We walked up an 800-foot trail leading to the next town, Hatiheu, passing a large mango tree covered in delicious fruit just there for the picking. In Hatiheu, there were small but attractive houses where French retirees from Europe lived. On the way back it was obvious – when my legs became useless – that the lack of exercise during our long Pacific passage had taken a toll on my body. I felt very old and grabbed a pole and my husband to help me descend the trail.

Stopping at the Marquesas after the long sail gave us a chance to catch up on the news of our cruising friends who had arrived before us. Anne, from *Oddly Enough,* liked to swim from boat to boat and strike up a conversation when in an anchorage. Harvey and Jean on *Island Express* and Dietrich and Pietr from *Guitar* showed up, having also crossed the Pacific from the Caribbean. We met an Australian boat, *Bagheera,* with Rod and Hilary, who had been sailing for seven years. Hilary said she was ready to pack it in. At least she was closer to home than we were. When we met acquaintances again, it was a chance to invite them on our boat for drinks, dinner, and conversation. There were also a number of Canadian boats from the West Coast who were "doing" the Pacific, but we lost touch with them eventually. Cruisers from the North American West Coast would sail down to Mexico, spend time there, and cross to the Marquesas, skipping the Galapagos, which shortened their sail by 1,000 miles. I began to call them the Mexican group, as apart from the Panama group. They were a friendly bunch, and I was sorry to have to say goodbye. Easter had come and gone and it was time to leave for our next destination.

CHAPTER 16

— ✀ —

The Tuamotus

WE WERE HEADING toward the Tuamotus, 750 miles west of the Marquesas, enough time to take an account of our boat's needs. My stove was a disaster, the sails needed readjusting, and our batteries had to be replaced. The engine vibrated on an unsteady platform, and the Winlink connection for ham radio communication should have worked better. We hoped to find competent, knowledgeable people to help us. This, we hoped, would come in Papeete.

The Tuamotus were also known as the "Dangerous Archipelago." All of the atolls were only as high as the tallest palm tree. Because of GPS and radar, the danger was not too great, but GPS was not the ultimate answer to safe navigation. Some 20 miles by 9 miles was a fairly average size for an atoll in the Tuamotus. A boat's charts didn't necessarily coordinate, since they came from limited information before there was GPS. It was necessary to enter an atoll according to the tides entering and leaving the designated entrance. I was busy reading Michael Pocock's book on the Pacific and trying to absorb it all before reaching our first atoll.

After a few days of rough seas of 10 feet, the winds calmed down just before we came to the Tuamotus. We slowed down in order to enter during daylight and slack time between tides. Al chose the atoll called Toau, more remote and less explored. The French government had placed directional markers to help entering. There were two white markers just opposite the entrance, on the other side of the atoll, that gave you the correct bearing, so that when entering the boat could avoid the reefs on each side. It took an experienced sailor to make this attempt, and my husband was now near that level. He was very careful, though as we looked at the churning water at the entrance after the tide had gone out, I didn't think experience was the only requirement. Just plain guts. The wind and waves tossed the water in all directions for 100 feet before us, hitting the fast-flowing water coming out of the entrance. How could we ever enter?

"Let's go!" said Philippe. "It's now or never."

It could be never, I thought.

"Hold on, I've got the markers just right." Al revved the engine, and in we went through the turbulent water. Our boat tossed and jumped around in the waves, and the rough edges on each side of the entrance became apparent. No way did we want to hit the reefs that were part of the wall around each atoll.

How quiet it was inside! I couldn't believe it. It was like a swimming pool, but miles wide. We could see 40 feet down, and carefully dropped the anchor between the heads of coral scattered about. All around were black-tipped sharks that fed on smaller fish, carried in and out of the atoll by the tides. A grove of palm trees lined the edges and protected us from the east/northeast winds. It was another paradise. The beauty of the place was unbelievable. I was sorry that we were only staying one night. Al and Philippe went snorkelling nearby, but I could see the fish as I swam around the boat and a large green turtle seemed to be my companion while I was in the water.

Early the next morning, Philippe took a swim, and in a few minutes we saw him speed back to the boat as if he were in some Olympic competition. His arms and legs were going as fast as his chubby body allowed, and he was yelling. "There's a shark after me!"

Sure enough, at least a 6-foot shark was heading his way.

"I looked up and there it was starting to swim right towards me. It had sharp beady eyes staring at me as though I was its next meal," Philippe quietly said after taking many needed breaths. He could have been right, but no one wanted to test that out.

CHAPTER 17

Tahiti

THE FRENCH SOCIETY Islands were very different than the Marquesas and the Tuamotus in configuration. This time, we had to find the marked entrance through the fringing reefs, but inside there were beautiful lagoons sheltered by the large formation of each island, and the outside reefs blocking the constant hammering waves, which sometimes foamed 10 to 15 feet in the air. Captain James Cook in the *Endeavour* landed in Tahiti in 1769 on his first voyage. It was impossible not to follow in his footsteps as we crossed the Pacific. His first job in Tahiti was to observe the transit of Venus across the face of the sun, which would give astronomers a more accurate value of the distance between the sun and the Earth. He also encountered a friendly welcome from the natives who encouraged him to stay for some time. We too were prepared to enjoy the Society Islands.

Our first stop was at Papeete where we expected to find help with our boat problems. This meant finding a place at the city dock, which I hoped would be temporary. It was too busy and much dirtier than the lagoon further to the east where we could anchor.

"I can't get onto the dock," I cried as I attempted to climb up from our dinghy. Throughout our cruising, most of my accidents were from our boat to the dock. We were tied Med-style (our stern to the dock) and there was no way to leave from that end because of our monitor (steering device). Al had put down the dinghy next to the boat for disembarking. I had to wait for help while Al and Philippe disappeared into town. Al had to renew our cruising visa and find workmen so I understood his hurry, but Philippe was contacting his girlfriend and forgot me. The tide must have been at its lowest and much further from the dock that morning. I had no choice but to wait and the excitement of Papeete with its busy pedestrian traffic, wonderful stores, and fragrant-smelling sidewalk food trucks called *roulettes* drove me mad.

Papeete was the "bustling, vibrant, noisy, administrative capital of French Polynesia," as stated in our *Pacific Crossing Guide*. Once on shore, I found several internet cafes, black pearl outlets, and designer shops, all very expensive. The food trucks set up tables and chairs in the downtown park where we would eat many inexpensive meals alongside the local people.

Slowly but surely, *Solara* became a usable boat again. A new regulator solved the problem of our stove. Apparently, the original one had been put in the wrong way, allowing saltwater into the device. Michel, the mechanic, did a temporary fix on the stove so I could bake. We had left the town dock the day before and moved east through a narrow channel which cut across the airport runway to an anchorage called Maeva Beach, a much cleaner lagoon but a bus trip away from Papeete. The fringing reef that circled Tahiti kept the lagoon's water quiet and peaceful from the powerful waves outside. We anchored close to the reef where the water was clear and sparkling blue as it crossed over the barrier. The vibration of our engine was solved by Marc, another "expert," when he was able to sit the engine right. Apparently, the large, heavy Yanmar engine had become dislodged from its platform and needed reinforcement. Our sails came down for repairs and new batteries had to be purchased. All this left us bound to our boat although we were anxious to explore the various Society Islands. I was able to find a *magasin* for very expensive supplies so we ate well.

Philippe would be leaving soon and invited us to have a meal in an expensive Papeete restaurant. "My treat," he said in his lovely French accent after we took our seats. "It's been a wonderful crossing experience on the Pacific, but I will be meeting my girlfriend soon in Thailand."

"You were extremely helpful on the boat and we'll miss you," Al said as I watched with a few tears in my eyes. Philippe had been a good crew, unpretentious and accommodating. We raised our glasses and made a toast to successful adventures to come. I had a feeling that we would not meet again.

The restaurant was called L'O a la Bouche, a very French restaurant owned by locals. Philippe probably asked around for the best place. The meal was excellent, including the wine, and an unforgettable ending to our friendship. We were expecting one more crew to join us in Papeete and I was very apprehensive. Did we need another crew? Gary would be coming in two weeks, the middle of June, which would give us time to finish up the boat work and be ready to sail again. It was nice to be by ourselves again after four months, even though Philippe had been exceptional.

It was time to have fun between work and waiting to go. There was an arranged trip to a beer factory which also sold local vanilla, coffee, and chocolate. That was somewhat successful but Pete, on *Sojourner*, arranged that we all meet at the local Total gas bar that also served beer and drinks. We hadn't seen *Sojourner* since Trinidad and were delighted that Pete was in Tahiti as well. He still found the best and cheapest beer in town, and these spots became get-togethers for all the cruisers. His wife Julie had decided to go home for a while, leaving Pete to solo. No one was sure when she would return. Later, Pete told us he almost lost his boat in Huahine, another island near Tahiti, when he was trying to enter a channel through the reefs during a storm and couldn't see in front of him.

We met up again with *Bagheera*, the Australian boat. We would probably see Rod and Hilary again in Fiji and from there they would finally sail back home after seven years away. Some year we would do the same but when I couldn't say. We also got reacquainted with *Guitar, Infidien, First Light*, and *Free Radical*. Ed and Julie on *Free Radical* were also circumnavigating and later we would travel together for part of our journey. We passed around boat cards again; I kept many of these cards as keepsakes. It was surprising, too, how many wives had left their boats to go home for a visit, leaving their husbands to carry on. These men seemed very lonely, but I wasn't aware that they found any substitutes as most of the women came back to carry on, sometimes reluctantly.

The work on our boat was almost finished. We had a little more provisioning to do. For our two daughters, we bought two black pearls that could be made into pendants. They were beautiful and I planned to take them back to Canada with me when I returned for a visit in the fall. French Polynesia was the world's largest producer of cultured black pearls, most of which were grown at pearl farms in the clean lagoons of the Tuamotus. We paid a modest amount, but black pearls could be very expensive according to size, purity, and colour.

Gary, our new crew, was continuing to email Al for information. He had many questions and concerns. Did I need the problems of indecisiveness or doubt? I was beginning to have concerns about this man who would soon join us. Finally, Al went to pick him up at the airport, and I made a cake to welcome him and celebrate his birthday which we found out was that day. When I saw them arriving back from the airport, I wondered how he was going to fit into our small cabin. He was well over 6 feet and carefully folded his legs to fit into places around the boat. He had a very thin body which seemed to stretch in all directions and a worn look on his face as though he carried the burden of the world on his shoulders. He was compatible though, and I hoped a good crew. I wasn't happy to give up my privacy but he was supposed to sail with Al to New Zealand from Fiji when I took a break later in the year.

CHAPTER 18

Moorea, Raiatea, and Bora Bora

HAVING EXPLORED TAHITI to our satisfaction, it was time to leave. We had visited the Lagoonarium, an underwater aquarium, which was very interesting in its layout. It contained reef sharks, sea turtles, and many tropical fish, but of course we saw them in nature right from our boat and weren't too impressed. The "truck" transportation that took us there dropped us off on the highway right against a 3-foot drop which meant jumping down the embankment so as not to get run over by the bus as it drove away. It was not a good scene. The Museum of Tahiti and the Islands, on the other hand, was very worth the visit. It was one of the best in the South Pacific. It gave a thorough story of French Polynesia and its history, as well as the geography, geology, and the sea life, flora, and fauna. I was most interested in the culture and handicrafts of their people.

We had a good sail to Moorea, only 12 miles away and a popular island for tourists to visit from Tahiti because of the regular ferry service between them. In contrast to Tahiti, Moorea was a very peaceful island. James Michener described it as looking like a dinosaur because of its jagged peaks of mountainous basalt. But it also had deep bays and emerald lagoons to make it one of the most beautiful islands in the Pacific. We decided to anchor just outside one of the bays in a shallow, sandy area protected from the seas by the fringing reef. We could see the fish below us in the clear, blue water. The snorkelling was superb, and the breeze kept us cool and free from bugs. Al wanted to stay there for a while but all the other cruisers had gone into the bay nearby. I felt like socializing again, and after two days convinced him that we should leave that idyllic spot. Why would I do that? I guess the need to talk to other people, have a meal away from the boat, or just get my feet on terra firma.

The morning we prepared to pull up the anchor, we saw the most incredible rainbow, brilliant against the background of the dark mountain beyond. It was a picture moment. Before leaving, I fed the box fish just below our boat that had been swimming around while we were there. Its protective fused plates gave it a square-shaped form and it seemed to have adopted us, temporarily chasing away any other fish coming near. It was obvious that we wouldn't find another perfect anchorage for a while.

It was a 62-foot deep drop just in front of the Bali Hai Club where we had to anchor. It took most of our chain, which was 200 feet long, to keep our boat steady. There were many boats around and we had a chat with Ed and Julie from *Free Radical* who were about to leave that day. So much for socializing! Our walk along the road near the club had busy traffic with its noise and pollution, something we came there to avoid. An evening trip on Saturday to see a so-so Polynesian show at the Tiki Village Theatre finished up our visit. Time to sail to Raiatea.

How were we to know that Gary would get seasick? Both of us seemed to take all kinds of rough seas and weather without taking medication. We were lucky. We'd had the English seasick pills just in case until they disappeared in the Galapagos. He was out of commission, and no help on our overnight passage to Raiatea. Once we got out of the shelter of Moorea, we had 20- to 25-knot winds and 10-foot seas. We were used to those conditions. *I'm surprised about that but after 18 months at sea it seems to be true.* But Gary was not. I admitted that the movement of the boat was irrational and my sea legs needed to be tuned again which made me somewhat squeamish. But Gary! His face turned grey and sweat formed on his brow. He was very seasick and spent most of the trip with his head in a bucket. Al had told him to bring medication for sea sickness but he didn't seem to have any, much to my disgust. I didn't cook a meal, and Al and I chewed on some French loaf to keep our stomachs full.

We covered the night watches together and the seas didn't let up, but there was the full moon which lit up the sky and allowed us to see clearly. Mother Nature at times was most helpful.

There was a pass through the reef into Raiatea and calm seas, thank goodness. We paid for a mooring ball just by the carenage, a large boat works near the town of Uturoa, the administrative centre. The guys rode to the dock with the dinghy to check in. While there, Al saw Pete on *Sojourner* who told him that someone had stolen his knapsack with all his money, credit cards, and important papers. That was unfortunate; no wife as well. He was such a nice man that I didn't like to hear about his bad luck. I found out later that the dock outside the town of Uturoa had no security and was the scene of a few robberies. It had developed a hostile atmosphere and become a dangerous place to stop. We were lucky to not have been robbed as well.

It was possible to tour around the island inside the reef, find shelter, and discover various sacred locations scattered here and there. Our first anchorage was at Vaiaau Bay, but we stayed only one night because of the very deep waters and strong winds coming down from the mountains. The shallow reef nearby made us nervous because if our anchor was dislodged the current would send us into the coral.

On our second day, we stopped in front of a *motu* (a reef islet formed by broken coral and sand) called Vaonao Island off the south coast of the mainland but close to great snorkelling. Soon the local fishermen shooed us away because we were in their fishing area. I should have asked if they had any fish for sale and maybe they would have let us stay. The most important stop we made in Raiatea was at Opoa Bay where we could visit the Taputapuatea Marae, one of the most sacred locations in all of Polynesia.

Opoa Pass offshore was the departure point for the discovery and settlement of both Hawaii and New Zealand, according to legend. As we walked around the large site, we saw the raised altar used for sacrifices to Oro, god of fertility and war, created by the Tamatoas, very powerful chiefs in their day who mingled religion with politics. Surrounding the *marae* were rocks with backrests used by the chiefs, supposedly for greater comfort. The entire complex was in a coconut grove on the shore of the lagoon. It was truly worth the visit, and looking out to the windswept waves of the Pacific through the palms, one could imagine what it was like many hundreds of years ago as boats departed for places unknown. Fires placed on the *marae* were used as beacons for ancient navigators.

Once anchored near the quiet village of Opoa, we saw a charter boat come swiftly by, between us and the shallower water on our left.

"A problem is about to happen," said Al quietly as we sat in our cockpit for our lunch.

Sure enough, their keel got caught on the coral below and the boat suddenly stopped. As we watched, the man tried to start the motor in his dinghy while his wife attempted to call the charter company who weren't answering.

"I think we'd better help," Al said to Gary. "He's not getting close to being free from the reef."

At first, the American was very proud and refused their offer to help, but I guess frustration took over. For almost three hours, they assisted the poor guy getting off into deeper water, using our dinghy and other knowledgeable methods that Al had learned from experience. I invited his wife, young daughter, and a friend over for some coffee, although a stiff drink would have been more welcome. Apparently, it was their first day on the water in the charter boat, and they had much to learn about anchoring and reefs. I felt thankful that we had passed that point and were able to help.

"How do you anchor in the ocean at night?" their daughter asked.

Although that was a silly question often asked, I answered. "We were never far from land but it's 5 miles below our boat." That was a silly reply as well. "But seriously, we keep sailing our boat, and take watches at night."

"That must be hard." She looked at me with wide, staring eyes, all agog. Right then, I felt proud of our accomplishments. One just needed reassurance from a stranger that what we were doing wasn't too insane.

Our discussion was mostly questions and answers, and I did my best to explain how we had crossed the Pacific Ocean.

Our last destination on Raiatea was the town of Uturoa where we could buy fuel and provisions. After we finished tying up at the dock, we saw a boat we recognized approaching. It was *Rag'n Drag'n* from San Diego. John and Diane had just arrived after sailing from Moorea for 20 hours and she looked beat. This was Diane's first passage, as she had flown to Tahiti from California. I wasn't sure what John had done crossing the Pacific, as I saw no other crew. Seeing Diane convinced me that I had made the best decision by making the long voyage and not starting from the middle of the Pacific.

Although the French had built an ultramodern dock and showcase shopping mall in Uturoa, no one was using it, and when I walked into the superstore to buy food the cockroaches were so numerous that I could see then scurrying around on the shelves. I had to be sure to fumigate each item by dipping it in a pail of Javex and water, as well as making sure no cardboard came onto our boat. The area surrounding the harbour seemed spooky: no tourists, no locals eating at the numerous *roulettes* scattered around, and just our boat tied to the dock. We were ready to seek out Taha'a, often called the Vanilla Island, on the other side of the reef circling both Raiatea and Taha'a.

It was quiet and beautiful at Taha'a where we found anchorages near *motus* and small inlets. Exploring the island by foot on a roadway which seemed to skirt the entire circumference, we discovered a small restaurant called Louise's. The owner suggested that we bring our boat to her mooring ball, and eat her dinner that night. She noticed that I was tired from the long, hot walk, and gave us a ride back to our boat. This was another example of island hospitality, and I was very grateful although the men were ready to decline, the testosterone showing up rapidly, but yielding for my sake.

Louise was a very astute lady and would have made her mark in the corporate world at home. Although she was most ready to give us a meal, she also had a cruising group of 20 arriving for dinner and was spending most of her time preparing it. We were given a fish plate of sorts but not much else, and realized we were secondary patrons and left on our own. Looking into the restaurant from her outdoor patio, we saw sparkling white tablecloths, fancy plates, and colourful flowers decorating each table. There was not much we could do but feel envious. Once dinner was over, Louise's granddaughter, about 10, plus two other women began dancing. They were dressed in flowery skirts, short coloured tops, decorative bracelets and necklaces, and sported bare feet. This will be a great show, I thought, just for the tourists, but we were invited to join the group. When the music began, it was obvious that the "show" was very genteel and non-professional, but that made it all the more interesting to my point of view. I wasn't sure how the men felt, but I think they enjoyed the swaying rhythm of the young ladies.

We stayed on the mooring ball two more nights until Louise made it plain that we had stayed long enough. But while there, she showed us her vanilla orchids which she had to pollinate by hand. The flowers later developed into seed pods which had to be dried out in the hot sun for a few days, producing the vanilla beans used to make the extract. It was no wonder that vanilla bought today was so very expensive.

While in Taha'a, we encountered a funeral procession as we walked on the local road. I heard lyrical music from a few instruments, and then saw ladies in colourful straw hats and stark white clothing. The men were in their formal best. I stopped to watch as they passed. Some of the women said *bonjour*, and others shook my hand as I stood by the road with my head bowed. They were walking the casket to its burial place in someone's property, which must have been the way it was done there.

As we approached Bora Bora, we could see the large castle-like silhouette of Mount Otemanu as it pierced the sky. It was never out of sight, a very conspicuous marker. It was considered to be the most beautiful island of all the Society Islands, with its tropical slopes and hibiscus-laden valleys very attractive to tourists. Our destination was the Bora Bora Yacht Club, using a very tricky entrance through the reefs, well-marked by the flashing green light. There was a free mooring ball right in front! How lucky we were, as they were scarce.

The "club" was actually a restaurant/bar with a dock, showers, and laundry machine – just what I needed. And many of our cruising friends were there: Pete, on *Sojourner,* who had probably found another cheap beer place; *Zephyr*, an American boat; *Free Radical,* our loyal Canadian friends; *Little Gem* from Victoria; and *Rag'n Drag'n*. Time for some socializing! We would be there a week and were happy because it was near the middle of July, just in time for the famous Polynesian festival. There would be competitions involving all the islands in traditional dancing, spear throwing, and other island sports, as well as culture and arts on display.

The Heiva i Bora Bora, as it was called, was an annual event and wonderful to watch. The traditional dancing was held in a large, open, sandy field with a grandstand, surrounded by grass and bamboo shelters serving food and running carnival-like games. The women dancers wore coconut-shell bras, grass skirts just below the navel, and flowers in their hair and around their necks.

"I wish I could wiggle like that," I said to Al. "It must take lots of practice."

"What was that?" he answered, his eyes glued to the dancing. I looked at my husband and there was no way he was paying attention to me. The dancers were young and pretty, and I must say very remarkable.

I had my turn later the next day as the young handsome men, with bare chests and some kind of native grass covering, had their competition for spear throwing, a tradition probably stemming back centuries as a means of combat or hunting animals. The target, a large coconut, was at least 100 feet above the ground. From a long distance, the competitors had to throw their spears to penetrate the coconut. Although it looked impossible, there were a few men who had no difficulty.

One cultural phenomenon we found difficult to understand was the rearing of boys in a family as girls when they had a shortage of female offspring. Maybe they were meant to be the caretakers in the home. Unusual sexual proclivity was the norm in Polynesian society. There was an abundance of male transvestites, homosexuals, and bisexuals. I saw a beauty contest where a number of men were dressed in gorgeous female attire, hoping to win. I must admit they were beautiful specimens, and looked very proud of themselves. In the bar after the show, the contestants took time to engage in conversation, and supposedly draw in tourists to the restaurant.

When it was time to leave Bora Bora, a group of cruisers gathered together at a place called Bloody Mary's for dinner. The original group of 12 grew to 20 with a bus provided by the restaurant. It was a fun end to our stay. Our next stop would be the most remarkable and unforgettable place we visited throughout the Pacific.

CHAPTER 19

The Cook Islands

IT WAS A 750-mile passage to the northern Cook Island of Suwarrow. Al estimated that it would take at least a week, but that would depend on the winds, of course. He and Gary fortified themselves with sea sickness pills in case of bad weather that was sure to happen before the week was over. We started with light winds, and took up our watch routine and boat chores as we had done before when sailing to the Galapagos. This time I had contact with a wonderful older man named Des of Russell Radio in New Zealand. Des could be reached by ham radio and give me the weather forecast, and I would, in turn, give our position, state of seas, wind force and direction, as well our bearing and boat speed. With all that information, he had a good idea if we were heading into a storm and would warn me how it could be avoided. Des was the guiding force for many of the cruisers on the Pacific, and a most important source of information.

It was on this passage that I wondered if I could be a friend to Gary. He apparently had some mental problem, either with his wife or something else. I never did find out, as my husband refused to tell me. I called him passive help as he only helped when he was told what to do. When we sat together in the cockpit, his legs began to move up and down, as though he was trying to get rid of something pesky. He conversed with Al but not much with me, and I was hoping he would offer to help with some of the domestic chores, such as cleaning up after our meals, helping prepare the dinner, or even taking over some of my tasks, since I was doing watches as much as he was. I was probably spoiled by having Philippe before him. Looking back, I feel Gary was more of a hindrance than a help. That would be the last time I would agree to have a crew; it just didn't work out.

By our third day out, we had flat seas, no wind, and very little movement. We literally stopped, and decided that instead of trying to sail we would just sit until the winds came up again. The sails were lowered so they wouldn't flap around, and we floated for two or three days. It was a very interesting experience. The seas rolled, with the swells becoming pink and blue hued from the sunsets and seemingly endless. We lowered our ladder and decided to have a swim, right in the middle of nowhere. We tied a long rope to *Solara* just to be sure we didn't get left behind if the boat started to move. I grabbed the line while in the water, but the men just swam a few feet away. It was an eerie feeling having no one around. We were an island in the Pacific.

"Look, I see a whale," shouted Al from the cockpit after our swim. Sure enough, you could see water shooting into the sky from its blowhole a short distance away.

"I think it's coming closer."

And there it was, a beautiful, dark-coloured minke whale about as long as our boat and sleek as a long submarine. It got closer to have a look at us, and tipped its body so that its huge eye was staring right at the three of us. The eye was as big as a saucer, with an intelligent gaze. Was it going to knock over our boat? Apparently not, but it was an awesome sight. Unfortunately, it swam away as suddenly as it had come. Unforgettable! We also saw three mahi-mahi swimming around and beneath our boat. They were a beautiful green colour with yellow fins. I thought they were trying to get some shade from our keel, as the sun was beating down relentlessly. We were now wishing for some breeze, and wind would have been very welcome at that point.

Finally, we could move the next day when the breeze became a 15-knot favourable wind. Only 175 miles to go, then we would enter the Suwarrow atoll the following day. After eight days of sailing, I was getting tired even though the winds kicked up to 25 knots. Al planned our entrance exactly on time. It was similar to entering the Tuamotus a few weeks earlier. The seas were very choppy, and our chart plotter showed us the way, as did my standing at the bow, pointing out the direction shown by the various colours of the water.

Once inside Suwarrow, we felt the peacefulness of the atoll. The vicious wave action outside had disappeared within the surrounding landscape. It was a national park and protected by two old Cook Islanders of 70-plus years who set up their "office" and establishment on one of the islands within the atoll. The office consisted of a rickety table and chair sitting on the sandy shore under a lush coconut palm. We went to shore on our dinghy and paid the small fee to enter the Cook Islands.

The 70-year-olds, John and Fernando, cousins, were there as wardens, and lived on that atoll year in and year out. While we were there for the week, we had many interesting evenings with the two men, especially John. A sturdy structure of treated wood had been built for their shelter, but it seemed that most of their living was outside, especially cooking and dining. Cruisers were welcome and an interesting diversion from their solitary life. Most nights there would be potluck, and we would bring food and drinks to the shelter, sitting around a campfire and listening to John's stories. Fernando was the cook, who made a delicious barbeque of coconut crab, lobster, homemade coconut bread, and real coconut juice, handing each of us a coconut with the top cut off. He said a short prayer before we ate.

We were one of four cruising boats that week: Larry and Lynn from *Zephyr*, the US boat that had been sailing with *Free Radical* (where had *Free Radical* gone?); a Japanese boat; ourselves; and a French couple, France and François, on *Atare*, who needed us to translate John's broken English which we did as best we could.

"See this scar," John said one night. "I was swimming with my granddaughter too close to the entrance of this atoll. Suddenly, a large shark came at her, and I attacked him with a knife, and it bit a big chunk out of my leg."

It was an ugly and deep scar with jagged edges, and I wondered how he had treated it so far away from help. He then showed us more scars on his upper body, also from shark attacks. We remembered that atolls were often filled with sharks which swam near the openings to catch the incoming fish from the tide, as well as enjoying the calm waters on the inside.

Again, John spoke about his past exploits. "I was a champion deep sea diver when I was younger," he boasted. "I could go down 80 feet with no air, and stay down for 10 minutes." He had been a pearl diver of distinction, and I thought he had every right to boast.

All of us were enthralled by his stories. Accompanying the stories and food, Fernando played guitar, and there were many jokes probably saved up for guests' enjoyment. We couldn't have asked for better evenings, no matter where we were going next.

The Japanese cruise boat that was in Suwarrow at the same time was much smaller than *Solara*. Ken had a lovely but quiet wife, who spoke no English, and two young children. It was a Juneau, a sleek French racing boat that must have been most uncomfortable in rough weather. Al and France helped him with his dinghy motor, which wasn't working, and he was most grateful. Let it be said that my husband knew dinghy motors much better now.

Ken told us that he left Japan the year before, and spent a year in Alaska where his children went to school and he had matters to attend to. The family left Alaska and sailed down the Canadian coast, planning to spend time in the Rockies to be part of a video on cliff-scaling in Yosemite National Park for Japanese television. After leaving Canadian waters, US Customs wouldn't let him land as he had already spent time in Alaska. He therefore had to sail down the US coast without stopping until he got to Mexico. I couldn't believe his misfortune, but also his lack of knowledge regarding US Customs which were very strict. I felt very sorry for his family, but they seemed to enjoy their time in Suwarrow.

One evening, the family set up a traditional Japanese meal of home-made noodles, mushrooms, fish and broth, rice with beans, and bean soup. Al, Gary, and I happened to motor in to see John, and were invited to join the group for dinner. The meal was very tasty, and I wondered how Ken's wife could make it all in such a tiny boat. Ken, on the other hand, was very upset because the noodles were ready before John appeared, and we had to wait. That was the last time we saw the family, and I hoped they arrived back home without any more mishaps.

Before the week was over, John invited all the cruisers to take a boat trip to another island in the atoll to find coconut crabs. These large, ugly creatures lived underground near the tree roots, but often climbed the coconut trees for protection. In order to catch one, John dug around its hole with a long sturdy pole, and pulled it out by hand. These crabs had a large, round body with six legs and front claws. He pulled off their legs and tied them to a tree until it was time to leave. The legs were put in a bucket to take back for all of us to cook. He found enough crabs to give us several legs to take back. Before leaving, John, whose skills could out-shine any young man's, climbed a coconut tree after tying palm leaves on his ankles. He boosted himself up the slim trunk like a monkey to knock down enough coconuts for everyone. His sharp machete was used to strip off the top, make a hole, and offer each one of us a drink. All these experiences that we had in Suwarrow and elsewhere made me glad that I had decided to cross the Pacific. The experiences couldn't have been duplicated.

"I hope you can get rid of all the rats, John," I said while saying our goodbyes. Apparently, a few cats had been brought to Suwarrow to kill the rats who loved the coconut trees. Unfortunately, the cats disappeared, and the rats got fatter. What was one to think! I couldn't imagine that that beautiful atoll was going to be spoiled by a rat infestation.

Samoa was our next destination. It was often called the birthplace of Polynesia since it was thought to be from the island of Savai'i that the original Polynesians set out to settle in the many islands of the Pacific.

This passage would be about 500 miles, a trip of four to five days if the weather was favourable. I realized, at that point, that having sailed from place to place on the vast expanse of the Pacific I had lost fear and apprehension of the weather we might encounter and trusted the sea-worthiness of our boat, as well as my husband's ability. All this after 18 months at sea!

So far Gary hadn't been sick and was able to do his watches. I was thankful for that. Our routine was set up again, and we learned to deal with the broken sleep necessary for watch-keeping. One night, we had a most beautiful vision of the full moon, which lit up the sky all around us. No rain and constant trade winds from the east pushed *Solara* through the rolling waves. I couldn't ask for anything more.

I was on our last fresh food except for some onions, potatoes, one cabbage, and a couple of apples. At least I had lots of cans of this and that which would be fine until we got to Apia on the island of Upolu, the main entrance to Samoa. There were another four days to go on our passage, but as we got closer to Apia the weather changed, as well as the wind which veered to the north. No more full moon, and the beginning of rain, which came with the cloud covering. This was the time which I liked the least. Variable winds, and the occasional squall, caused us to make many sail changes. There was no time to relax. Finally, when we were 14 miles away with no wind, Al conceded to motoring those last miles. Thank goodness. I was ready to get off the boat and see why Robert Louis Stevenson decided to end his last years there.

CHAPTER 20

❧

Samoa

SAMOA WAS ORIGINALLY a German colony, but after the First World War the country became a British colony, administered by New Zealand. It was now an independent nation, but the British traditions were very evident as we walked around Apia. We had to pass through a reef, well-marked by lights, and found a place to anchor near Aggie Grey's famous hotel. Aggie opened the hotel in 1943 to accommodate US Marines training there. It had been replaced by a modern, but charming, Victorian-style building, with verandas trimmed in gingerbread fretwork. Looking about after anchoring, the beautiful building immediately drew us in, and we were anxious to check into the country and explore the town of Apia.

"I've got to buy one of those," remarked Gary when he saw the Samoan men dressed in their *lavalavas*, a long wraparound skirt sometimes fastened with a leather strap, accompanied by sandals, and very cool and comfortable looking in the heat of Samoa. And off he went shopping for the day while Al and I did boat chores, which were always necessary every time we were in port. Even the local police wore these "skirts" when they lined up early each morning and marched to the main square to raise the Samoan flag in ceremonial style, while everyone nearby stood silently at attention. I convinced my husband to take our dinghy into town early one morning so I could take a photo of this picturesque tradition.

One didn't go to Samoa without visiting the Robert Louis Stevenson Museum at Vailima, where he lived his last years trying to repair his lungs, ravaged by TB. It was in a beautiful setting up the slopes of Mount Vaea above Apia, giving a wonderful view of the ocean. He lived there with his mother and wife Fanny, who had children from a previous marriage. When RLS died four years later, in 1894, she went back to California to live. This beautiful house then became home to several families, mainly government officials, but in later years it was badly damaged by a hurricane. Finally it was repaired, and beautifully renovated into a museum by using photos taken at the time to match the fine house that Stevenson originally made for his family.

It was in the museum that we felt the sense of the author and the wonderful tales he wrote such as *Treasure Island* and *Strange Case of Dr. Jekyll and Mr. Hyde,* as well many stories and poems for children. He continued to write steadily at Vailima and was called Tusitala, "the teller of tales," by the Samoans, who loved him dearly. When he died, 200 Samoans tracked up the hill and placed him in a grave on the hillside with the view he cherished.

Al and I planned a trip by bus to Savai'i, the other large island comprising Samoa, where we would spend a night and the next day exploring its picturesque setting, with the population living more modestly and settled in small villages. Much of the island, we read, was covered with deserted lava fields after numerous volcanic craters erupted many years ago.

The very crowded bus from Apia drove to the dock, where we took a ferry that went across the channel to Savai'i. The ferry was very comfortable, but the TV which sat prominently for all to see was playing a Hong Kong kung fu movie, a truly awful one, but which seemed to be enjoyed by all the local passengers who outnumbered us 100 to two.

My husband thought we had a car waiting that we could drive around the island the next day. In a small town near the docks, we grabbed some breakfast in an attractive open-air restaurant and proceeded to walk to the car rental place.

"It's too far," said one man when we asked him the way to the car rental.

"I'll just keep walking," Al replied, continuing on, but it was very hot and there was no sign of the place.

"Go ahead. Don't wait for me and come back with the car." After saying that I saw a market nearby, and decided to buy a large piece of material that I could wrap around myself, feeling very conspicuous in my shorts. All of the women around me wore colourful *lavalavas* and seemed very comfortable in the heat. The salesgirl wrapped it around me and fitted it like a pro.

"There, now you look beautiful," she said with a big smile. I was now ready to explore Savai'i.

There was no rental car, we learned. It had been in an accident, we were told. I wasn't too sure about that, but fortunately I found a taxi in town to meet up with Al. We were able to hire a man to take us around, which turned out to be a much better arrangement, except he couldn't speak English and we had to rely on an old map showing all the sites. It was a much cheaper way to go, costing us only US$40 for his time.

I was impressed by the *fales* (Samoan houses) which dotted the landscape. They were of all types, most open, with screens that came down to protect them from the colder breezes or hot sun. All were supported by heavy vertical beams on cement flooring. A thatched or metal roof and beautifully carved ceilings of wood and branches made a decorative pattern. Unfortunately, such traditional houses were disappearing. How comfortable they looked, although they had no walls for privacy. Family life was an open book, but as we passed these homes we looked away to give the privacy we felt the people would want.

We spent the night in a small inn in the north end of the island. The seas were much calmer than on the south and southeast coastline. The inn was built like a *fale*, but with filled in walls and, especially to my liking, with a hot shower. There was a lovely tranquil beach for swimming as well. Oh, how I liked staying away from the boat once in a while and being a tourist.

Each village had a large, well-constructed church looming over the small *fales*. The wealth of the church bothered my husband and me, as tithing at 10 percent was compulsory in each village. But we loved the people and their culture. The *aiga*, as it was called, was the extended family unit, which could include thousands of relatives, in which everything was owned collectively. These *aigas* were ruled by high chiefs who settled disputes and made sure that everyone was provided for. To us, this arrangement was the epitome of democracy. But we were bothered by the fact that the oldest male member of the family was more secure in his position in this hierarchy, which meant many younger male members of the same family left the country to find their own places in the world.

At 14:00 we left Savai'i by ferry and went back to our boat which had been well looked after by Gary. We were planning to leave Samoa in two days' time, with plenty to do beforehand. It was the beginning of August now, and we wanted to sail to Tonga and then Fiji before the cyclone season began in mid-November. We had been enjoying reasonably good conditions, but as it happens good things come to an end, and before we knew it another storm was brewing west of Samoa.

CHAPTER 21

⚓ Tonga

IT WAS STILL dark when I heard Al pulling up the anchor to cast us away. What a way to wake up! He was anxious to leave once we were ready, but I couldn't see around me, and then I heard a loud noise from a tanker's whistle leaving at the same time.

"Let's follow its path," I said. "It will be easier to find our way out through the pass in the reef, even with the markers."

We had 180 miles to go to Niuatoputapu in Tonga, which would take about two days if the winds were good. "New Potatoes," the name used by cruisers, was at the top end of the chain of islands comprising Tonga, and part of the Vava'u group of islands. Captain James Cook called them the Friendly Islands when he visited in 1773 and 1777. It was said that the friendliness was all a ruse in order to attack Cook the next day and eat him, but fortunately he sailed away before that could happen.

The first day was always the hardest after being at anchor for a week. The routines weren't yet set, and the disruptive sleeping patterns for watches didn't give us enough rest. We would only be sailing for a short period, and because of the favourable winds we reached our destination the next day.

Just before entering the bay at Niuatoputapu, the rains came down and obliterated our view. We needed help from the electronic chart to enter the pass, dropping our anchor just in time as the weather worsened. It was obviously the beginning of a front. Since Tonga was in the same time zone as New Zealand, we had skipped a day across the imaginary dateline. It became Saturday, not Friday. Being the weekend, we couldn't check in and had to stay on the boat.

We tried to collect the rain in pails, as it was constantly pouring all that day. But the rains washed off the salt that had accumulated on everything above the waterline. As I looked around, I saw many anchored boats through the mist surrounding us. One in particular anchored very close to our bow after we had settled in.

"There's *First Light* just ahead of us," I remarked with concern, as it was too close. It was an English boat captained by Richard, whose wife was a former policewoman. We had met them some time ago. When we bedded down for the night all seemed well, but at 04:00 the winds shot up to 40 to 48 knots (force 9-10 on the Beaufort scale) and other boaters reported that they had gusts of 50 to 60 knots. I woke Al up because I felt something was terribly wrong. We soon discovered that *First Light* was dragging right toward us and would possibly push us into the reefs close to our portside. Al put on our motor to try to move away, and called to *First Light* on our VHS.

"*Solara* to *First Light*," he called. "You're dragging right into my boat."

At that time, I could see their boat alongside ours, which was really scary. Richard also turned on his motor, and for two hours manoeuvred his boat to keep it away from ours. It was a tense night, and too windy and dark for him to try to reanchor. Also, Richard was crisscrossing our anchor line, and we were worried that it would be yanked by his dragging anchor. Finally, in early daylight, he found a new location and we could finish our lost sleep.

Because of the storm, no one wanted to take their dinghy ashore to pick up the local officials who would check us into Tonga. Another day to relax and read! The following day, Al made several trips to bring all the officials to our boat: customs, immigration, health, and agriculture. Shades of Cuba, except they wore no shoes! Agriculture wanted to see all my fresh food.

"I washed all my fresh food in bleach. Is that OK?"

Responding with a shrug, he answered, "As long as you keep the food in your fridge." That was good enough for me, but I had to cover our bananas with a clear garbage bag. I could understand Tonga's concern to keep all foreign fauna (which included bugs) and such from their very isolated country.

"Have you had measles?" asked the health official. Apparently there was an epidemic of measles in Vava'u, our next destination in Tonga. That happened from time to time, and the World Health Organization would start an immunization program. I didn't know what the official would do if one of us hadn't had the measles. Once all the paperwork was finished, we were free to explore the town.

On the 3-mile trip in to Niuatoputapu, it was apparent that we had arrived in a third world country. As we passed neat but tiny homes, we saw strips of pandanus leaves hanging outside on fences to dry. The leaves would be used to make their mats and ta'ovalas (woven mats wrapped around their skirts) which were used every day. The ta'ovala was also worn for ceremonies such as funerals and special occasions. Some were very old family heirlooms, and beautifully made. As I passed one community building, I saw several older women weaving a large mat together. It reminded me of my grandmother many years ago, sitting around making quilts for winter. They very kindly let me take a picture, which I now cherish.

I was sure that we were in a third world country when I came across the "communication centre." The Australian government had given the town a large satellite dish, but no equipment to work it, so there it sat, looking very modern but useless. There was also a telephone booth in front of the building that had no telephone. They should have called it "the non-communication centre." On the bright side, there was a school with many happy children playing in a field nearby, an old-fashioned bank, and one store, which carried a very limited supply of non-perishables. I was able to give my supply of extra toothbrushes to the local dentist who, in turn, gave my husband and me a lift back to our boat in his old car.

The town and surrounding countryside seemed to have had a pig invasion. They were everywhere, and probably communal property, foraging with their very long noses and digging up roots. When the tide was out, we would see them on the beach finding treasures from the sea and rooting around in the sand and seaweed tossed up on shore.

Because there was a weather window, we decided to leave for Vava'u, 160 miles to the south. Vava'u was well known for its great cruising amongst the various small islands and inlets where one could anchor in splendid solitude. We headed for Neiafu, the main headquarters for Moorings, a popular chartering company who made their in-house guide to anchorages available to all cruisers. Although the anchorages were numbered, taking away the romance of discovery, the guide was a blessing. The small town was also where I found provisioning, and places where we could have a meal away from the boat. I was always for that.

On our way out of the harbour at Niuatoputapu, we saw two humpback whales spouting high streams of water very close to our boat. Tonga was the breeding grounds for these whales between July and November, and before we left Tonga for good we would see many more. I could never get enough of the sight of those large mammals slapping the water with their flat, wing-shaped tails.

Again, it was hard to be on the open seas where the waves were 7 feet high right on our beam, and since we were close-hauled (almost right into the wind), *Solara* had to pound her way through the waves all through the night until the next day, when the wind changed to a more comfortable direction. We were passing through a front that had never moved away. Rain dogged our passage all the way. Twenty-four knots of wind, although uncomfortable, gave us a faster trip than we anticipated. *Solara* was a strong boat, and easily tackled the weather and direction we needed to reach Vava'u. On our approach, two more whales appeared, and one breached near us, showing its large and broad tail high up in the air. It was a great welcome to Neiafu harbour.

"There are a lot of cruising boats of friends anchored here," I cried happily.

I saw *Free Radical* with *Zephyr*, who seemed to sail together, and Pete from *Sojourner*, who was still sailing alone. *Would he find the best drinking place?* The next day *Sunshine*, a boat from Australia, and *Tien Sie*, from Singapore, arrived. They had taken the southern route of the Cook Islands, and had been hammered by the stormy front. It looked like a party ahead of us as we headed for the Mermaid, a hangout near Moorings. It was a great gathering of old acquaintances, sharing stories about passages and landfalls, discussing our plans for the next few weeks, and just enjoying the fact that all of us had come through a good part of the Pacific.

At the Mermaid, we saw a transvestite parade. In Tonga, families also encouraged one of their male members to turn female for reasons I could never comprehend. Nevertheless, the winner of the contest was present in all his finery, and looked very proud of himself/herself; I couldn't tell which.

While we were there, Al and I took walks down the main road away from the town, just to get our land legs back in shape. One day, we saw a funeral for a very important person, as all the people marching down the road wore black woven mats, black being a sign of respect. There were at least 200 mourners and a band to mark the event. I couldn't find out about the deceased, but I was sure everyone was there because all the establishments in town were closed for the day. It made me realize how important the close relationship of the community members was, which we also saw in Samoa. Although poor, the people had a richness of self-worth and belonging, something not always found in our Western culture.

We finished up our visit to Tonga by visiting some of the anchorages recommended by Moorings Yacht Charters. They were all delightful, sheltered, and quiet. There was a chance to swim, and in one place to explore a hidden cave, which had to be found after swimming 10 feet under the water and through an opening in the grotto. I had no interest in trying that since my swimming skills were minimal. Even though Al was a good swimmer, he went down 20 feet, got disoriented, missed the opening, and came up after a very long time, scaring me completely.

We tied up at very rickety steps and a decrepit dock at our last Moorings-recommended place, and then went up a hill to an Austrian restaurant situated among lush vegetation, overlooking the ocean. Now that would be a good place to eat, we thought. It turned out not to be the case.

"I wonder why the waitress is crying," I quietly whispered to Al.

"How should I know?" he answered. I wasn't sure why I asked him that, as he wasn't paying any attention to her situation. We were also made to sit outside on a patio for our meal, which would have been fine but the cold wind blew at us from that side, and it was hard to keep warm. The restaurant had a new owner who seemed to make life difficult for his staff because the food was so poor. He had made the pathway up to his place very inviting, which brought clientele like us up the stone steps and into the fox's lair.

We decided that it was soon time to leave Tonga. The weather beyond our sheltered anchorages in Vava'u was blowing winds in the '20s, and whitecaps were forming. We would have a fairly long sail to Fiji and needed to do some last-minute preparations before heading out. I wanted to wait for calmer weather as well.

We had a chance to say goodbye to some of our cruising friends. Some had left already, but others were soon ready to part at the same time as us. And there was *Hallelujah* which had arrived while we had been away.

"We're glad to see you," said Al with enthusiasm. "Never thought you would make it out of the Panama Canal." There were hugs all around in the local Neiafu bar.

"You know me," answered Kim. "I just had to cross the Pacific."

I also talked to a lovely Norwegian couple who had an interesting story to tell. When I asked her how many children they had she said, "We have three, but one came to us very late in our lives. We were sailing from Spain to the Canaries to cross the Atlantic when we saw a body in the water near our boat. It was an African, wearing a lifejacket but floundering in the water. We picked him up. Apparently, he had been thrown from the ship that he stowed away on, trying to leave the poverty of his country. We sailed back to Spain and after much paperwork put him in school there and adopted him as our own."

That was a wonderful story.

CHAPTER 22

Fiji

When we left Tonga at first light, our friends on *Free Radical* and *Sunshine* weren't far behind. There wasn't much wind at first, so we put up our beautiful blue spinnaker with a large sun appliquéd across the centre. It pulled us along like a parachute with the breeze at our stern. Ed, on *Free Radical*, took some wonderful shots of our boat on his camera and sent them to us later, but soon he motored away, leaving us far behind. We were grateful for the gesture, but I was sorry we didn't make haste as we ran into a terrible storm before arriving in Viti Levu, Fiji, and its capital Suva.

Gary, as usual, got seasick with the rocking of *Solara* on its spinnaker. We should have left him behind, I was thinking, but I couldn't do that again to a crew.

We ran into a nightmare of a front that never moved away. The barometer kept going down, but fortunately stopped before it showed a hurricane low. Low pressure meant stormy and unstable conditions. Because the front never moved away, we were subjected to heavy weather for days, with gale force winds and waves up to 13 feet. The worst was the large occasional wave that broke over our boat, filling our cockpit. Even though our hatches were tightly locked, the seawater came in and soaked my bed in the middle of the cabin, pushed the window through on our dodger (the canvas over the companionway), ripping away the seams, and tossing away our full 5-gallon tank water jug, leaving only the handle which had been tied down. Gary hadn't fully closed the hatch to his cabin which was behind the dodger, so the water poured down onto his bed just as he went to sleep. That was a hard lesson, and obviously we weren't as well prepared as we should have been for such a bad storm.

I was beside myself. Even though I had gone through some bad weather, this one was trying my patience. Why did Al keep using our mechanical steering device instead of quickly moving straight with our automatic steering? *Solara* handled the rough passage well, but with our mechanical steering we veered back and forth 10 to 20 degrees each way which added many more miles to our trip. On top of that, the monitor broke after three days and we had to hand-steer the boat. The rain belted down in buckets, and the dark and gloomy sky made the atmosphere completely depressing. You couldn't see more than 30 feet around the boat. It was as if the storm god had unleashed all its anger in those few days. I had been in touch with Des, our weather man from New Zealand, who had been helping us across the Pacific by radio contact twice a day. He was most apologetic as he had predicted much calmer weather, but we had to take what was given. Was I now an experienced sailor, ready to handle the storm? I still relied on my husband to make the decisions, but became aware that conditions like those didn't scare me like before, and experience showed that our boat was seaworthy.

I put on my storm clothing and took my watch from the companion-way, which gave me some shelter. I checked our instruments from time to time, while Al put on all his gear – heavy rain pants, boots, and two jackets – and braved the weather in all its fury. He was always ready to go to the bow if necessary, and of course all of us were always clipped in with our safety harness once leaving the companionway. Gary was a big help now that he was acclimatized, and took his turn at the wheel. No one was really hungry, but I was able to make soup for lunch and pasta for dinner. There were always cans to open, and I didn't want to use the stove very long at one time as it was very tiring while cooking. Relaxing at a meal wasn't in the works. With time off, we tried to rest or sleep, as the storm took all our energy and focus.

"OK guys," said Al. "We'll put on the autopilot as you've been asking. We're getting closer to Suva, and winds have gone down to 30 knots."

Thank goodness. It was late in the day and I wanted to get into shelter as soon as possible. We had to manoeuvre our way through a complicated string of small islands and reefs before coming to the island of Viti Levu and the entrance of Suva harbour. As we neared Suva, we had been in touch with a few of the cruisers already there and they were anxious because the harbour was full of derelict vessels waiting to be dismantled, plus large metal buoys for ships to attach to. Working one's way around that mess really needed daylight, and we had no more. *Sunshine* and *Free Radical* had been looking for us, and listening to the VHS for our call. Al had been so busy navigating that he forgot to call our friends, and Julie from *Free Radical* was getting ready to call security in case we had run in to trouble. After slowly motoring through the narrow entrance bordered by reefs and into the harbour, Ron on *Sunshine* put on his powerful searchlight and guided us through to a spot for anchoring. What a relief! How lucky we were to have concerned and helpful friends!

After talking to other cruisers the next day, we learned we had been lucky to arrive in one piece. One boat had capsized and lost all its rigging. Others came through the storm by going bare poles; that is, they took every sail down and carefully steered the dissembled boat; not always a good tactic in heavy weather. It was time to check in the next morning, but as I looked around after getting out of my warm but damp bed, the boats that had been near us last night were many feet away. It meant only one thing. We had dragged through the muddy bottom all night as we slept, but fortunately were stopped by the shallow bottom we were now sitting on. Did anyone notice? Hopefully not, as it was embarrassing to not have one's anchor set, but we were so tired that Al must have just let it drop. No problem though, as it was easy to motor back and anchor in a better spot.

The authorities called us on our VHF and gave us a time to check in. No fooling around in that country. We took the dinghy into shore at the Royal Suva Yacht Club, which had a very convenient dock and place to leave our dinghy. It was only a dollar taxi ride into the busy city, which was bustling and had signs of former British rule. There were a few art deco buildings such as the old cinema, some ugly modern buildings, and an infrastructure of colonialism in a now independent country. The main population was of indigenous Melanesian heritage and culture, very different from the Polynesians we had met in the rest of the Pacific islands. They were much darker, very large, and stockier with frizzy hair, looking fierce and foreboding. Less than 100 years ago, they were noted for their cannibalism, but now they were a very friendly people making us most welcome.

The other populous group came from India, descendants of the indentured labourers recruited a century earlier. It was apparent that there was a conflict between these two main groups. The Melanesians had control as administrators and holders of property and heritage rights, while the Indians ran the commercial enterprises but had no chance of owning land; some were forced out of farms they had leased for decades. Villages outside of Suva were governed by hereditary chiefs who had full authority over the running of the village.

While in Suva, we were busy with arranging our stops and cruising permits for our sail along the south coast of Viti Levu to the west side where I would be taking a flight back to Canada a couple of weeks later. I caught up on email to our family and did some last-minute shopping. Souvenir shopping included *tapa* cloth from a tree bark, decorated with beautiful designs, a large shell necklace with pink delicate lining strung on a woven coconut fibre cord, and, even though heavy, a small decorated wooden *kava* bowl which, in that culture, was used for special ceremonies. *Kava*, a narcotic drink given to the guests of the house, would be passed around ceremonially. Cruisers who were planning to visit villages on their travels would, as suggested, bring dried roots of the "grog" plant in case they were invited as guests of honour.

We hadn't checked our email since Samoa, and after checking our bank account Al found that our Canadian Visa numbers had been compromised, and three items put on that totalled $9,000. Fortunately, Visa credited the amount to us, but we had to get new cards. At the time, we didn't know how both our numbers – which were different – had been used. After a few delicious Indian meals and more socializing at the yacht club with our friendly cruising group, we were ready to leave.

Our first stop was at Bega, a small island surrounded by an atoll which we sailed to in a fresh breeze and calm seas. We arrived at Vaga Bay on the west side, protected from the southeast and east winds. It was good to get away from the garbage smells, mosquitoes, and the derelict trash in the harbour of Suva. There we could rest and relax before heading west again.

Our next stop was Vunaniu Bay, arriving early afternoon and carefully motoring through the narrow channel lined on both sides by reefs into a much protected anchorage. *Free Radical* and *Sunshine* arrived about the same time. Suddenly the sky got very dark, the rain belted down and lightning flashed constantly, lighting up the sky. It was obvious that we would be there at least another day. Our view was obliterated and the Fiji radio was giving a warning to all small craft.

"We might as well relax," I said. "There's no point in killing ourselves in this weather."

The other two boats must have felt the same way, as all three boats remained in the protected bay. We could do some reading and enjoy our meals without rushing. The weather on the radio talked about a clearing on the weekend, but the rains came harder, if that was possible, and the winds were unrelenting. What stinky weather! We could at least party with the others, so Gary rowed Al and I over to *Free Radical* to play a popular card game, and then picked up Trish and Ron on *Sunshine.* The party went on into the evening, and when it was time to go, the winds picked up from brisk to gale force; we were only protected there from the waves, not the wind. It was a problem trying to get back to our boat, but Gary and Al struggled hard to keep the dinghy directed to *Solara,* finally making it.

Since the weather calmed somewhat, our captain decided to leave that anchorage and head over to Cuvu harbour, 25 miles west. The winds came up later and we triple reefed our main sail as they went from 20 to 40 knots (force 8 on the Beaufort scale) giving us a fast sail to the entrance of Cuvu.

It turned out that there was a fancy resort here, and suddenly we heard: "Boat entering, boat entering, we have a good spot for you to anchor. If you wish to come to our restaurant, we can pick you up." This message came from a VHS call on shore. As usual, that sounded good to me.

"Say yes," I pleaded. "We might as well get away from the rainy weather."

With that a small powerboat arrived and showed us the place to anchor, and then gave us a ride to the resort. When we stepped off the boat, we saw a large group of well-dressed people, apparently from New Zealand, who had come to celebrate a wedding. How disappointing it must have been that the weather was so miserable. Rain was dripping off their heads as they went from place to place between the covered areas of the resort. Nevertheless, the wedding party didn't seem to mind the rain, and they all appeared happy and carefree. After a delicious buffet, we had a wet ride back to our boat, feeling very satisfied.

It was now rainy day number six, and past the middle of September. My plane reservation was for September 28, and the airport was close to the far western corner of Viti Levu in Nadi, a large town relying on tourists. I was becoming impatient with the weather and anxious to get our boat to Musket Cove, just off the mainland of western Fiji. We finally left our sheltered anchorage, and had a good sail to our last destination before I was to leave the boat.

Musket Cove was a wonderful and relaxing resort that tolerated all the cruisers stopping by. We could attach ourselves to a mooring ball, use the facilities such as showers, laundry machines, and grocery store, and swim in the adjoining pool if the beach was too hot. This was, of course, at a decent price. We gathered again with some of our cruising friends, but most of the American boats had left for New Zealand from Tonga or sheltered their boats in Tonga and flew home during the cyclone season.

Gary decided to leave our boat once in Musket Cove and go home to solve some problems, leaving Al to sail to New Zealand with another crew, an Englishman named Glen who had answered an ad from a crew-seeking website that Al had placed. Glen seemed like a mature, responsible person. I did not want to leave my husband to manage the boat without good help. It was well known that the sail from Fiji to New Zealand could be a difficult one, weather-wise, and that was part of the reason why I decided to visit home for two months. As it turned out I wasn't wrong, and never heard the end of Al's passage.

Al was very annoyed when he found out that Gary had joined another boat going to New Caledonia, not going right home and breaking his commitment to help Al sail to New Zealand. By then, I had tired of Gary, and concluded that I would have no more crew for the rest of our journey once we left New Zealand.

PART 4

Down Under

CHAPTER 23

❦

New Zealand

IT WAS A difficult visit home after two years. The mail had piled up at least 2 feet on the kitchen counter, but at least the condo was still standing. I talked about my experiences with friends.

"Oh the beauty of the Pacific Islands, and the incredible vastness of the ocean," I would say. They would just look at me and try to understand. I couldn't adequately describe the experiences I'd been having so that they could relate to my feelings.

It was a joy to see my family after such a long time. They were leading busy lives and thankfully didn't need me since I was about to leave again. It was hard to find out that others had died. My brother-in-law and friends I knew in Collingwood were now gone. Was this circumnavigation worth not having the chance for a last visit? It was as though Al and I had disappeared from the face of the earth. At times, I felt like a stranger from a distant world. The supermarket especially confused me. I was perplexed by all the choices that were available to me. I was ready to go back to a simple life again.

When I got off the plane in Auckland, I breathed a sigh of relief. The anxiety slipped away, and I was truly back where I should be, with my husband. There was my second home, *Solara,* securely tied to a slip in Gulf Harbour, a very luxurious marina near Auckland. We would be there until April, with lots of time for boat work, travelling, and preparing for further adventures. We bought a car. Now we could explore both South Island and North Island, do our food shopping more easily, and, of course, make the necessary trips to marine stores for boat supplies.

After getting settled, Al described his passage from Fiji. Apparently it had been a terrifying experience, but in some ways he was excited about it. He was glad that I wasn't there, and wondered if I'd want to sail in the Coral Sea. The canvas from the dodger and the main sail had torn. Water had swamped the cabin below, damaging the batteries, and the electronic autopilot. He didn't talk about it again, but I'm sure it stuck in his mind long after.

Our daughter, Vicky, arrived soon after my return to be with us for Christmas and stay for a month. I was excited about having her with us and exploring New Zealand together. As Vicky was unpacking her bag, she pulled out a small package.

"What do you have there?" I asked her.

"It's a Christmas tree," she said. She began to blow on the tube attached to the package, and there was a cute little green tree covered with coloured plastic balls, topped off with a yellow star. "That will set the mood. I'll attach it to your stern."

On Christmas morning, in spite of the surrounding green grass and flowers in our marina, we felt a connection with our family in Canada. We exchanged gifts, ate a delicious dinner, and finalized our plans for an extensive road trip.

New Zealand was like a playground with deep valleys, ocean vistas of startling azure blue, winding paths over grassy fields, and forests of strange trees that looked like they came from a Dr. Seuss book. The country invited us to explore it all, in a kayak or by hiking when the mood suited us. For the next three weeks, we tried to see everything that was possible to see. New Zealand was amazingly beautiful. From the rich apple-growing and wine region of Nelson, to the mountainous area of Queenstown, with its glacier valleys and deep fiords, we took in the spectacular scenery.

From Te Anau in Fiordland, we drove on the Southern Scenic Route through the Catlins and found sea lions, elephant seals, and an abundance of birdlife. We tasted wine in Nelson and in the Marlborough region near Christchurch. Between these two cities, Vicky found time to swim with the seals, see penguins and albatrosses, and go whale and dolphin watching. What more could she ask for? At a cultural museum near Wellington, we learned about the Maori: their independence, their culture, their migration, and settlement in New Zealand (the vast majority of place names were of Maori origin and a puzzle to pronounce). Then, unfortunately, it was time to go to the airport to see our daughter off. We had had a marvellous visit and sightseeing tour with Vicky, and said our goodbyes with heavy hearts, not knowing when we would see her again.

Before leaving Auckland, I said to Al, "Let's drive down to Tauranga and see Derek Hatfield, before he leaves for the Southern Ocean. His next passage will be very difficult."

The Around Alone race, held every four years, was very serious business. Canadian Derek Hatfield had one of 11 boats that had entered the race and were sitting in the harbour, where repairs or maintenance could be done. There was only one woman there, representing England; all the other boats were skippered by men. Tauranga was one of five stops they would make, and we were lucky to be in New Zealand at the time.

It was exciting seeing all the boats, from many countries, preparing for their next passage. I looked at Derek's boat, which was so different from any cruising boat that I was familiar with. The hatch to the cabin below could be fastened shut like a submarine to keep out water in case it "turtled." There was no doubt that he or any of the other racers would encounter storms. Both of us were impressed by the ultimate endurance the race enacted on each skipper. It took a great deal of courage to face the wild storms and fierce oceans alone, with no help in case of breakdowns or before 40-foot breaking waves. Later, we read that Derek's boat suffered a serious dismasting near Cape Horn, but the *Spirit of Canada* did reach the final stop in Newport, Rhode Island, some weeks later.

Before going to Tauranga, we watched America's Cup, which was being held in Auckland. There was staunch support for Team New Zealand, as evident in the newspapers and in talking to the Kiwis we met. Being stationed in Auckland harbour, the race was right on our doorstep every day. At the beginning of the final challenge races, hundreds of crafts from all over Hauraki Bay, including Gulf Harbour, piled high with friends and goodies and motored out to the race area. For most races, they returned a few hours later, with sober and confused faces. Many times, the race was cancelled because of too little wind, too variable wind, or too much wind. Because these large, fragile racing boats could only race in winds of certain strength, the weather wasn't cooperating. Of the best nine races, there was only one truly competitive race where *Alinghi* from Switzerland won in the last seven seconds with the very talented skipper Russell Coutts who, remarkably, was from New Zealand, as well as many of his crew. Team New Zealand had a boat that kept falling apart. A very devastating time for the host country!

On March 15, we finally left Gulf Harbour, untying all our umbilical cords, electricity, water, and phone. After our long stay, we felt the boat was ready to go offshore: her bottom was cleaned and painted with anti-foul paint, all systems checked and repaired as necessary, a thorough rigging inspection completed, and new varnish on all her topside wood. We sold our car almost at the price we paid in November. It was sad saying goodbye to new friends and old.

I loved New Zealand, and understood why some cruisers wished to stay and live there. But we needed to get the feel of water under our keel again, and headed out to Great Barrier Island, stopping first at Kawau just off the mainland for a couple of days to check our gear. The Barrier, as it was sometimes called, was located about 61 miles northeast of Auckland. Captain James Cook circumnavigated New Zealand between 1769 and 1770 and named the island for how it acted as a barrier from the stormy Pacific to the east. We saw the small brown teal duck, which was almost extinct, as well as the historic kauri dam, which helped to bring the huge trees down the river to be picked up by boat. After taking hundreds of years to grow, the kauri tree had almost disappeared from New Zealand. Its immense, tall trunk was used for lumber and spars on tall ships. I was saddened by the disappearance of the trees, as well as so many species of fauna, such as the kiwi. How wonderful it must have been to see this country before man arrived, when only birds were there and the huge kauri trees were still standing.

Our final plan before leaving the country was to stop in Opua in the Bay of Islands area in northeastern New Zealand. We were able to say our good-byes to a few old friends on our sail north: Dave and Di on *Amoenitas*, and Pete and Julie on *Sojourner*, in a small marina at Tutukaka. Both boats would be spending another southern winter in Fiji. We probably would not see either couple again. That was the pitfall of cruising.

As we continued our passage, the weather wasn't in our favour. We got choppy seas, strong winds, and continuous rain. We spent a week in Whangaruru, north of Tutukaka, although we weren't protected from the north winds coming at us in gale force. The fresh water pump, which we had just bought in Gulf Harbour, stopped working. So out came the buckets, and the canvas covering the cockpit was angled to let water run off and fill them. Our only solace was that the rain was unrelenting. It was impossible to see beyond 100 feet most of the time. I thought that sailing off the coast of New Zealand would be easy, but we were not having a good time at all.

How was it like to be just the two of us again? Wonderful! I was so tired of the extra person in the boat, especially Gary, who seemed to me to be mostly a burden, and not much help. My husband and I worked as a pair like before, each with our own tasks, but I was glad to leave the responsibility to my husband and take orders as he saw fit. I guess that I knew as much about the boat as he did, but I was unable to physically perform some of the tasks, like pulling up the last of the anchor chain or beginning the task of furling in the large genoa.

In quiet waters, after the stormy week, we sailed past the "Hole in the Wall," a small passage through a large rock, on our way to the Bay of Islands, named by Captain Cook, with its multitude of small protected bays and islands. The well-known lighthouse welcomed us as we drew near, standing beautifully alone and sparkling white on a rocky precipice at the entrance.

We stayed at the Bay of Islands for 10 days, hiking the hills, visiting friends at the marina in Opua, and doing necessary tasks before leaving for Australia. We visited Des in Russell, and said we'd keep in touch when we sailed across the Coral Sea. He was much older than he sounded on our SSB radio, and showed us his small radio room surrounded by weather charts and other devices he used to keep us informed. The stormy weather "outside" the sheltered Bay of Islands continued, and delayed our departure until April 10.

The marina in Opua, where we spent our last few days, was a mixed bag of permanent members, and those like us who were preparing to leave the country. Al had time to see about a tooth problem and decided to have it extracted. Then Mike, on *Hallelujah*, arrived while we were here.

"Are you planning to leave soon? We're also sailing to Australia," he told Al.

"As soon as we can," Al replied. "It depends on the weather. We could sail together if you'd like."

It was amazing that *Hallelujah* was there and ready to go. I chalked it up to Kim, who had an agenda like my husband. Nothing could stop her. Three of us left Opua at the same time – *Solara*, *Hallelujah*, and *Adriatic*, an Italian boat – heading for Sydney, Australia.

The New Zealand officials were most diligent. "Where are you heading? You must not stop anywhere in New Zealand once you leave Opua. We are going to take a picture of your boat before you leave so we can check by air that you won't be stopping." Finishing with, "Here are all your papers and good luck."

What a departure! In spite of the officials, we had felt very welcome in their country, and left with many fond memories.

It would take 12 days to cross the Coral Sea to our destination of Bundaberg. And what a passage! It had been a long time since there had been only the two of us on a lengthy passage. I kept in touch with Des for the weather, checked with *Hallelujah* each day about our positions, and radioed Ed and Julie on *Free Radical* who were going to meet us in

Australia. It was difficult at first, with three-hour watches and much less sleep than when we crossed the Pacific and had an extra crew. We knew that perfect weather wouldn't stay with us. We were expecting at least three fronts while at sea.

In fact, after two days of benign and favourable winds, where we could enjoy the sea around us and get accustomed to the gentle swaying of the boat, we got the first front heading our way. Since it was just behind a low, it made the cold front more vigorous. The winds went from 20 to 22 knots from the east, with 7-foot swells, to 30 knots from the southeast and 7- to 10-foot seas. We could handle these conditions since Des had warned us about the front and we were prepared. He had also suggested that we head more west, and try to get above 30 degrees south latitude. The Coral Sea was an imposing body of water, which was more formidable further south, if one were to go to Sydney. I couldn't believe the large swells. Solara would ride 40 feet up the slope of the swell, and 40 feet down again in the trough. At the top of each swell, I looked down into the trough below, and wondered if we would ride down head first, but our boat stayed solid and steady, a real seaworthy vessel. It was like a roller coaster. The sea there was immense, since the waves and swells were coming from far away, across the Southern Ocean, with no land mass to slow them down. We had to hope that no breaking waves would come our way and fill up our cockpit with water.

The first front was followed soon after by a second. I was feeling scared and alone. The winds had risen suddenly above 24 knots, and the waves looked ready to wash over the boat. I hated a dark night when there was no moon or stars to keep me company, and I couldn't see beyond 10 feet.

I called down to Al reluctantly as he needed his sleep.

"Al, I'm scared."

I wasn't sure what he could do, but I didn't want to face the seas by myself. He put on his storm gear and slowly came up from below. He looked competent and ready to tackle anything, and I felt guilty for waking him.

"What are you afraid of tonight?" I knew he felt excitement and exhilaration from the wind and waves. *Why couldn't I feel the same?* "Let's talk about what might happen, but likely won't."

"Well, the boat could be knocked down by a breaking wave, a passing ship might not see us and collide, or you could be swept off the deck, and I'd be left alone." All these possibilities came to me. I had read in sailing magazines that they had happened to others.

"I have confidence in *Solara's* stability and performance," my husband replied. "We have gone through rough weather before, and nothing has happened. And don't forget we use all safety precautions."

Al always had the ability to calm me down, and I told him to get back to bed and that I'd be OK until my watch was over. I listened to some favourite music on my Walkman such as James Taylor, Eric Clapton, and Jimmy Buffet. That was always soothing, but I had a feeling that my husband didn't get to sleep right away.

Our head stopped working a few days into our passage. What a drag! One of our buckets took the place of the toilet.

"I'm using the bucket," I would call to Al, and he stayed below until I was finished. Actually, it was quite comfortable. With the bucket between the two benches, and a narrow cockpit, I could hold on, and prevent any loss of balance. The fresh air around me was most pleasant.

I was having an intense pain in the tooth that was supposedly fixed in the Marquesas.

"I can't ignore this problem," I commented to Al. "I'd better take some antibiotics."

I was afraid that the bacteria in the tooth would affect my whole body. That was the second time I felt the need to medicate myself with antibiotics. Thank goodness we had them with us. The medicine did the trick temporarily, but I would have to deal with the tooth in Australia.

We had another front soon after the second. This time, Al was on a night watch. I think he was aware of my fears, and proceeded to shorten the sails, which would give us a more comfortable ride. Maybe he was a little fearful himself, or he caught it from me. I woke up with the wind screaming around the boat as though it had full control. Then the full force of the rain pounded down upon us. I felt that I had to get up and help my husband. Although he seemed fully in control, I was sure he would be glad to see me. On went my storm clothes, my boots, my harness, and lifejacket, before dashing up the companionway. We then proceeded to put in a third reef in the main sail, which slowed our speed and gave us more control. It was wild in the cockpit with the rain, the darkness, and the splashing swells, causing *Solara* to pitch and rock. Al then put the first and second washboard over the companionway stairs, remembering the time when water had poured down into the cabin when he had sailed to New Zealand with Glen.

Now, I looked around me at the vast wild ocean, and all I could see were the high swells topped by breaking waves. The waves were as high as a three-story Rosedale mansion, and looked ready to pound down on top of us. The night didn't seem to end, but the storm let up somewhat and I could send my husband to his bed and take over. I plugged my Walkman into my ears, and Bob Dylan helped to calm me. Al told me that if he heard me singing away to the music, he could relax and know that all was well. The Italian boat *Adriatic*, which was heading for Sydney, contacted Des to tell us that they were getting 60 knots of wind in the second front, and for us to be prepared. We were 4 degrees north of them, which gave us a better position for lighter winds. How wonderful it was to have the concern of a fellow boater!

Finally, after 10 days we were north of 30 degrees south, out of the Tasman Sea and into the Coral Sea.

One quiet morning, *Hallelujah*, who had been in daily contact with us, showed up next to our boat. Mike called over, "Can you take our picture?" He stood in his cockpit, camera in hand. "I've taken yours. It will be fun to exchange pictures that have been taken in the middle of the ocean."

Of course we would. Mike and Kim had first planned to sail to Sydney, but realizing weather would be a problem, decided to enter Australia at Bundaberg like us.

We started listening to the Queensland coastal weather report. We were only 80 miles from the coast, but learned about a ridge which caused strengthening southeast trade winds every four days. How difficult it would have been for Captain Cook. He would have had no weather reports, no navigational aids, and no idea of the large barrier reef that protected the coastline of Queensland from the furious waves to the east.

I was getting tired from lack of sleep, using a pail for a toilet, and running out of fresh food. It had been 12 days since we left New Zealand, and it also happened to be Easter Monday. The weather was worsening after a few days of steady winds. We kept two-hour watches since we were close to the entrance of Hervey Bay, and the stormy conditions meant constant surveillance. But once in the bay, there seemed to be no shelter. We had 33 knots of wind right on our bow, and 10-foot waves as we approached the entrance to Bundaberg harbour 60 miles away. We kept getting swamped with water, and the heavy rain made visibility poor as we slowly motored all that day.

"Australia Customs," called Al on our VHS. "We are approaching the entrance to Bundaberg and would like to come in."

Did we ever, I thought. I wanted to get out of that madness and have a good night's sleep.

"It will cost you $200 extra, since it's Easter weekend, but if you wait until five this evening you can pay the normal fee of $120," answered the official-sounding voice in a strong Australian accent.

We were almost within shelter, and I felt like crying. We were cold and wet, and had been in that bay since five in the morning. That would mean another five hours heaving to.

"What a bum deal," said a stranger's voice on our radio after our discussion with the customs man. At least we had some support nearby. Al set the sails for heaving to (the boat basically rides with the waves and wind and gives the crew some needed rest), but that meant we drifted a long way from the entrance and didn't get into shelter until about 19:00. We finally anchored in the dark, but mistakenly in the main channel, where we almost got rammed by a large freighter. That was close! We finally anchored again, and collapsed for the night. Those last 12 days were finally behind us.

CHAPTER 24

Australia

ONCE THE CUSTOMS, immigration, and agriculture procedures were finished in Bundaberg, we were left with no fresh food, canned meat, or honey. It was all taken away. Australia and New Zealand were very particular in what food they allowed. I could understand their concern, being very isolated in the Southern Ocean and not wanting any foods that would contaminate their own produce.

Solara always needed care and replacements. The marina in Bundaberg was very modern, and had all the services we wanted or needed. I loved Bundaberg, maybe because the area made rum from its sugarcane. We saw the Australian boat *Sunshine* sitting on the hard. It belonged to the cruising couple we had met in Fiji, and was finally home after eight years. Kim and Mike on *Hallelujah* said goodbye the next day as they were staying at a different marina down the river from the coast, and visiting friends in Sydney. Perhaps we would see them again on our travels.

As we sailed north up the Queensland coast, the ugly fronts hit us again every four days. They seemed to keep a constant schedule, as though they were following a weather clock. We often anchored in rivers that ran into the ocean from far inland. The tides along the coast and in the rivers were 12 to 18 feet. We had to have enough anchor chain out when the water level rose. The currents were strong too because of the tides, which moved our boat back and forth. Our bow would face toward the river mouth when we anchored in the evening, and face upriver in the morning. Anchoring took some practice, but since there were no ac-cidents, I guess we learned. We were also told not to swim outside the boat as the river had many saltwater crocodiles that would have loved to have us as a meal.

Some of the good shoal water areas for anchoring were closed at the time we were there as a naval exercise was going on for the month of May. We heard guns from time to time that reminded me of the waters outside the Meaford range area in Georgian Bay, near our home in Ontario. The protected rivers away from the turbulent seas were beautiful and quiet, but often better for small powerboats and shoal draft sailboats due to the sandbars and shallow depth. Large trees lined the banks and turtles could be seen swimming by, oblivious to the crocodiles. Because of the hazards of anchoring in the rivers, we decided to find places among the various small islands just outside the coast, sheltering there when the next storm came up.

The first island anchorage was Hexham Island and was supposed to shelter us from the southeast high winds, which were now 25 knots. I also saw my first water spout near a big black cloud as we sailed along. It looked like an upside down tornado. It was so scary and I hoped it wouldn't come our way. It could have disabled our boat with no trouble.

Once at Hexham Island, it turned out there were other problems with this "shelter." Firstly, we were getting swells from the northeast, and the high tides here caused an unpredictable anchor setting. We were surrounded by rocks and reefs which bothered my husband, since there were the remnants from wreckage on the beach. It took three attempts to secure the anchor before Al was satisfied. Otherwise we could have been pushed into shore, hit the sand and rocks, and become part of the wreckage.

"That could be us if we're not careful," said Al. "Since the winds haven't changed we'll be here for a while."

Was I going to be able to sleep? I was thinking that we could end up on the rocks and there was no one nearby. We were all alone except for an eagle's nest just above our heads, sitting precariously on a large branch. We watched the parents constantly feeding the hungry new ones with fish from the surrounding ocean. It was like watching a nature pro-gram on TV.

Although the winds were still high after a week, Al convinced me that it was time to leave Hexham. Both of us had read enough and were thor-oughly rested. We sailed to Curlew Island 40 miles away, which from our pilot chart showed a good anchorage. We had to avoid many shoals and small islands on our passage, as well as the hazards entering the shallow entrance to the anchorage. There was only a small German boat sitting there, but we didn't know them and kept to ourselves. After such an in-tense sail watching all the time for rocks, we were too tired.

The next day we finally found a secure marina at Mackay "Reef" Marina after passing the largest dock in the South Pacific, where eight large freighters were waiting to unload. It was comforting to be in a ma-rina after such an uncomfortable sail. I was glad to step on shore after nine days in a stormy sea, but as usual there was boat work to be done, and provisions to buy. We continued making stops as we headed north. The passage along the Queensland coast seemed to take forever. There were the Whitsunday Islands, a popular cruising area, Goldsmith Island, Cid Harbour, and Sawmill Bay, all overnight anchorages. The weather was cold and rainy most of the time, unfortunately, but winter was approach-ing in Australia, and it was sure to be warmer further north.

"We'll go to Townsville instead," Al suggested, feeling very frustrated when he found out that a new wind generator, recently ordered, hadn't arrived as promised. "We can find another technician who can install the generator once we arrange to have it sent there."

Consequently, we sailed to Townsville for an overnighter. Before dark the rains came. It was the most torrential rain we had encountered in our two years of sailing. In fact, we were told it was a weather record. Before that, I had looked at our radar while on watch and saw the screen develop a dark area, which got bigger and bigger just before the storm. The storm followed our passage for hours, accompanied by high winds of 25 to 30 knots. We hadn't been warned about the weather change or we wouldn't have left that night. The visibility was nil, and it was scary because we couldn't see around us in the busy offshore shipping lane. How relieved I felt in the morning to see the entrance to Cleveland Bay, where Townsville was situated. It was 11:00, and I was tired, wet, and anxious to rest.

"I'm afraid you'll have to wait until 04:30 when the tide goes up, and you can enter."

This was another disappointment, reminding me of our nearness to Bundaberg harbour and not being able to enter a few weeks before.

Townsville was a delight, with its beautiful setting on the shore of the Coral Sea. Our marina was situated beside Anzac Memorial Park, a name commemorating all the Australian and New Zealand heroes and veterans who fought in the wars, including Gallipoli, Turkey, in WWI. In the park, we saw our first crested cockatoos and ibises poking around the mile-long beach, bordered by an ocean walkway called the Strand. A children's water park was situated halfway down the beach, full of frolicking youngsters. This newly built park was a wonderful place for the multitude of people enjoying themselves on the weekends. On Sundays, the town centre was filled with food and craft stalls. I couldn't imagine leaving Townsville right away. There was too much to entertain us. One of the highlights of Townsville was a trip to Billabong Sanctuary, where I cuddled a koala bear and Al a 4-year-old crocodile. Cuddling the koala bear was much nicer than Al's cold and slippery crocodile. I could have stayed all day feeling the soft fur against my neck from the young animal hanging on.

Al calculated that the Queensland coast was as long as travelling from Florida to Maine in the US. We continued to make many stops due to storms or just needing a rest after a night's sail. We anchored in Mourilyan Harbour, a commercial harbour mainly for freighters. The next day, towards Cairns, we approached Cape Grafton near Fitzroy Island, Captain Cook's first anchorage on arriving in this new land. We had read that the Aborigines were so unfriendly that Cook never set foot on the mainland. Although it was approaching nightfall, we were able to see the red and green buoys and use the leading lights to find our way through the dredged channel to the marina at Cairns, trying to avoid all the high-powered tourist boats coming back from Fitzroy Island.

"There's *Adriatic* close by," exclaimed Al after we had tied up in the marina. The *Adriatic* was the Italian boat that had warned us about the coming storm while we were crossing to Bundaberg. I was pleased to see them again.

The marina in Cairns wasn't yet finished. It gave us a good price per day since we had to scramble over debris and barriers to reach the washrooms and office. After a number of visits to boat repair shops, Al found someone to fix our boom in Port Douglas, 30 miles north, as well as have the new wind generator delivered. The large boom on our boat had cracked and bent when it suddenly swung around in a gusty wind before we could stabilize it. We could only blame ourselves for the disaster. Thank goodness we were in Australia and not Indonesia.

We had a week in Port Douglas while our boom was being repaired and enjoyed the friendly atmosphere and intimacy of the town. Many tourists came to Port Douglas to visit the nearby popular reef sites and the Low Islands. I often saw small powerboats leaving the town's harbour with tourists for snorkelling and scuba diving. There was also a local market with all kinds of interesting crafts where I found some cool dresses.

As we sailed north toward the equator, the heat was becoming oppressive off the boat. It was now the end of May, and we had to make it around the top of Australia before the middle of July in order to be in Darwin for the rally to Timor. There wasn't too much time to waste. Our boom was cut apart, reinforced, welded, painted, and finally attached to *Solara*. Our wind generator also arrived, and we were ready to tackle the northbound sail to Cape York.

It was in Port Douglas that we heard from our daughter about serious calls and letters that were arriving to our Collingwood address about money owing to various bulk stores, banks, and other institutions, all places we never used and of course weren't there to buy anything. It was obvious that our identity had been stolen. Al made a few calls to our bank to handle the matter, and we hoped that the problem could be solved. That was the last thing we needed halfway around the world.

We continued on after Port Douglas, stopping here and there. Low Islets, Hope Island with good anchorages and clear waters, and then Cape Flattery on the third night where we saw many prawn boats with their huge booms jutting out like an octopus anchored in the bay, sometimes a good indication of proper shelter. We also saw our first dolphins after a long time, not having them around our boat since crossing the Pacific.

Our most interesting stop was Lizard Island, named by Cook since he noted that all he could see were lizards. Lizard Island was also famous for Cook's Look, on the high hill overlooking Watson Bay. We climbed this hill, mimicking Captain Cook when he was looking for a passage through the many reefs to head out to the open sea. All I could see were the various shades of the water beyond the island, and wondered how Cook had managed to find his way. There was excellent snorkelling near our boat to see the large clam garden holding clams as large as a dining room table. It was possible to see the clams from our boat in the clear water below. .

It was on Lizard Island that we learned of the research being done at a laboratory nearby. Australia was concerned about the coral reefs and their preservation. They were also trying hard to protect more of the Barrier Reef from fishing and keeping many parts of the reef free from the public. One of the worst predators was the crown-of-thorns starfish. We saw a specimen which had clamped onto the coral and literally digested it. I hoped that Australia would be successful in their efforts as the beautiful area of the Barrier was one of the wonders of the world.

Reluctantly, we left Lizard Island in foul weather to Ninian Bay. Weather was always on our minds, but we couldn't just sit at anchorages or harbours. As we continued our passage north we saw: our first dugong, a large water animal similar and as vulnerable as the manatee in Florida; a mother ship which plied the waters, feeding the trawlers fuel and other resources; constant stormy weather with high wind and waves; and a lone palm tree on Morris Island, which was the last tree to stand after the British Admiralty planted many palms and sisal trees (which could knock down the coconuts), along with goats, to support any shipwrecked vessels that might land there. We passed isolated reefs and remote flat coastlines, anchored in shallow rivers with submerged rocks, saw the local Aborigines for the first time, and finally viewed a beautifully clear picture of Cape York with its surrounding islands. It had taken us two months to reach the most northerly point of Australia.

Cape York Peninsula was supposed to be the largest unspoilt wilderness in northern Australia. The stark white lighthouse at the cape sat on top of a craggy pile of rocks above a windswept rise of land. We dropped our anchor into the current of the channel at Horn Island after rounding the top of the peninsula. Across the channel from us was Thursday Island, or "TI" as it was called. Torres Strait at Thursday Island was considered to be international, and our boat was treated as a foreign boat and subject to the same restrictions as when we entered Australia in Bundaberg. TI attracted many tourists because of its location and being surrounded by Aborigine land. There was a Memorial Church nearby which commemorated the loss of 133 passengers from the British steamer *Quetta*, which struck a rock near Cape York in the 19th century and sunk in three minutes. There was also a cemetery with the graves of 700 Japanese pearl divers who first arrived in 1878. They had taken greater risks than the local divers and paid the ultimate price. The locals, called Islanders, lived easily on what the sea provided. They caught crabs, oysters, clams, and prawns, which were there in abundance. Most of them were Aborigines or of mixed race.

"Did you know Russell Crowe had his honeymoon here?" I said to my husband after we had settled in *Solara*. "And his boat was anchored almost in the same spot as where we are now." I looked at Al for a reaction, but his face told me that he couldn't have cared less. Russell Crowe probably sailed with a professional crew on a much larger yacht than ours. At least it made me feel that we were in a very special place.

On leaving Thursday Island, the Australian Coast Guard called us from a plane overhead and asked for our particulars.

"What is the name of your boat? What is your call sign and name of your captain? Do you have a cruising permit?" These questions came from an authoritative voice above us. Australia kept a close watch on boats coming and leaving their waters, as it was often the case that refugee boats attempted to enter the country from Indonesia or New Guinea.

"Maytag Gulf" is what cruisers called the Gulf of Carpentaria, which would take us to Gove Peninsula, a distance of 320 miles. The large gulf separated Cape York Peninsula from the Northern Territory. Although we could have crossed the expanse of the gulf, we decided to head south to Gove, where there was a marina with showers and some shopping, always a priority on my list. Why was it called Maytag? We soon found out as the weather cooperated to give us a very bumpy and uneven sail like we had never experienced before. The 10 to 14 feet of waves hit us on the beam every few minutes, accompanied by 20 to 25 knots of wind. It was almost impossible to stand straight, and I wasn't into meal planning.

"Oh God!" I said from our head on the last day. "The toilet has spilled all over the floor."

A sudden lurch of the boat, stronger than most, had caused the water to overflow before I could pump it away. I heard a laugh up above.

"What's so funny?" I replied, disgusted, knowing that the mess was mine to clean. Thank goodness we were getting close to Gove, and I hoped that it was worth all that trouble.

Al was busy figuring out our entrance into Gove in the dark, memorizing all the lights into the harbour. Usually we tried not to enter an unfamiliar harbour after dark. There were too many lights to confuse us, too many freighters anchored around, and it was difficult to find our anchorage. It took us two to three hours, fortunately in quiet waters, to finally find other cruising boats, drop our anchor, and immediately get our needed sleep.

Gove had a small yacht club, and the first thing I wanted to do was to find a proper shower after three weeks. The club seemed to be a meeting place for the Aborigines living nearby. They didn't have completely free reign at the club, but they took over the bar and drank beer all afternoon. They were a strange bunch, very slight, emaciated looking, with a swarthy complexion and kinky hair that seemed to have its own way, and, a laissez-faire attitude. When the day was over, the ones we saw seemed to disappear into the bush where they slept. They seemed to be happy with very few belongings, maybe because of the liquor they consumed with gusto.

Gove was a company town, and relied on the company for all its resources. The area around Gove had a large source of bauxite, which was the ingredient for making aluminum. Alcan, a Canadian company, had recently bought the large plant. That was part of the continuous wave of information we got from our driver, who picked us up and took us into town, 5 miles away. He was a talkative sort of fellow, and delighted in meeting people from far away.

"Let's hitchhike back," said Al, when it was time to leave. We had done all we could do in the small town of Gove. A local policeman picked us up on the outgoing road and proceeded to give us a lecture about hitchhiking and being careful, but at least he drove us back to the marina.

For the next week, we hopped across the north coast of Australia to Darwin. There was no comparison between this passage and that off the coast of Queensland. There would be no stopping on land as we were in the Aboriginal territory and out of bounds. We encountered strange tidal patterns, currents running against us, and fickle winds. The area around us – small islands, small coves, shoals, and isolated countryside – was all we could see. Al's charts and tide tables were very important for navigation.

I delighted in Somerville Bay at the top of Croker Island. It was quiet and peaceful with a sandy beach. There was no one around except for some turtles swimming, accompanied by a leaping dolphin near the boat. It was star-gazing time as the sky was sparkling with stars, no moon, nor clouds, to obscure the vista. Mars was at its closest distance from Earth that year. It looked like an approaching vessel from a distance, but then later we could see it rise through the sky. These beautiful nights on the boat were worth the many others I would like to forget.

Tipperary Waters Marina in Darwin was located northwest of the city, but in an area subject to very high tides. It was necessary to enter a lock at high tide, and be lowered to the level of the marina. First, our boat had to be "sanitized" (blowing out our through hulls), and then the lockmaster called Al on his radio.

"I'll talk you through the channel before the lock. I've only lost two boats in my time," he joked. He was talking about the narrow channel entering the lock that had no markings. Because this channel had a shallow depth, we had to wait until high tide.

"OK," replied my husband with trepidation, since we might be the third boat to be "lost."

Thankfully, we entered the small lock and tied up to the chamber, where our boat was lowered to the depth of the marina ahead. It was a small marina but with the necessary conveniences, and close to boat services down the road. I sighed with pleasure after setting my feet on land. It had been 10 days on the water and that was long enough.

Darwin was a great city to clear up our problems with the boat, as well as my tooth that seemed to have been aching forever. I went to a recommended dentist for help.

"Would you be able to look after my toothache?" I asked. "I'm only here for a short time, and I need a dentist to help me." The older, experienced dentist had a full load of patients, but introduced me to a young, recently Australian-trained girl from Sri Lanka, who looked as though she had just finished her last exam.

"This is Dali," the receptionist said, introducing the young dentist. "She is very competent and will look after you very well." *What choice did I have?*

Well, I must say that she was the gentlest dentist I'd ever had, and treated me for a root canal in a way that, I'm sure, I'll never experience again. Although Dali consulted her superior often, he didn't have to take over at any time. Unfortunately, it meant many trips to the dentist office before she was finished, which cut into my time to enjoy Darwin.

Darwin turned out to be the delightful Northern Territory capital. It had recovered from WWII and the Japanese, as well as a devastating cyclone in 1974, where more than half of the buildings were destroyed. But looking at it then, we saw little remnants of the war or cyclone. The surrounding countryside was very parched because of the dry season, but we could walk the waterfront around the perimeter of the city passing the beautiful capital buildings, the new commercial pier, and the long beaches of Mindel, where twice a week they had a market of crafts and tasty food stalls.

Our main goal was to be ready for the Darwin to Kupang rally.

"The boat and I are ready," I said to Al after my last visit to the dentist.

There would be 48 boats altogether to cross the Timor Sea, either to Kupang or Bali, Indonesia. It was the end of July, and we expected the crossing to take four days despite the warning we had from Australians that we were heading for hostile territory and could expect robberies or life-threatening attacks.

PART 5

South China Sea

CHAPTER 25

❦

Indonesia

WHAT A SIGHT! Our group of 28 boats in the rally left Fanny Bay, Darwin, all at once, our flying spinnakers on a run up the Beagle Gulf and out to the Arafura Sea. At first our boats were close together, but the faster yachts drew ahead and we became part of the middle-sized group, reporting twice a day to the organizers in Darwin. Al and I had decided to go on the rally because all the paperwork entering Timor would be handled beforehand – visas, passports, cruising permits, etc. Indonesia, we'd heard, could delay our passage if we had to do the entry on our own. The rally was a promotion by Indonesia to encourage tourism, but we began our passage in an atmosphere of misinformation, rumours, and fear brought on by Australians we had met in Darwin.

"You shouldn't go. I've heard you could get boarded and robbed," someone remarked to us in Darwin. The trial of the perpetrators of the Bali bombing was in process during our time in Australia, and stories of Indonesian or Muslim hatred and violence were published daily in the newspapers. Nevertheless, Al had decided we would go anyway.

"You can't believe all the stories you hear. Rumours run amok in the cruising community."

The first day and night we had a decent wind, but after that the wind died away and everyone started their engines. This continued for the next three days. As our boat approached Indonesian waters, I saw uncharted gas wells and oil derricks, unlit long-liner fishing trawlers dragging enormously long-hooked lines, invisible nets strung around, and, near shore, hundreds of small unlit fishing boats. We didn't reach the Roti Strait into Kupang, Timor, until it was dark. What an experience that was!

We entered a narrow 10-mile strait at the western tip of Timor. It was a harrowing experience for my husband, and for me as well. I was terrified. I felt helpless sitting in the cockpit with my husband and not being able to help him. There was no use in telling him that another boat was approaching and to watch out. I had nightmarish visions of hundreds of shadowy motorized fishing boats bearing down on us in the dark from all directions. I wasn't prepared for the sudden shock of these boats crisscrossing the strait at high speed all around us. They turned their spotlights on only when we came within a few feet of them. And they moved fast. We, of course, dropped our sails and tried to motor on a steady course in mid-channel, where the wind and current swept us through at about 10 knots. I heard their noisy, thumping, belching motors come very close to us in the darkness, and then felt them move around or pass us like scary, jumping shadows.

It was 02:00 when we finally dropped our anchor in Kupang harbour. But at 04:00 we were wakened by our first Muslim call to prayer. Looking around, I saw our boat surrounded by hundreds of anchored fishing boats, cargo boats, floats, buoys, and harbour debris. Where were all the other cruising boats? In the dark, we had miscalculated the anchorage and needed to find a more welcome spot among friends. The waters around us couldn't have been dirtier. I wasn't willing to stay in Timor very long. I had been spoiled by the developed countries of New Zealand and Australia, where we could be sure of help for our boat and feel secure about our safety. That wouldn't be the case now that we were in Indonesia.

Al checked in at Teddy's Bar where Dick McClune from Bali Marina welcomed the rally cruisers. It was an easy procedure due to being part of the rally, and also entitled us to sail westward to Bali at our leisure. It was difficult trying to land our dinghy in the dirty, sandy shore at Kupang harbour. The waves would fly up the beach at high tide, and on the last day our dinghy was swamped by the sea and sand, which damaged the propeller on the dinghy motor. The propeller damage kept us away from visiting many places through the Indonesian islands, but perhaps we were safer that way.

Kupang showed remnants of former Dutch and Portuguese colonial times, but was now part of Indonesia. It was famous for being the final destination in 1789 of Captain Bligh from the *Bounty*, after he was set adrift in an open boat for about 4,000 miles. Kupang was an old commercial port city established centuries ago by the Dutch as a trading outpost. The people were poor. I saw mostly men walking around dressed in the typical T-shirt adorned with commercial logos. The town was dirty and crowded. A strong military presence dominated. Most people drove motorbikes and rode *bemos*, vans that operated like a bus and played very loud music. We walked the sidewalks, broken and narrow, usually filled with hawkers of various things. There were many bike repair shops, old glass bottles full of gasoline, plastic junk, fruit and vegetable sellers, and stores selling cell phones, the only form of communication. How different it was from the clean and trim streets of Australia's cities. Bargaining was the only way to buy anything, whether to catch a *bemo* or get souvenirs at the market.

We took an informal one-day tour outside the city, where I saw many rice fields and pretty houses tucked inside small garden properties. The old original homes had grass or thatched roofs, and many sat on stilts. We visited an old Raja's pool built in the 16th century that was now being used by the local women to wash clothes. I noticed plastic garbage everywhere. How sad! If you had plastic garbage from the boat, how would the people in the villages get rid of it? Lastly, we visited Pak Pah and his family who made the *sasando*, a traditional string instrument made from lontar leaves and bamboo, and played like a harp. While there, I listened to a young man play on his *sasando*. Such beautiful music came from his competent hands.

Then it was time to go. I'd had enough of the city, dirt, and noise. We tried a local restaurant which served rice with a small bit of chicken or fish and a slice of tomato and the local Bintang beer. I wasn't too impressed, except for the price (US$2). Because of the problem with our dinghy motor, we missed the last cruising party the night before leaving. I had no more interest in Kupang and we nervously prepared ourselves for the passage west.

Most of the boats leaving at the same time as us travelled north to Flores, 90 miles away, but we went west to Rinca, a couple of days sail across the Savu Sea. Now we were alone! I wasn't sure how we would manage: no help for a troubled boat, little security, no stopping to shop, unpredictable weather, and anchorages that were questionable. Nevertheless, there was plenty of fuel and water to take us across to Bali.

Early in the morning, we arrived in the south bay of Rinca Island that had a protective small island on its south side, giving us a beautiful spot with a mooring ball to tie to. There were reefs for diving, a sandy beach for spotting Komodo dragons and other creatures. It seemed like paradise. We planned to spend a few days there, but the authorities felt otherwise. Soon park rangers on a large patrol boat arrived.

"Where is your permit for the park?" one asked in strong, broken English. "You can't stay here and must leave."

Al tried to give them the cost of a permit. I was hoping they would feel sorry for us, being from so far away. But no such luck.

"You can stay one day, but must anchor," the ranger continued in a strong, authoritarian voice. "We will come back to make sure you are gone."

We reluctantly anchored nearby, and decided to enjoy the spot for the day. By now there were a few tourist boats and divers, who wanted our mooring ball. Would our passage through Indonesia be a problem? Except for good maps and navigation by my captain, we were on our own.

The same park rangers came back the next day and suggested that we go to Komodo, an island nearby, where there was a ranger station. We decided that we'd better follow their suggestion. On our way there, we felt the full force of the tidal currents between the two islands. There were violent eddies and whirlpools that caused us to temporarily lose control of our boat. They turned out to be from inter-island currents, which were irregular, and so fast-moving they exceeded our boat power speed.

We finally reached Komodo. On nearing the ranger station, I was approached by several men in dugouts selling souvenirs of dragon carvings. Of course, I had to buy a little "something." After we were settled and anchored, two young men came by in their large wooden fishing boat with a noisy putt putt engine. Sitting in our cockpit and beginning to relax, I could hear them long before they got to our boat.

"Do you want to visit the park?" said one. "We can take you in our boat." We looked at each other and agreed that would be suitable. Although their boat looked very unseaworthy, we wouldn't have to use our unpredictable motor.

"I have a brother with a bad injury that is infected," added the other man. "Do you have any medicine?" I wondered if the story was true but offered some antibiotic pills from our stores. The young fishermen were thin and wiry, muscles tight from fishing many hours each day. Who could blame them for trying to make a living from tourists such as ourselves?

The next day we left on their fishing boat for the park, hopefully to see the Komodo dragons. Their boat was a large, wooden craft with no seats. Al and I scrambled on and sat uncomfortably on a large wooden platform, hoping the ride wouldn't take long.

After walking through the park area for two hours, I saw only wild chickens, deer, and pigs. But, oh yes, I saw two sleeping dragons near the park office. They were huge and menacing, but while sleeping looked very calm and satisfied. Apparently, dragons used to be fed live goats as a tourist attraction, but that had been discontinued. *I wonder why!* After some conversation with the rangers at the park, we were told the number of tourists had dropped considerably since the Bali bombings in October of the year before.

Our next stop was Gili Banta, sailing north and west from Komodo. We passed hot, dry, and hilly areas with signs of former volcanic eruptions until we found our next anchorage. There were a number of fishing boats in the shallow waters. One boat was just leaving and its crew gestured to Al that he might like the spot. Looking in the water below our boat, I saw beautiful clear water with many colourful fish swimming around the coral.

"Let's anchor here," I suggested. "It's wonderful to see all the fish. And look, there is a stingray!" Its large bluish back was covered in small spots. It had burrowed in the sand below our boat but was easy to see as it moved back and forth with the waves. We got *Solara* settled, but soon a small dugout with an outrigger approached the side of our boat. A father and son wanted to come on board. They looked harmless so I invited them for some tea, which they took with lots of sugar. They looked around the boat with intense interest, and I began to feel somewhat nervous. Our "conversation" was mainly gestures as we didn't speak a common language. I had a small Malay dictionary but it wasn't much help. One of them pointed to Al's cap with a gesture that seemed to indicate that he wanted the cap. This was a baseball cap that Al wore all the time to keep protected from the sun. Al shook his head and the hat stayed on his head. The old guy picked up one of my sandals and had it on his foot. He wanted to take them back to his boat. I shook my head. They were my only shoes.

After trying to have us give them all the things they wanted, I began to feel that their visit should come to an end. At that moment, the old father left to pick up his granddaughter. I guess he wanted her to see our boat. We weren't free from their curiosity yet. The young girl, about 4 or 5, was very shy. She clung to her grandfather and peeked over his comforting arm at the two of us. I offered her some milk with chocolate syrup but she wouldn't drink it. Even so, when the family finally left, they had only the milk and chocolate in their hands. Thank goodness.

During the night, the winds came up and the currents began to push us towards the nearby reefs.

"Let's pull up the anchor and leave," I suggested. "The boat is rocking too much, and I'm nervous about the intense interest our neighbouring boat had in our things."

So, at 02.00 we left, and struggled through the strong current trying to pull us into the island to our south, and headed west again along the islands of Indonesia.

For two weeks, we sailed towards Bali, stopping every night in suitable anchorages. We were never threatened or felt in danger. I was getting used to waking up to the Muslim call to prayer from the mosques in nearby villages. "Time to leave" they seemed to say. Once in a while small outrigger canoes would come close to have a look. I saw all manner of local fishing craft. Some were amazing vessels. They were sturdy and seaworthy, obviously built to withstand any storm with the highest pounding waves. Some were ingeniously fabricated canoes pieced together with sticks and twine.

It was impossible to miss the high mountains rising up from the mist in the early morning, especially one called Mount Tambora, at more than 9,100 feet. The mountain was originally 13,100 feet, but in 1815 lost its top in an eruption that rose 28 miles into the air, resulting in death and aftereffects from the blast that affected at least 75,000 people. I tried to forget that we were in a very volatile volcanic region, and as we passed Mount Tambora it was a beautiful, sunny day with calm seas belying its history.

We sailed passed the island of Lombok after a harrowing experience across the strait between Lombok and Sumbawa because of disturbing winds off the mountains and the local conditions causing high waves and wind speed. It seemed that we would never make any headway during the night and finally had to anchor in a quiet bay away from the turbulent water. I saw more and more fishing boats, with their colourful sails of rainbow hues.

Lombok was famous for Gunung Rinjani, the highest mountain (12,225 feet) in Indonesia, outside Irian Jaya. It stood proud and majestic, silhouetted against the azure blue of the sky. The mountain was climbed often, especially by Indonesians at full moon to seek the curative powers of the hot springs below the summit.

I began to see more evidence of tourism the closer we got to Bali. Efforts were continually being made in Indonesia to draw tourists away from Bali. Tourists who went only to Bali were missing the miles and miles of palm tree lined beaches, incredible coral reefs, and fascinating waterfront fishing villages. I had seen no other white people on our two-week sail between Komodo and Lombok.

The day before we left Lombok, we had stopped and anchored in a small quiet bay in front of a charming and delightful village called Gili Asahan. It was obviously a predominantly Muslim village, as the local mosque had the only light shining at night and the call to prayer seemed to continue all day. The people were very curious, and we were constantly surrounded by local dugouts. One small dugout arrived at our boat paddled by a woman with her two small children. When I looked down at her, it was obvious she was asking for something, but I couldn't understand her gestures.

"Would you like some sugar?" I asked as I held a bag of sugar for her to see. She took the sugar, but I was sure that wasn't what she had asked for. "Buku," she kept saying. How frustrating it was that I didn't know the word, and I wanted so much to know what she wanted. She was a pretty woman who had made the effort to bring her children to our boat. Many days later, I was told by a local Balinese that she was asking for a book. How easy that would have been, as I had a number of books and magazines that I had finished reading.

Between Lombok and Bali, we passed through the "Wallace Line," named after Alfred Wallace, a geographer in Charles Darwin's time, who divided two ecological zones. East of the line, Lombok was dry and desert-like, with fauna resembling those in Australasia. West of the line, in Bali, the flora and fauna appeared of Asian origin, with its lush foliage and plentiful crops. It was just a matter of sailing from one zone to the other, and finally reaching Bali. This we did amongst the hundreds of small fishing outriggers with their beautiful, coloured sails heading towards us from Bali, moving with the winds and current. It was a wonderful sight! At last, we were approaching Bali and would see so many of our friends again.

CHAPTER 26

Bali to Singapore

It was great to finally see old friends again. Some of them had sailed straight to Bali from Darwin, missing the Indonesian islands altogether. I felt that they had missed the beauty of the islands to the east, but I could understand their concern about safety. Perhaps we had been lucky not to have had any problems.

After sailing through a treacherous channel, we finally entered Bali marina which was so rundown there was no way it could last many more years. But it was the only marina in town. To compensate for the listing docks and crumbling structure, the bar was fun and the people friendly and helpful. The bombing had affected tourism immensely; it was obvious that the Balinese were still recovering.

Bali was extremely different compared to the rest of Indonesia. For example, most of its population were Indonesian Hindus. The vegetation was lush compared to the dry and desert landscape of the other islands to the east, and Bali's main income came from tourism. I was able to provision well, and Al got a temporary fix on our dinghy motor propeller. A friend, Julie, and I took a visit to a well-known town called Ubud where the craft industry was fully established. Of course, we shopped for souvenirs. On the way back, we visited a monkey temple full of macaques. They were so interesting to watch: intensely grooming each other, feeding their young, and scrambling over the many temple structures that made up their "home." We were discouraged from getting too close to them as they were known for responding with vicious bites.

We left the marina in Denpasar, fully loaded with food, fuel, and water, and sailed to an anchorage at Ambat further north, a good starting place to make our way to Kalimantan, the Indonesian part of Borneo. We were three boats, *Solara*, *Free Radical*, and *Duetto*, a ferro-cement pilothouse and motor-sailer from New Zealand. I couldn't imagine a boat made from concrete, but after being invited on for refreshments I saw a comfortable and cosy interior. Geoff and his wife made Al and I most welcome, and we were glad to share the passage with them. Ed from *Free Radical* was always helpful when we had problems or questions needing answers. This would be the first time that we had sailed in a group since starting our voyage. I had seen groups sailing together before in our travels and always envied the companionship that they offered.

Our three boats couldn't keep together, but each night we met at a designated anchorage. We struggled through contrary winds and waves as we sailed through the South China Sea, passing Java to our west. The sea was filled with large ships coming and going on their missions, carrying cargo or on serious fishing excursions. One almost hit us during a night passage. Al had to hand-steer quickly in the opposite direction with full sails to avoid a collision. *That was a close one.* The commercial vessel wasn't going to change its course.

After another four-day passage in quieter waters, the three of us met at the mouth of the Kumai River in Borneo. This was the beginning of the most interesting part of our time in Indonesian waters: I was going to visit an orangutan sanctuary. Al was anxious as the Kumai River had few navigational markings and close attention had to be made to avoid obstructions. Rolling brown waves flowed past us as we wound up the river through thick bush and jungle. I watched logs, branches, canoes, and local *pinisi* fishing and cargo boats move past us down the river toward the mouth and the open South China Sea. Birds screamed from luxuriant green foliage on the shores beside us. I felt the haze and the burning ash from the log and bush clearings. We watched for stakes marking shallow places, for changes in water colour and in the water ripples. I watched our depth gauge intently. I looked at Al's face as we moved up the river. The concern and discomfort was obvious. Was I taking him on trip away from his need to move to more civilized waters?

I was excited to see the orangutans. Long ago, I had seen Julia Roberts on TV as she visited the sheltered Camp Leakey sanctuary for these most endangered apes. It had been a very interesting program.

We anchored on the river beside the town of Kumai and were introduced to two young men who would take us to the camp. It was the next day that the six of us were in two small riverboats motoring up a narrow, winding branch of the Kumai River lined with green vines filled with chattering birds and monkeys. Our fast boat trip up the tributary of the Kumai was very scary. The driver had to stop many times to clear his propeller of small twigs, leaves, and other junk. There were saltwater crocodiles in the river, and the area boasted over 200 kinds of snakes, most fatally poisonous. But I wanted to go. There were a few stilt houses along the shoreline. The Dayaks, known as fierce head-hunters years ago, at one time lived in these houses along the rivers of Borneo.

"I'll just clear the propeller," our driver would say.

I sat quietly, careful not to rock the small and shallow boat in case a crocodile lurked beneath. A young Englishman had been grabbed and eaten by a crocodile the year before at Camp Leakey. He had carelessly decided to swim in the river.

Once arriving at Camp Leaky, we were directed to a pathway that would take us to a feeding platform for the orangutans. The encroachment of agriculture and human need for more living space had endangered these wonderful creatures. The camp was there to protect the jungle that was left. The apes were living in the jungle, and only came out to eat when they couldn't find food elsewhere.

Oh, their faces! So human, their expressions! How beautiful to see the mother orangutan care for and protect her infant. It would be in need of its mother's care for at least six years, almost like a human child; it clung to her constantly. The older, independent "teenagers" seemed to have no cares in the world, swinging from branch to branch deliberately and expertly. Our small group sat on benches nearby and watched the antics of the orangutans. I took Al's hand, I was so excited. Once in a while, one would sit down close to us. We were told not to touch them, as they were very strong, but to sit quietly and enjoy their presence. Although they were wild in some senses, they were also used to humans looking after them.

I heard a loud rustling in the trees, and coming towards the feeding platform was the dominant male, huge and powerful with large black cheek pads and red hair that seemed to flow around him. All at once, the families busily feeding left the platform to allow this male to feed without hindrance. No question about it, there was the top of the pecking order.

When I looked at Al, I was glad to see that he too was fascinated, and would be grateful that I had insisted on making this wonderful visit – the highlight of Indonesia. On the way back from Camp Leakey, we saw proboscis monkeys in the trees at the river's edge. How funny they were with their long, hanging noses. Altogether, I saw three wonderful animals that day: orangutans, proboscis monkeys, and gibbon monkeys. What a day!

"Thanks for insisting we go," my husband said sincerely.

It would take almost 10 days to reach Singapore Strait from Kalimantan. Our three cruising boats stopped in several anchorages in the South China Sea, but we stayed away from Sumatra, and especially Aceh which, we were warned, was dangerous. There was a history of boardings of merchant ships, and we weren't taking any chances.

On the way to Singapore, Al and I celebrated our passing through the equator again, going north this time. We had a drink to Neptune, and finally viewed the Big Dipper in its entirety. I was glad and relieved to be in the Northern Hemisphere. From then on, I hoped we would get better weather conditions for sailing, and more experienced help with equipment failures. On the other hand, there was uncertain territory – pirate attacks in the Gulf of Aden, and an unforgiving Red Sea – to navigate. I seemed to be constantly worrying.

Our last stop before Singapore was at Bintan Island, Indonesia. Al chose to sail up the eastern end of Bintan, as rumour was that going through the Riau group of islands to the west was dangerous that year because of pirates. We anchored in a beautiful bay in front of a busy resort on Bintan Island, full of Singaporeans who had no beach of their own. From our anchorage, I could see the busy Singapore Strait with all its heavy boat traffic, controlled by unseen forces. We would have to cross this east/west moving traffic "barrier" the next day. It seemed like a formidable task, especially since our motor wasn't charging and it could "conk out" anytime, leaving us with no electronic instruments. Al determined that it was the regulator that wasn't working, which was affecting our motor. *Why do these things happen at the worst possible moments?*

It was like moving through Toronto traffic at rush hour. Vessels of all sizes, big merchant ships, cruising boats, small fishing trawlers, and ourselves, going in the opposite direction from the shipping lanes of the Singapore Strait. We heard constant communication between ships, harbourmasters, police, and coast guard. We spent our time avoiding collisions, keeping our course, watching for buoys and markers, and generally keeping our wits about us with no chance to converse. We were anxious to have this part of the passage over as soon as possible and reach Raffles Marina.

It was like heaven when we finally checked into the marina at the northwest area of Singapore, not connected to the famous Raffles Hotel downtown. Sir Stamford Raffles was the founding father of modern Singapore in 1819. Because we had been on the Darwin to Timor rally, the marina had a special rate, 10 days for the price of one week. It was too good to ignore. We would be there until the middle of September. That would give us plenty of time to stop in Malaysia and Thailand before Christmas.

Raffles Marina was a high-class facility. They offered golf carts to move from the clubhouse to your boat, in case you had heavy loads, a beautiful swimming pool, restaurants, workout rooms, and fancy bathrooms. There was also a free bus to the LRT (light rail transport) stop, which would take us to downtown Singapore. As we arrived, I experienced my first Sumatra coming from the northwest. It brought high winds, black skies, and very heavy rain. It was almost impossible to see through the curtain of wind-driven water.

I worked my way to the shelter of the clubhouse. In spite of the rain, I wanted to have a hot shower, my first in many weeks. When I entered the ladies section, I was stopped by an attendant who asked me if I had any flu or cold symptoms.

What was that about?

"I'm healthy," I replied, still not understanding about the question.

"We're just being careful because of the SARS epidemic," she answered. That was the first I had heard about SARS. It occurred to me that we were isolated in our little cruising world, and from the hazards of city life and crowded conditions that caused epidemics. That was the lucky condition of sailing.

After arranging for boat repairs and waiting for a new regulator, Al and I explored Singapore. What a city! The bustling metropolis was scattered with groups of high-rises amidst parks and greenery. It was most impressive as long as one behaved. No spitting, no gum chewing, no this and that, but it led to a very clean and ordered city. I discovered parts that hadn't been taken over by modern buildings. A few blocks of Little India and Chinatown gave me an idea how Singapore looked in the past. When I took the LRT, it was my first look at people with their cell phones, busy playing games or talking to their friends. We took advantage of purchasing electronic gear from a vast high-rise retail mall. The most important device we bought let us play DVDs when we plugged it into our boat. That would give us a "movie night" when anchored somewhere.

Singapore was pushing all its land boundaries, which concerned Malaysia considerably. "We'll just add more land" was the motto, and then more dredging would occur. I couldn't see how Singapore would find any more space, but it did. Singapore was a very special place in my estimation. Nevertheless, talking to those who lived and worked there, I learned it was too expensive, with high taxes and rules that were hard to deal with. Some of the workers who were employed in the marina lived in Malaysia across the river to the north for just that reason.

Soon we were ready to leave for a cheaper country: Malaysia.

PART 6

Strait of Malacca

CHAPTER 27

❦

Malaysia

Our passage along the Malay Peninsula toward Thailand was in the infamous Strait of Malacca, which was a busy important shipping lane for large vessels going from Asia to the Pacific. For many years, the Strait of Malacca had been subject to attacks from pirates and boardings. I wasn't ready for pirates, the nasty weather, or numerous fishing vessels, but we needed to sail to Thailand.

Our first major stop was Port Dickson, about 140 miles north. We were day sailing due to the hundreds of fishing boats, lines, and buoys that had to be avoided. It was impossible to see the lines strung between the floats, often made from plastic bottles or any material that was handy. Our sailing guide suggested that cruisers sail at the 100-foot depth of water in order to avoid most of the mess, but we also had to watch for the large ships in the shipping lanes to our west, which would have run over us with no hesitation.

We got hit with another Sumatra our first day, heading right into it with 40-plus knots of wind, lightning, and thunder, and waves right on our nose. It meant motoring into the waves, which entered our cabin in spite of our precautions. I read later that this area of the strait experienced thunderstorms more than 300 days a year.

Despite motoring most of the way, I was looking forward to Port Dickson and the chance to visit Malacca, a city with a most interesting history. Our first anchorage towards Port Dickson was Pulau Besar, a good shelter from the western rollers on the strait. Nearby, there was a deserted resort that had been built a few years earlier. We took our dinghy into shore and saw an empty pool and restaurant. Whatever must have happened to close the place which had a beautiful beach overlooking the mainland of Malaysia and a ferry leaving for the town of Malacca a few times a day?

We approached Admiral Marina just outside Port Dickson by carefully following waypoints through a dredged channel. It was built only a few years before and looked very grandiose, but lacked the refinement of Raffles. We planned to stay for a month and to do some travelling inland. After settling ourselves in the marina, we had to check into Malaysia by taking a public bus to the town of Port Dickson.

Looking around, it was obviously a predominately Muslim country. The women, young and old, wore colourful headscarves, fastened with fancy pins to cover their necks. Their other clothing, usually long pants, lacked style, and were obviously meant to cover the rest of the body. Many stores sold these scarves, which made me think that the scarf was the young woman's way to show individuality and colour. Walking along the busy streets of Port Dickson, I saw happy people going about their business. We couldn't buy alcohol except in Indian and Chinese restaurants. Pork was not sold anywhere. I had to travel around to many places before I found some frozen chicken in a Chinese store. The open market was more promising. It carried wonderful fresh vegetables and fruit. We also found an internet cafe, which was one of our more important finds in every port we visited. Al was always anxious to check his bank balance and I always contacted family and friends.

Port Dickson was important for its good transportation link to other places. We could get a direct bus for US$5 to Kuala Lumpur, a two-hour trip, or a connection through the town of Seremban by a fancier bus line. Because we were planning to go to the Andaman Islands of India, we had to process our papers in KL ahead of time. During the weeks we were in Port Dickson, I saw friends that we had met in Darwin, which seemed so long ago. Boat work could be done while there, including varnishing, a dreadful job as far as I was concerned, but *Solara* had so much beautiful wood on the exterior Al wanted it to remain in good condition.

Long ago, before our voyage was even in my husband's thoughts, I met a woman on a public golf course in Toronto.

"Do you live nearby?" I had asked her.

"Not right now," she said. "I'm just taking a break from our boat, which is in a marina in Malaysia."

"That sounds exciting," I exclaimed. "It sounds so far away." I was full of questions, and overwhelmed by her account of life on a boat. How was I to imagine that one day I would be one of those cruisers doing the same?

Al and I decided it would be worthwhile to visit Malacca and stay overnight. It was such a historic city. Because Malacca linked China and India for the maritime trade hundreds of years ago, it had tremendous importance. It had also been a very wealthy city, ruled by the good administration of various wise sultans expanding into the Malay Peninsula, and spreading Islam throughout. The area was first conquered in the 16th century by the Portuguese who built a massive fortification called A Famosa, which helped control the city for 150 years. In 1641, the Dutch captured Malacca after many battles and rebuilt the ruined city. The Dutch East India Company needed Malacca to control the Strait of Malacca, but in 1795 turned it over to the British, who ruled until Malaysia became independent in the middle of the 20th century. Consequently, while we walked around the city of Malacca, I could see remnants of Portuguese, Dutch, and British rule. There was A Famosa saved from complete demolition by Sir Stamford Raffles, and the Stadthuys, a Dutch governor's official residence, now a museum. I walked on Jonker Street, a haven for antique collectors and bargain hunters, set amidst the narrow and winding streets of the old city. Unfortunately, I could only look with envious eyes, as most of the antiques that I liked wouldn't fit in *Solara*.

After a day of sightseeing, I had my first night in a hotel after many months on our boat. I was going to get a night in a real bed! It was a budget hotel situated in the old part of town, retaining much of its charm as a wooden crafted structure dating from the 17th century. I tasted local Baba-Nyonya food, such as a meat dish flavoured with many hot spices and satay sticks that could be dipped in a spicy sauce. For a cooling effect, I drank fruit-flavoured coconut milk and *cincau*, a dark grass jelly drink. I felt no need for beer or wine. I enjoyed all the flavours of the delicious dishes, but Al wasn't used to the strong and pungent spices, and preferred a less intense meal. I hoped he would come to like Malay food and not rely on my cooking every day. The next day we took the bus back to our boat, as it was time to continue up the Strait of Malacca.

Between inevitable boat work, we took more inland trips, one to Kuala Lumpur, and another to Taman Negara National Park. In KL we picked up our visas for India, after all the paperwork the Indian Government felt it had to do. It was a beautiful city with its famous Petronas Twin Towers, the tallest twin buildings in the world at the time. We also made an appointment with a private hospital to have our skin checked out for precancerous spots, which could be burned off. The cost for that procedure was next to nothing compared to US prices. That was why we did not carry health insurance while we were away. KL also offered wonderful shopping opportunities and delicious Indian restaurants.

Taman Negara National Park, established in 1938-39, was first called King George V National Park, and was now promoted as an ecotourism park. How appropriate! I felt the need to see the "wild" part of Malaysia, and looked forward to some jungle, wild animals, river boating, and a look at the local natives called *orang asli*, who lived on the shore in primitive shelters. It was a day's drive by bus from Kuala Lumpur, and a two-hour boat ride in a peroque up the Tahan River to the resort where we were staying.

The riverboat ride was interesting, seeing how the people lived in the area by fishing and foraging for food, but when we got to our "resort" it was very tired looking. There was only one other couple staying in the very large hotel, and walking outside, after checking into our room, there wasn't much to see. We started to hike into the jungle on a marked trail, but when I picked up leeches on my ankles, it was time to turn around. We had a so-so meal, and retired in a very damp bed, probably wet from the monsoons. The next day, I encouraged Al to take the canopy walk amongst the trees. Although the scenery around me was very pictur-esque, I saw no birds or wildlife.

"This is a waste of time and money," complained my husband.

I couldn't agree. "It's a good change from sailing," I retorted. And that was where we left it.

There was time to fly to Cambodia, as it was only a two-hour flight from Kuala Lumpur. It was a memorable visit to a sad, war-torn country. We planned to stay four days, and arranged our trip with a local agent in KL. That way we could ignore the innumerable touts at the airport.

"Take my taxi. I have a good hotel for you," I heard constantly in bro-ken English once arrived at the airport in Phnom Penh. The people were poor and anxious to have our business. All around me I saw beggars and war victims with missing limbs, often caused by the millions of landmines left behind after the conflict during the Pol Pot administration.

We only had that day and evening to see the sites in Phnom Penh, the capital of Cambodia. But what a shock it was to visit the Khmer Rouge S-21 Prison. Nothing was left out in the story of the treatment and torture of the prisoners, and extermination of the anti-government regime that had been in power in the '70s. Victims were from all parts of the country and all walks of life, but mainly educated people. Families of these victims were also exterminated. The Pol Pot regime was ruthless, and my heart went out to the people of Cambodia. The memory would be forever with me. It was thought that 2 million Cambodians died either through geno-cide or starvation. What made it worse was the fact that the party now in power included former Pol Pot followers.

It was a shock to see what Cambodia had gone through in the '70s. However, the people of Phnom Penh were surviving. Temples and markets were full, and tourists were welcomed with open arms.

"Are those small birds for sale?" I pointed to the crowded cages of sparrows that were being sold at the market.

Al noted, "I think that they're sold for food."

It was hard to imagine that anyone could get much meat from such a small bird, but I also saw insects and other unrecognizable "food" for sale at the sidewalk stalls. For the tourist, though, the cuisine in the restaurants was very tasty, with some influence of Thai and Vietnamese cooking.

The famous cultural heritage of Cambodia was the ancient ruins of Angkor Wat, a boat trip from Phnom Penh on the Tonle Sap River. The modern, fast, and comfortable boat gave us a marvellous view of life on the large river, flowing out of the Mekong River in Vietnam. The local people literally lived on the river in stilted houses or on houseboats that moved with the season. In October, while we were there, the Tonle Sap River changed direction back toward the Mekong River, and was celebrated by a colourful festival. Twice a year, the northbound river filled the Tonle Sap, and six months later flowed southward out of the lake, bringing with it millions of fish that were caught easily with nets for a year's supply of food. That was a reason to celebrate! The celebrations also included famous canoe races and fireworks. I saw long canoes filled with a least a dozen men practising their skills, similar to dragon boats, but slicker and narrower. Whoever reached the Mekong after many days would be the winner for that year.

After that most interesting river trip, we finally reached Siem Reap, the city which would be our stepping stone to Angkor Wat. Climbing up and down and through all the ruins of the famous heritage site of the many *wats* (temples), and filming the weather-worn stone carvings throughout the temples kept me busy all day. Although built in the 12th century, it remained untouched until recently, when the encroaching jungle was cleared away. Many walks throughout were not open to visitors because of the numerous landmines, which hadn't been cleared away since the war. Nevertheless, the *wats* were spectacular, and Cambodia made full use of this cultural heritage and the flood of visitors who came.

After our trip to Cambodia, we were back to sailing, avoiding fish nets and hoping for good weather. We made three anchor stops before reaching Penang, an island that we didn't want to miss because of its interesting history. It was now recognized as a UNESCO World Heritage

Site. I was most interested in seeing the remaining historic homes and buildings left from many years ago. Penang's population, largely of Chinese descent, gave the city a rich and multicultural flavour. It was considered to be among the top 10 great street food cities in Asia. I would be joining the many famous people who had visited the island such as W. Somerset Maugham, Rudyard Kipling, Noel Coward, and Her Majesty Queen Elizabeth II. We couldn't enter George Town's harbour like most tourists, though. We were directed to a fairly new marina that had been erected just south of the high bridge that crossed to mainland Malaysia from Pulau Jerejak. It was a tight fit just to get into a spot as most boats were small powerboats. But after some manoeuvring and help, we tied up to a slip.

"Hey, there's *Free Radical* and *Duetto*," I exclaimed to my husband as I looked around. "I wonder how they managed the Strait of Malacca." There were also boaters that I had met many months ago in Darwin. It would be good to catch up on our travels, and hear about their experiences.

After a long walk and crossing two highways to a local bus, we had a cheap ride into the city. We were fortunate to be in Penang for a special Indian festival where the streets were decorated top and bottom with garlands of flowers, flower petals, leaves and vines. The royal couple of Malaysia were coming for a visit, and everyone around us was excited, lining up well ahead of their arrival to get the best view. The flowers were not just decorating the streets. The Indian women wore their best colourful clothing – azure blue, cadmium yellow, and crimson – all embroidered with complementary patterns. I looked at myself and felt that I should hide behind a pillar, so as not to contrast so boldly with the display of the women in their finest. There I was, brown cotton shorts, T-shirt, and sandals, topped by a hat to keep out the sun.

Instead of joining the crowd in the park where all the action was, we decided to explore the old part of George Town. Cheong Fatt Tze Mansion was the most interesting house I visited and Penang's most prominent attraction. It was originally built by a wealthy merchant, Cheong Fatt Tze, in 1880. The house represented beautifully the style preferred by the wealthy Straits Chinese of the time. The front edifice was strikingly blue, a large courtyard inside filled the entrance, and the polished mahogany staircase flowed upward to the second floor. Colourful windows of inlaid glass lit up the rooms and intricate furniture with sunlight. My visit was highlighted by the guide who showed us around. He made himself more interesting than the house by telling us stories of the original owner, who seemed to me to be quite the man with many wives.

Langkawi was 40 miles to our north, and to make the trip easier we anchored in Junk Harbour just off George Town, and a small bum boat (a sort of taxi) away from the downtown. At 02:00 in the dark, as usual with us, we left Junk Harbour. Our engine seemed to be working overtime, and I sensed vibrations on the wheel. Since Al didn't notice anything, we motored on to Langkawi.

After settling into the Royal Langkawi Yacht Club, I said to Al, "I think we should check the propeller. It didn't feel right when we left Junk Harbour."

"OK, if you think so," Al replied.

I was glad that he always listened to me. Probably now he was aware that I had a feeling for our engine, and could detect things out of sorts. Sure enough, after diving with scuba gear in the murky water under our boat, he found the shaft completely wrapped around with a fishing net picked up from the bottom of Junk Harbour, well-named as it turned out.

Langkawi was another place for last-minute repairs and provisioning. The bay was made up of many rugged and beautiful islands. I could see a number of boats that were cruising between the various anchorages. How was I to know that almost a year later the area would be flooded by a tsunami? It was formerly a haven for pirates, but now it was a duty-free location for visiting cruisers. Consequently, we shopped well as it was the last place to buy cheap liquor for many months.

John, a New Zealand cruiser stationed at our dock, found us soon after we had tied up. He asked if we needed any boat repairs. He was a typical offshore cruiser, living the casual life away from the bustle of the city, who needed to top up his income. His shorts probably could stand up by themselves, and his grubby T-shirt had seen better days, but one couldn't tell by appearances if he was the real thing.

"Hi mate, I'm John," he said with his strong New Zealand accent. "If you have any repairs to do, I'm the man for the job."

"Well, we have a pump that doesn't work and a windlass as well. The anchor won't go up all the way. I have to pull it by hand the last 10 feet," Al said.

For more than a year, I had seen my husband struggling with the very heavy anchor. Would John be able to do the job? When we asked around about John's work, we found out that there was no one in town who had the patience and knowledge that John had. His fee was also acceptable. His knowledge about boats was vast, and we were well satisfied when he was finished.

Kuah, near our marina, was an interesting town, very relaxed with little formality. One day we passed a community potluck put on by some local women. The various dishes were laid out in a buffet style. I couldn't identify the different, colourful foods, but they all looked very tasty. The women drew me in to join them in their festivities. Suddenly Al disappeared from view. I figured he didn't want to have anything to do with a women's buffet. Nevertheless, I took up their friendship, and had a taste of the delicious food. This was just an example of the friendliness of the Muslim community that we encountered in Malaysia.

Sitting around the dock to relax and chat with other cruisers, we met an older Dutch-American man who had a young Thai woman living with him. He had a very interesting story to tell.

"I was sailing alone from New Guinea toward Indonesia when I had a stroke and couldn't move. I can't remember what exactly happened next, but I found my boat sitting in sand on an unknown island. I learned later that some Indonesian fishermen found my boat floating aimlessly and me lying in the cockpit unconscious. All my goods were stolen and I had no money. I was found by other islanders and taken to a clinic where a doctor diagnosed the stroke. Once I got a cell phone, I was able to contact people I know in the US, who helped me claim insurance for my loss. After spending a few days in the hospital, I was able to sail my boat with help from friends to Malaysia, as I'm now without use of my left side. So here I am enjoying the companionship of this lovely lady." He seemed very content living on his boat, and not interested in sailing anymore.

"Weren't you angry with the fishermen?" asked my husband.

"Not at all. Don't forget they saved me and my boat. They were very poor, and I don't blame them for taking what they could. I'm glad to be alive."

What a story.

CHAPTER 28

Thailand

OUR NEXT DESTINATION was Phuket, Thailand. It was known as a beautiful tourist destination because of fine sandy beaches, many bars and restaurants, and high-class hotels. On the way, we had to make a few stops among a series of islands with very deep anchorages. I couldn't imagine putting down our anchor to 100 feet, but that was we did in Ko Rok Nok. It was a good thing that our anchor windlass was now working. It seemed to take forever to bring it up in the morning.

Our last stop was at Ko Phi Phi Don just before entering the harbour in Phuket where we were to check in with the authorities. Ko Phi Phi Don was hit by the powerful wave from the tsunami the following year, and most of the crowded conglomeration of shops, restaurants, and diving establishments disappeared.

Once we had anchored, I went on shore with the French couple we had sailed with from Langkawi. We wanted to watch a special rugby game between France and New Zealand. Al chose to stay behind on our boat. I couldn't get over the crowded streets and noisy tourists that wandered around half-dressed, often carrying beers clutched in their hands. The island had two bays with a narrow isthmus separating them. This bit of land held all the narrow streets, alleyways, and back lanes that could possibly fit in. I couldn't blame my husband for not wanting to go. I wish I could say who won the game, but the crowds and the noise blew my attention away.

"Well, was it worth the trip?" Al asked when I got back.

"Probably you'd say no. But it was worth the visit. Where else would one see such self-indulgence and impropriety in one place?"

We were going to stay another night but the bay was so filled with ferries, tourist boats, and fast powerboats that we decided to leave for Phuket in the morning. Al had to check into Thailand through Phuket which meant a stop in Ao Chalong, where the winds whipped around and made the anchorage very uncomfortable. The muddy bottom also caused an anchor holding problem. When the tide went out, our dinghy could only go so far into shore, and then I had to wade with bare feet through the mud which sucked through my toes. My progress was very slow as though I was walking in deep, snowy drifts. Some cruisers who were living on a restricted income spent all their time in this bay as it was free. I was very glad that we could afford some time in a marina.

The checking in took at least two days as the officials – customs, immigration, and port authority – didn't keep a time schedule and we never knew when they would be in their offices. Some offices weren't even in the same location; some required a short tuk tuk ride. However, the officials were most pleasant, and helped Al fill out the papers. It seemed very casual, and we were allowed to stay in Thailand for a month, which would give us plenty of time to celebrate Christmas before we set out for the Andaman Sea.

Al had made arrangements to stay in Boat Lagoon marina, which had a number of boat services and other worthwhile conveniences like a spa and restaurants. *What more could I ask for?* Our cruising experiences were often enhanced by these arrangements, and I realized I was lucky that we could afford the occasional luxury. Our daughter Vicky had some time off from work and was joining us in Phuket to sail across the Andaman Sea to Sri Lanka and the Maldives. She was a very competent sailor and would be helpful in our ocean passage. Oh joy! I would once again be able to bring out the plastic Christmas tree that we had used in New Zealand.

Arranging to enter into Boat Lagoon was an interesting experience. First, we had to wait for high tide and daylight in order to see the faint signs marking the narrow, winding channel, and then it took at least an hour to make the trip. Once inside, I saw a remarkable facility. The marina catered to high-powered boats probably owned by wealthy Thais. Besides the boat services, there was a large hotel with a spa for guests and pools for swimming, which drew my full attention. Unfortunately, we had to leave the marina for 10 days during our month in Thailand as there was going to be a boat show during our stay and the marina needed all the slips. I hoped they'd take us back again. There weren't many transient boats like ours because of this inconvenience, but I was going to make the full use of it while we were there.

I arranged to have our Force 10 stove completely overhauled. Interestingly, the stove came from Vancouver, and the parts we needed, and had ordered, hadn't arrived in Langkawi when we had wanted to leave. A German cruising friend on *Hanto Yo* left there after we did, and he brought them to us in Thailand. Thank goodness we were never without help from cruisers. I found an enterprising Chinese man in Phuket who took the whole stove out of the boat and drove it away in his truck. All I could do was trust his work and hope that our stove would give me no more trouble until our trip was over. On the positive side, we had to eat out all the time the stove was in his hands, and that was no problem for me. There was a special coffee shop nearby which served tasty pastries, and a roadside fish barbeque stall where we could have a whole fish baked in banana leaves. There was nothing better than that.

The bus into the town of Phuket was so tiny that when you sat down you couldn't see outside as the windows were too high. Unfortunately, that was the problem on our first trip on the bus when we almost missed our stop. Al had more paperwork to do in Phuket which also had everything we needed: provisions, boat parts, internet, restaurants, and bars. Too bad Pete on *Sojourner* wasn't there to let us know the best place to buy cheap beer.

We went to Nai Harn Beach for the 10 days we were away from Boat Lagoon. It meant sailing around the tip of Phuket through Ao Chalong and up the west side. Al wanted to avoid the northeast monsoon and felt that we would be protected in the bay. At first it was quiet and beautiful. The beach was lined with restaurants, and one hotel dominated the western side. We could take our dinghy to shore, being careful to pull it far up onto the beach or the waves would sweep it away. Then we could explore the area to find a favourite restaurant or two. There were many cruising boats and tourist longboats anchored in the bay, as well as several large, crewed yachts participating in the King's Cup race that week sponsored by the king of Thailand. It was fun to be here, and a good change from the marina. Out in the bay, we could pick up the fresh breezes, while in the marina there was little wind. As the week progressed, the bay became very rolly due to a severe weather system in the Andaman Sea, which was later discovered to be a cyclone. Because of the high rollers, Al found it impossible to take the dinghy on shore. Nevertheless, I was glad that we had those few days in Nai Harn Beach before leaving for Boat Lagoon again.

We followed the same route on our way back, through Ao Chalong and up the east side to the entrance to Boat Lagoon. The wind was right on our nose all the way until we reached Koh Rang, a small island just outside the entrance to Boat Lagoon. This time, Al decided we would dinghy over to shore and join the many tourists visiting the place. On Koh Rang, I saw an interesting pearl museum and farm. Many types of cultured pearls were being cultivated, the best being the large South Sea pearl which was larger and rounder than the other pearls. Having seen the beautiful pearls in the South Pacific, I had no need to buy any more.

There was a large group of Asian tourists enjoying the day on the beach nearby. Groups of people would come from the mainland in longboats for the day, and kayak throughout the small islands in Phang Nga Bay, famous for the James Bond Island (Ko Tapu) seen in the movie *The Man With the Golden Gun*. The numerous islands had *hongs* or caves that could be explored. I realized that we were lucky to be in this area on our voyage, having the experience of a lifetime, whereas tourists spent thousands of dollars and traveled many miles by plane to see what I casually took in as a cruiser.

We were back again in Boat Lagoon with all the wonderful amenities. Vicky arrived by plane the next day. She always had an interesting agenda for her visits. After she arrived, we went to Phuket to see the opening of the last episode of *The Lord of the Rings*. Interestingly, we had seen the first one in Wellington, New Zealand, when Vicky had been with us the year before. It just seemed right to duplicate the experience. Before the movie started, the audience had to stand up for the national anthem with a large picture of the king projected on the screen. That was probably better than having many advertisements pushing their products in our faces.

The remainder of the time was spent preparing ourselves, and the boat, for our next ocean passage to the Andaman Islands. Vicky seemed anxious to get going, and I knew all of us had had enough of marina living, despite its luxury.

One day, Al said, "Let me treat the two of you to a Thai massage at the hotel." He pointed across to the other side of the marina from where we sat in *Solara's* cockpit, having an afternoon cocktail. "That will be my Christmas present to you both."

Vicky and I looked at each other and nodded our heads, vigorously agreeing to the suggestion. It was just a matter of making an appointment and then spending half a day getting pampered. Nothing was better than a Thai massage.

Al was anxious about this new ocean passage. He told me just before we left Boat Lagoon, "We are facing long passages between strange and distant ports. I am worried about possible engine and equipment breakdowns in remote, mysterious places."

Before he said that I had been feeling very excited about our next destination, and now he had me worried.

He continued, "We'll be entirely on our own in these places. I've read news clippings about bombings in Sri Lanka, about pirates in Oman, Yemen, and Somalia, and about skirmishes in Eritrea and Sudan."

How could I answer? I was less a worrier and was getting excited about new countries to visit. Nevertheless, he was right to be prepared. We were leaving Thailand with a ready boat, all breakages repaired, provisioning complete, our fuel and water tanks topped up, our safety gear checked, and our rigging and electrical and engine systems working well. My husband had the responsibility of the boat and the crew – me and our daughter – so I could understand his being concerned for our next long passage. We couldn't stay in Thailand forever, or leave our boat and fly home. We were committed to going ahead.

We sailed *Solara* to the brown choppy waters of Ao Chalong, anchored in the swells near the fishing boats, and readied the dinghy for a wet and muddy ride to shore in order to clear out of Thailand. I saw many tiny desks in a small room dedicated for boat clearances. It looked very official. After a long wait, Al finally cleared out, having made many trips to the copy shop, a few blocks away, to duplicate the papers given to him by all the various officials sitting at those tiny desks. Would we ever get out of there? Finally, the immigration officer in his bemedaled uniform, looking like a US Navy admiral, said a pleasant goodbye with a big smile on his face.

"Good wishes for your next destination."

We were allowed to stay in the country for a few more days which we needed to sail up the west coast, before heading out to the Andaman Sea.

Things didn't start out as well as we had hoped. Just as we were leaving Ao Chalong and putting up the main sail, Al discovered a foot-long tear in the leech of the sail. His expertise in sail repair was going to be tested. Once anchored again near a sandy beach resort, it took several hours for him to expertly create a nearly professional sail repair. Thank goodness we could now leave. But no, I discovered the mainsail traveler coupling (a 3/8-inch stainless steel shackle) had shattered. Fortunately, Al found a spare shackle that he pounded and bent into the fitting, which amazingly worked. I was getting more and more impressed by my captain's abilities. Nothing could go wrong that he couldn't fix, I thought.

Finally being able to leave Ao Chalong, we sailed up the west coast of Phuket, passing Nai Harn Bay to Kata Beach, another popular hangout for tourists. As we passed Nai Harn, our friends on *Free Radical*, seeing us sail by, pulled up their anchor and joined us in Kata Beach for the day.

I was glad to see them again. They were going to stay in Thailand for Christmas and New Year's, when there was going to be big fireworks at Patong Beach nearby. As for me, I was tired of the sleaziness of that part of Thailand, a tourist trap if there ever was one. Patong, where I had a quick visit, was a tourist Mecca, explained the brochures. It was "ideal for party and play"; "a partying hotspot," said another. I didn't like the crowds and noise, although the shopping was good. The beach in Patong was extremely popular if you could find a spot to sunbathe.

I was ready to leave for a quieter place, which would be the Similan Islands about 60 miles west of the Thai coast. It was now Christmas Eve, and the third Christmas away from family. I would miss the family party, opening of gifts, delicious food, and companionship of friends. How time did fly!

At 03:00 we left a quiet anchorage on the coast of Thailand for the 60 miles of sailing to the Similan Islands, which were now a national park. There was fantastic snorkelling and diving around the limestone boulders strewn around each island, as though a giant monster had thrown them from afar. When we arrived, there was a mooring ball available for a small fee, and we could spend a few days there swimming, snorkelling, and walking through the large boulders.

On Christmas morning, I blew up the plastic tree and the three of us celebrated in the Peters' tradition: orange juice cocktails with champagne, and crepes made by Vicky, who was the master of the stove for that dish. There was an exchange of presents, and a relaxing day of swimming on the beach. It was a beautiful spot to celebrate. The water was glistening in the sun, the sand below our boat could be seen clearly from above, and the fish surrounding *Solara* were seen as though they were in a large fish tank. I wondered where I'd be in the following year: 2004. It would be hard to top that. Nevertheless, I missed seeing the rest of the family at that special time of year.

Ahead of us was the unknown.

PART 7

Andaman Sea to the Red Sea

CHAPTER 29

❦

The Andaman Islands

THE ANDAMAN ISLANDS are very remote and beautiful, but only a few are available to cruisers. We were visiting the most interesting one, Port Blair, on the South Andaman Island. Despite the endless paperwork in Kuala Lumpur beforehand, the bureaucracy of the Indian government didn't end once we arrived in Port Blair.

We had three days of comfortable sailing along the Thai coast, through stunning offshore islands ringed by large palm trees, sandy beaches, and rocky shores, and then across the Andaman Sea. A peculiar phenomenon happened in those waters. One morning, I looked over to the port side at the bow and saw ripples of water coming toward our boat, as though a large underwater creature was heading our way. *Solara* began to rock to a fro with the large waves. There was nothing that Al could do but to let the boat bounce along for the next 20 minutes. Soon after, the strange phenomenon was over. After crossing many oceans, that was the first time we had seen such strange currents.

Port Blair Harbour Authority wanted a six-hour notice before our planned arrival. Al called on the VHS to the harbour very early in the morning, at 02:00.

"We should be at the entrance at 08:00 and we'd like to come in."

There was no response. At 04:30, we received a call telling us to radio again when we reached the harbour. Hey, they finally knew we were coming!

We arrived at the Port Blair harbour and dropped our sails just inside. We called the authorities again. A new voice replied, "Turn around and wait outside the harbour as you don't have permission to enter." Al, Vicky, and I looked at each other in confusion but hastened to turn around. We then motored about 500 feet back and waited for five minutes. The voice came on again, "You now have permission to enter and to anchor." *If the entrance procedure was that bad, what more could we expect?*

After anchoring in the muddy water of the large bay, we inflated the dinghy, dropped it into the water, lowered and attached the motor, and prepared to pick up the first of several sets of officials. The immigration officers in spanking white uniforms waited for Al's arrival on a sloping ramp used as a dock a half a mile away. Soon after, I saw Al and the officers in our dinghy with their papers to be processed, bouncing through the waves as they approached *Solara*. I hung over the gunwale preparing to meet them and offer them tea or coffee. It took no time for the officers to climb on board with Al's help. They seemed quite used to climbing onto yachts. Vicky and I watched while all the papers were being filled out, and poured tea for those who wanted it. It all seemed very boring, but I sat like a dutiful crew and said not a word. The procedure took about an hour, while the wind outside our boat started to whip up the waves in the harbour to an intolerable level. Their trip back to the dock was a very wet one, and everyone on the dinghy got soaked. Other officials waiting their turn to visit our boat joked and laughed at the wet immigration men, but they were good sports about it.

Next, it was the customs officers' turn. One of them came with his little boy, who seemed scared at the process of the dinghy ride. He was wearing his father's uniform hat which came down over his ears, causing us to think that this visit would be less officious. Of course, this group got wet as well. I offered them tea, and a cold drink for the boy. That went very well but it didn't shorten their visit, which took a long time as they wanted a list of everything on board. Al started to make a list in a deliberately slow way, writing down everything in long hand, and making a copy on carbon paper. I looked at him with an amused expression, hoping not to look too obvious that I understood he was doing it so that the officer would get impatient.

The customs officer's son looked very restless and bored while this was going on, and finally his father said impatiently, "Just give us what is important: portable equipment such as cameras, jewellery, etc." We had never been asked to make such a list in any of our previous ports.

Procedures weren't over yet. After Al took those men and the nervous little boy back to the dock, three coast guard men arrived in their large boat, which was faster and sturdier than our dinghy. They were interested in our safety equipment, our log book, and the radio book. That was also a first.

Before they left, I asked, "Could you please give me some frequencies or numbers that we can call in an emergency?"

"Well," one answered, "here are some numbers but they can only be used on a landline, and our radio frequency is secret." We really would be alone on the Andaman Sea, the Bay of Bengal, and the Indian Ocean.

Now it was our turn to take the dinghy to shore and fill out the last entry papers. Our daughter was planning to take a short visit to nearby Havelock Island, where there was a resort. While she was making her plans, we were going to "soak up" a bit of India. Sacred cows, abundant on the crowded, dirty streets, wandered wherever they wished. Colourful and beautiful saris were seen on the women, and the traffic consisted of many small tuk tuks (three-wheeled motor vehicles). It was a busy, dirty, and congested city, not what we expected to find in such a remote island. It was difficult to find a decent restaurant serving Indian food, but we found the market with a variety of fresh vegetables and fruit. I had filled up our boat with provisions from Thailand, and wasn't too worried about the lack of good shopping. There were other interesting sites I wanted to see in Port Blair.

The Cellular Jail, built in 1908 by the British, was one of the most interesting. In the 19th century, the British annexed the islands and formed a penal colony for Indian freedom fighters. It became a place of horrendous atrocities for more than 30 years, and an important shrine for the former prisoners who had died there. Many Indians from the mainland came by ship from Calcutta to visit the jail. As we were wandering around, peering into the various cells, the Indian tourists were looking at us. We were an oddity to them. They wanted to take their picture with us.

I could just imagine a family member looking at the picture back in India and saying, "And who are those people?"

"Oh, some tourists from Canada who were visiting the jail. We had never seen anyone from Canada before."

The Indians were very friendly, and wanted to chat and find out more about us. I felt like a celebrity for a while. Our time visiting the Cellular Jail took up most of the day, but while we were away from the boat, the port authority was busy trying to reach us on our boat radio. Apparently, the tour operator who arranged the trip for our daughter wasn't aware that Vicky didn't have the green card tourists received at the airport, as she had come by yacht. When the ferry arrived at Havelock, the authorities wouldn't let her land, and consequently sent her back to Port Blair. She got her money back, but had no idea how to let us know she had returned. A bright idea came to her head. "Mom needs to pick up the laundry that had been left. I'll just wait there." That was a full afternoon wait while we were happily sightseeing. Poor Vicky. I felt really sorry for her and angry at the Indian officialdom, even though they were very apologetic, and blamed each other for the confusion.

The other interesting place we visited was Ross Island, close to Port Blair by ferry. We were the only North Americans among the large group of Indians visiting that day. Ross Island had once been the administrative headquarters for the British. But since 1941, when an earthquake destroyed most of the buildings, Ross Island had been left to the trees and plants, which grew over all the former buildings. We could see the remnants of the old ballroom, bakery, boiler room, officers' club, church, and other smaller buildings. Once called the "Paris of the East" I looked at the remains of Ross Island, somewhat disgusted that the British lived in such opulence compared to the local people in Port Blair. Most visitors quickly skimmed over the rocky remnants and enjoyed the large beach instead, desolate but beautiful as nature took over, scattered with foliage and broken branches from the jungle rimming the edge.

Leaving the Andaman Islands was just as difficult as arriving. The paperwork for leaving was done in antiquated offices, situated in Port Blair. It took a good part of the day to be able to leave. In one office, I looked around at the dusty shelves filled with old files piled high in disarray. The official saw my curious gaze and said, "We have to blame the British for all this bureaucracy." He smiled, and wobbled his head like all the Indians we met on our visit there.

Leaving the harbour was even more dramatic. As we were putting up the sail to head out, the first boat in the Phuket to Andaman race had just arrived. It was *Schtormvogel*, a large and beautiful yacht of at least 60 feet accompanied by eight crew members. They were trying quickly to lower their sail, not noticing *Solara*, and heading right towards us. *Schtormvogel* was the boat used in the movie *Dead Calm*. I was sorry I had seen the film before sailing on the ocean. It was about a young Australian couple who were becalmed on the ocean, boarded by criminals who professed to be in need, and went onto a dramatic ending with the couple fighting for their lives.

While we were busy trying to leave, our sail tore as I was raising it, and worse, our motor was heating up and had to be turned off, at the same time as *Solara* was heading for the reef around Ross Island. I heard a groan above me where Al stood by the mast.

"What's the matter?" I asked.

"I've wrenched my back and it's very painful." Oh, I thought, that's bad, especially right now. He continued, "We'll have to turn the motor on anyway, or we'll go into the reef or get hit by this approaching yacht."

"Let's head back to the harbour and fix the problem of the motor," I answered with what I thought was the best solution.

"No way," replied my husband quickly. "Do you think I want to go through all that bureaucracy again?"

So there we were, just outside the harbour, evaluating the motor problem. Vicky and I looked at the manual and suggested that we needed a new fan belt. Al was ready to tear the old one off but, looking at the manual again, I gave him a clue how to take it off an easier way. A female cruiser had no qualms about using a manual, while a male cruiser, like my husband, often liked to show his muscle. The new fan belt was the answer to the motor problem but, although Vicky and Al tried, the torn sail couldn't be properly mended while we were sailing to Sri Lanka.

CHAPTER 30

❧

Sri Lanka

IT TOOK A week to cross the Bay of Bengal with our reefed main sail. We were a crew of three, which made the sailing easier, especially with the winds of 20 to 25 knots at our back. We developed a good system of watches, meals, and free time as we approached the southeast coast of Sri Lanka. As we neared shore, we got fog and heavy rain, and no visibility. It was time to use our radar. Interestingly, a Sri Lanka warship passed us going north along the coast, but didn't indicate seeing our boat. As soon as we put on our radar, I noticed the ship quickly turn around and head towards us.

When the ship got closer, I saw a beat-up looking vessel blowing out black fumes and polluting the air, like a storm cloud. It was formidable looking, black and menacing. Someone of authority called us on the boat to boat radio. "Name your vessel and your purpose near our border."

"We are a Canadian registered vessel, and we wish to enter Galle harbour," Al replied, also with authority.

"You may anchor in the outer harbour today and wait until morning to receive permission to be escorted into our inner harbour." With those words we continued south, being careful of the fishing boats with their long, almost invisible lines spread out along the coast.

We were in Sri Lanka during a ceasefire between the government and the Tamils, who wanted independence. But the situation was very tenuous. The officials were being extremely careful about who could be close to government property, which was in the main harbour of Galle, where the navy was docked. Hopefully, the old ship we saw was just a border vessel as I was sure the country had to have a more sophisticated navy.

That night we spent anchored outside the harbour and waited until morning to get permission to get into the inner harbour. In the morning, a police boat arrived at the side of *Solara*.

"We have come to escort you to a dock where you can tie up," said one of the crew on the boat. There was a barrier set up to stop ships from entering the inner harbour at night, and that was why the police were there to take away the barrier for the day. The Sri Lankan government had very tight security measures, as during the war with the Tamils the harbour had been breached by underwater scuba divers coming in to bomb facilities. For that reason, underwater bombs were set off several times a night in the harbour to discourage divers, unsettling for the yachts in the "marina." The police escorted *Solara* over to the inner harbour, where we were going to get help docking.

"Docking" didn't really explain how our boat was fastened to the facilities set out for cruise boats. First, our bow was tied to a heavy buoy, shared with several other cruisers, and then our stern was tied on a cleat to a floating dock. The cleat for our stern line was very flimsy, and actually came off one night. But we had to put up with these peculiar arrangements.

Before the police left us, one of them said to Al with his hand out, "How about something for our effort?"

That was a first for us, and my husband seemed quite flabbergasted. "I don't pay bribes," he answered, hoping that would be the end of the matter. He received an unfriendly look by the policeman who walked away.

When leaving, his partner said, "I haven't anything to do with that. It was his business." We hoped that we wouldn't have to deal with them again.

Al used GAC Shipping to process our entry into the country. We were fortunate to have Nuwan Bandara as our agent, who could procure diesel and water for our boat, as well as process our entry. Most agents had to deal with large freighters and international shipping, but he was most helpful and pleasant working with us. Nuwan was always dressed impeccably in uniform and polished shoes, accompanied by a wide smile for all his charges. We paid him US$200 for entry fees, which seemed high but we were going to stay for more than a week and planned to take a trip inland.

Nuwan gave us a flimsy piece of paper that would allow us to leave and enter through the police-protected gate out of the harbour. After attempting to secure our boat properly, it was a balancing act to get onto the floating dock and walk carefully to solid footing on shore. My balance was never very good after a long passage, and I always needed help from my husband. The dock and my equilibrium didn't match, and it was like walking on air with nothing solid below my feet.

Vicky, Al, and I walked across the wide cement pier, past large freighters docked tightly against the side and a few cows and chickens ambling around, and out through the gate. *What were the cows doing in the supposedly secure harbour?* After showing our papers at the gate, we were aggressively approached by various men wanting us to give them business. A tour? Do your laundry? Take you shopping? Each man had a tuk tuk, but Al and I decided that the 20-minute walk into town would do wonders for our legs. Or at least Al did.

The town of Galle was Sri Lanka's most historical city, and used to be the major port before Colombo. There were traces of Portuguese influence, but most of that had been destroyed when the Dutch took over in 1640. The fort they built was now a World Heritage Site. Looking down from the high walls, I could see the beauty of the rocks far below and the Indian Ocean. It was an excellent means of protection from outside forces, until the tsunami the following year.

As well as sightseeing, boat work, and provisions to be purchased, we wanted to take a four-day inland tour to see the highlands, tea plantations, and beauty of Kandy. A neighbouring cruiser, *Volovent* from Vancouver with a crew of three – Andre, Alex and Miaco – were interested in joining us on the tour. They seemed very compatible, and would help with the cost of using an agent, Marlin, who arranged the van and driver. He gave us an itinerary that he felt would give us a good picture of his country. While we were away, Al had found a young man who could repairs sails. Well, he said he could repair the sail, damaged almost beyond repair from the sun and salt. We had to trust that his skill matched his bravado. After Al jury-rigged a canvas to protect him from the hot sun, he was left to do the work and hopefully we would return to a sail that didn't have to be replaced.

The first stop recommended by Marlin was Yala National Park. On our way, we stopped at a roadside stand to taste coconut water. Marlin thought it would cool us down but I wasn't sure; the temperature in the south part of Sri Lanka must have been at least 40 degrees Celsius. The roadside owner picked out the coconuts, shook each one to make sure there was liquid in them, and chopped the tops with his large machete. My, that tasted good! Manna from heaven!

The park was a long drive away on bad roads, and I was beginning to think it had better be good or the trip would be a waste of time. Open scrub, lagoons, and lakes covered a vast area, and from afar we saw only a few specimens of wildlife: groups of buffaloes, crocodiles, deer, and a few elephants. Perhaps I was spoiled by having visited Africa a few years earlier. Our first night was spent in a hotel near the park gates, but in the morning we would travel to the hill country, a beautiful highland area where tea was grown.

The weather in the higher plains was a welcome relief from the heat further south in Galle. And the scenery was well worth the trip. The dark green tea plants covered the undulating hills. They were a patchwork of various hues, and amongst the tea bushes I saw small figures of colourfully clothed women harvesting the leaves. The large baskets sitting on the ground nearby would eventually be filled to the brim and carried carefully on the backs of each woman to a waiting truck.

While in Kandy, we visited the Temple of the Sacred Tooth Relic. It supposedly contained a tooth of Buddha. More importantly, whoever guarded the tooth symbolized the right to rule in Sri Lanka. Consequently, the temple became a target for those fighting the government, with the most recent bombing in 1998. There was serious security, such as one goes through in an airport, to enter the building. But it was worth the necessary inconvenience. The interior shone with gold and rich materials. The tooth relic lay under an elaborate golden canopy. I felt I had to trust that there was a tooth hidden somewhere in the seven caskets, one inside the other, all engraved with precious stones. The Sinhalese visitors reacted to their visit with reverence and humility. Buddhism was worshipped

– governing politics as well – but I was there to enjoy the beautiful country and tried not to discuss the conflict with others.

The last tour was to an elephant orphanage sanctuary. I have always had a soft place in my heart for elephants. Consequently, our trip to the orphanage was a highlight. We stood with all the tourists on a high plat-form and watched the keepers take about 30 to 40 elephants to a water-ing hole. There they could drink, roll in the mud and sand nearby, and play in the water. The most interesting part was watching the babies having a wonderful time rolling in the water. The older elephants would watch over the little ones and make sure they could get out of the mud. After the bath, the keepers took the group back to the feeding area where the babies were fed by bottle. It was sad as the young ones had lost their mothers, so there was no mother to feed them anymore. The elephant orphanage stop finished our inland trip. I felt it was well worth the time. Sri Lanka was a beautiful country, too lovely to have such a long conflict happening to the population.

Nuwan, our agent, invited us to have a meal with his family in Galle. The invitation was a wonderful treat. We would experience the traditional family meal and see how the middle class lived. I got dressed in my finest (skirt and blouse), and Al changed into long pants (I think I tried to press the wrinkles out of them). Nuwan came to our boat and we walked together up a hill to his house. It was a modest one-storied clapboard house with a long, wide porch in front. The front door opened onto their main parlour filled with various knickknacks sitting on open shelves amongst large, heavy but comfortable furniture, framed in local wood. The large dining room table sat a few feet away, but one step up, perhaps to delineate it from the rest of the sitting room. Family photographs sat on the shelves with faces of various ages. Nuwan probably had a large family well-established in Sri Lanka.

We were invited to sit down and were offered a drink, either a fruit drink or beer. Nuwan had invited some of his relatives to meet us but their English was basic; there was no discussion about the unrest in their country. All of us were having a nice friendly evening, and I was looking forward to the meal ahead. We sat down at the long, carefully decorated table. I noticed that there was no cutlery, and we were going to eat like locals, with our fingers. I looked over at my husband, questioningly, as I knew he didn't like using his fingers. We were then given bowl-shaped pancakes that were to be used to pick up the food. I learned that eating with one's fingers was an art, and I carefully watched the others. You could pick up food with your right hand only, and used your thumb together with your middle fingers which acted as a scoop. So, there I was with my fingers making a scoop, trying to take enough food to satisfy my hunger, but nothing compared to Nuwan's family. Al managed to procure a fork. He couldn't throw away his Western culture for a minute. Vicky was better than me, having eaten like that before.

The food was delicious. There was banana and pineapple roti, vegetarian, fish, of course, and a curried mixed dish. All were cooked as though there had been a gourmet chef involved, but I knew that it was Nuwan's mother who had done all the work. We had brought them a gift, but nothing we could have brought them would compare with the pleasure we had to be invited to their home.

Of course, cruisers can't be on the seas too long before an accident happens. Al was just cleaning up a mess that occurred from the multitude of birds that sat on our bow sprint all the time we were sitting in the harbour. He had the cover raised on the chain locker at the bow. When he was closing the heavy lid, it slammed down and crushed his finger. I heard a cry from the galley, where I was cleaning up after our last meal.

"Oh! The top of my finger is gone. Blood is pouring out."

Vicky hurried to see what had happened. I stood back numb and scared, perhaps looking stupid. I did get our first aid kit from the locker, but we soon realized a bandage wouldn't be enough. Al quickly went from eager to leave to thinking he'd better get it taken care of.

I quickly called Nuwan to let him know that we wouldn't be at their dock to get diesel and water. "It's a medical emergency. Could you bring your vehicle to our dock?"

Vicky moved quickly down the concrete pier to get the tuk tuk driver who had been driving us around for the week. They both came scurrying back to help Al get to a clinic for treatment.

From then on, I just hoped someone out there would help my husband. I was told to look after our boat in the meantime. I counted on our daughter to do the right thing, as she thought and moved faster than I did. Everyone – the driver who took Vicky and Al to the clinic, Nuwan who found his own doctor, and all the hospital staff – showed me how thoughtful and caring they were. Al finally got the emergency care he needed, but the doctor suggested he stay put for a few days. I had a feeling that the doctor was talking to a lost cause.

Later, I heard about the hospital experience. Apparently, the first clinic the tuk tuk driver stopped at wouldn't take him because Al's injury was too serious. The three of them headed for the hospital. By then, Al was feeling very weak and, knowing him, was probably about to faint. The staff told him to lie down, and he did faint with the blood continually pouring out of his wound. One nurse asked the tuk tuk driver to lift up his legs (yes, the lovely man had continued to be of help). Then the driver also fainted. Vicky was making mental notes. The doctor cleaned and sewed up the end of Al's finger. Amazingly, he also put a bit of nail at the top and into the stitches, hoping that it would eventually grow. He sent Al back to our boat all bandaged up, with antibiotics and instructions for cleaning the wound. The surprising end to this terrible accident was a total cost of US$65. It was a good thing that we weren't in America.

When it was time to leave, I looked at my husband's fragile appearance. It was apparent that he was in great pain and not able to take command of *Solara*. I suggested that we stay there another day until he felt better, but he insisted that we leave the next day, "no matter what."

Vicky and I had to take control of our boat. After only one day of recuperating, we set off. Vicky and I took charge of the boat, following the recommended route to the Maldives. Although the women were in charge, Al sat in the cockpit with his arm held high, giving orders.

All he needed was a black eye patch and a sword to make the perfect picture. Perhaps he didn't trust us to pick the correct sail combination or know how to follow the GPS coordinates. Fortunately, the weather was in our favour with very light winds, which meant we could motor most of the way.

CHAPTER 31

The Maldives

AFTER SEVERAL DAYS motor sailing, Vicky and I entered the most northern atoll in the Maldives and found Uligan, a small village. You could walk around its perimeter in less than an hour. It was our only stop before heading west on the Indian Ocean, but what a delightful experience. The only way to visit was by boat. Many cruising yachts, apparently, came here for a little R&R, as there was nothing to do but relax.

We checked in with an agent called Ahmed, who also arranged diesel for us which would be put in our jerry cans. Throughout our travels, there were several ways we got fuel. In developing countries, there would sometimes be a dock and a fuel pump with a gauge. We could also buy fuel from a barge, which would motor around with a load of diesel tanks. That fuel had to be filtered before going in our tanks. In other cases, we needed to buy fuel by carrying our jerry cans and filling them up at a pump in a local gas station. In all cases, the purchasing of fuel was a job that had to be done, but which was not exactly enjoyable.

Once officially entered into the Maldives, it was apparent that I was in a very conservative Muslim country. Al was handed an information sheet on what not to do when visiting Uligan. Rules included not allowing local people on or near your boat, dressing properly in the strictly Muslim village, no alcohol to shore, and not giving anything to anyone without permission. It was a very comprehensive list.

Nevertheless, the three of us motored into shore and made our entrance into the village. Immediately, we were welcomed in a very friendly manner and invited to take part in their special play day. I looked around at the happy crowd who were playing a type of baseball with a tennis racket and ball. The young girls were bare-headed, but the older women wore colourful headscarves and long skirts. I didn't see any men in this group of players which made me realize this was only for the women, while the men had other activities. I saw coloured, patterned pants and matching tops on the girls, and on the feet sandals or no shoes, since the warm sand where they were playing was soft and cleared of debris. It was a beautiful setting among the tall, swaying palm trees.

They asked me to play and I declined at first, but later took up the racket at "home plate" in front of the group, who looked at me with anticipation. "How will this stranger hit the ball?" their looks seemed to say. Suddenly, the small ball came whizzing by me and I missed, consequently making a fool of myself. I looked over at my husband standing there, trying not to laugh. Where was Vicky? She was probably smart enough not to get herself embarrassed. Another ball was tossed, my racket contacted, but a young girl quickly caught it and I was out. The game was all in fun though, and I did try to do my best to take part in the festivities.

We walked around the small village on clean sandy "roads." No vehicles were allowed. The houses were made of dead coral or cement blocks. The local store was tiny and limited to what they could receive from a freighter that came, perhaps once a week. As we walked back to the main event at Uligan, we were invited to join their banquet at a small cost, which we did, of course. The whole experience was a wonderful moment for me. My heart went out to the people in this small atoll. The coral was dying, and all I could see was the brilliant white colour below our boat. The land was too low to survive any tsunami or global warming, which would raise the sea level to heights that would roll over the Maldives. I hoped that wouldn't be the case, as the area was so beautiful, a paradise in that remote atoll.

Vicky left us in the middle of the night in a small boat operated by two local men, happy to take her in the dark across the water to an airfield two hours away. From there, she had arranged to fly to a resort for a few days. Al and I were once again alone, but while we were anchored at Uligan, *Klondike*, an American boat, was anchored nearby. We had met Katie and Don previously. Fortunately, Katie was a retired emergency nurse from California. What more could I ask for but to have her look at Al's finger and take out the stitches?

"Katie," I called over from our boat. "I can't deal with taking out the stitches on Al's finger. How about a bottle of wine to do the job?"

Katie took off the old bandage I had tried to carefully wrap around the damaged finger. The digit looked raw and sore; black thread hung out of it in small pieces, and the tiny bit of nail that had been put at the end was still there. Katie diligently took out the stitches, cleaned the wound carefully, and gave me advice on continuing treatment. That meant that Al still couldn't handle all the boat work, and it would be up to me to do much of the sailing. Would I be able to? I didn't think I had much choice. Soon we were on our way to Oman, no matter what might happen.

A new passage always took three of four days to acclimatize to, especially a long passage of 1,200 miles that would take us to Salalah, Oman.

We were heading for the dreaded Gulf of Aden, with its unpredictable pirates. I was on edge the whole way, not knowing how we would handle the passage since Al was still recuperating from his injury. In the meantime, we would have 10 days to make our plans. Fortunately, the weather was on our side, light winds coming from behind. That gave me time to relax with little sail changes to make, our bearing straight ahead, and my not having to bother Al too much for his help.

CHAPTER 32

Oman and the Gulf of Aden

As we neared Oman, I saw the dry, mountainous landscape in the distance, looking like a brown mirage. The temperature was hot, and the blowing sand mixed with the salt air encrusted our entire boat with a red sandy "paint." Soon we approached Salalah, the main harbour. It was time to take down the main sail, but something was caught on the track of the mast. I couldn't send Al up with his injured hand, but I could make a call on our VHS to our cruising friends, who would be sure to be in the harbour.

We passed the commercial harbour with large tankers, cargo ships, and huge container vessels, tied up on the wharf, and then into a smaller section for anchored boats. On entering, our main sail was only partway down, flapping away and looking very unprofessional. Al was annoyed at my asking for help and assured me that he could very well fix the problem. But quickly, one of the cruising captains on a nearby boat got in his dinghy and motored over to *Solara*. The problem was solved easily as a screw on the track had partly come loose and stopped the sail from being lowered.

I looked around and found so many of our friends: *Free Radical* and *Volovent III* from Vancouver who had travelled with us in Sri Lanka, *Honey Moon* from Australia as well *as Revision II*, a French yacht. There was also Katie and Don on *Klondike*. It was great to see them all there in Salalah, along with about 15 other yachts. They were all waiting for the proper wind to leave.

All of us were anxious to head west to the Red Sea and try to protect ourselves from the pirates. It was important to reach the entrance to the Red Sea in the next couple of weeks, before the end of February, as the contrary north winds kicked in by March and April. All the fancy yachts contrasted sharply with the dirty, rusting coastal freighters and large Arab fishing boats tied to the high concrete dock. The fishing boats were huge, open steel or wooden boats, about 60 feet long and crewed by 10 or 12 rough looking men. Were those pirates ready to rob our boats once we left the security of the Salalah harbour? The harbour was heavily guarded by Arab police in smartly tailored uniforms in British military style, well-armed with modern weapons. Contrasting with the fishing boats were the large open freighters which plied the seas around the Middle East, taking cargo from port to port. One was packed with about 800 live goats filling the air with a foul smell. It smelled like we were in the middle of a barnyard.

Our agent was Mohammed, a tall 6-foot-2 man with an open smile, happily ready to help all the cruisers for entry to his country. Any needs we had would be looked after in a very professional manner. Mohammed strolled around the harbour in his flowing white *dasha* and colourful head wrap. You couldn't miss him. It was too bad that he couldn't help us through the Gulf of Aden.

Oman was also our first developed and rich country since Australia, and I found good provisions, except for alcohol and pork. In order to leave the harbour, we had to go through a security gate and show our passes to visit the city of Salalah, the largest and most important port in Oman. Our passports would remain with Mohammed until we left the country. I found these security arrangements necessary but difficult to live with. There was little freedom, and strong controls over our movements throughout our time in Oman.

Al rented a car for a few days so we could do some sightseeing around Salalah and shop more easily, as the stores were far apart. We went to the local *souk* to buy frankincense and myrrh, both famous perfumes sought after in the ancient world. At one time, they were more valuable than gold. Frankincense and myrrh came only from a few places in the world from an aromatic gum on special trees that grew in that southern Arab country. It would be fun to take them home and perfume our house with the rich aroma. The local people, we were told, would burn the spices in their houses, and pass the smoke under their garments to perfume their bodies.

It bothered me to see AK-47 weapons also for sale in the market. Should we have a weapon on our boat? Not for us, but some American boats felt the need for protection.

I enjoyed watching my husband getting his hair cut from a Pakistani barber, while I sat nearby drinking tea. For little cost he not only got his hair cut but a special massage treatment. Following my spouse around, watching him get his hair cut, letting him drive the car, made me feel somewhat like the women of that Arab country. Unfortunately, there were very few women in town. I saw them sitting in the back of luxurious cars hidden behind black *chadors* with only their dark eyes peering ahead, or walking quickly behind a man – husband or family member – to do necessary errands in the market.

While Al was working on our boat, always a continual task, I took a day's outing with a few other cruisers with a guide and van. The excursion was very interesting, especially since I had not travelled in the desert before. I looked around at the desolate, scrubby landscape and the wild, parched mountains in the distance. Our group saw Job's tomb some miles away, protected in a small building just near a large mosque far into the hills beyond Salalah. The tomb was a single, long grave set into the floor, covered in ornate shrouds embroidered with verses from the Quran. The tomb was considered a sacred place, and all of us dressed appropriately. Job is mentioned in the Old Testament, by the Jews in their sacred writings, and is a prophet in the Quran. Who knew where the real Job belonged?

Travelling inland from the Arabian Sea, the guide took us to a Bedouin campground. They were nomads living in tents and tending camels used not only for transportation, but for milk and meat. Plastic garbage lying around took away the drama of seeing a way of life so contrary to how I lived in Canada. We passed by an oasis where some local boys were swimming in the water despite the sign in English and Arabic that read: *Danger, snails in water will give you a bad rash.* On the way back, the guide showed us the ruined site of the ancient city of Al Balid situated on the coast of the Arabian Sea. The city had sat above a beautiful harbour long before 2000 BC as a key stop on the frankincense trail, where camels loaded down with the precious incense travelled beyond Oman to Rome and China. Now migrating birds had taken over the ruins.

After the tour, it was time to prepare for our trip through the Gulf of Aden, or "Pirate Alley" as it was known by the many cruisers we talked to.

Every time we took the dinghy from our boat, over to the high iron ladder fastened against the concrete pier in Salalah harbour, I nervously anticipated the difficulty I would have when I reached the top of the long ladder and couldn't raise my body from the last few rungs to the level landing. It took muscles I didn't have as there was nothing to hold onto. Al always climbed behind me in case I slipped as there was no one at the top to give me a hand. Sometimes he would boost me from behind, but usually that was more embarrassing than practical. After a few such incidences, Ed on *Free Radical* began coming over to give me a hand up from above, and often helped Al with the heavy containers. We had to fill up our water tanks and diesel tanks from a source on the pier, and then lower each container by rope down to the waiting dinghy. This meant a high number of trips from the ladder to our dinghy, and then to our boat. That was one provisioning I hated but there was no other way. We had 700 miles to our next destination, Bab-el-Mandeb, on the southern tip of the Red Sea, and we needed the fuel and water.

Meanwhile, all the cruisers met to discuss how we would pass through the area of the Gulf of Aden and avoid the pirates. In 2002, the previous yachting season, boardings by pirates were numerous and affected about 10 percent of the yachts. All of us sat around the "Oasis Club," as we called the room provided by the harbourmaster, discussing our plans. It was obvious that the new season was about to start. While there, I noticed a number of fishing crew listening to our plans. Could they understand? Did they have plans of their own? People in the area around Yemen and Somalia were poor, and our yachts were like gifts from heaven. We feared the 60-foot open fishing boats, however, as they roamed the entire gulf and could outrun most sailing yachts.

The final plan was to go in small convoys, meet at a designated way-point during the dark, and motor through the historical 150-mile-long piracy zone at night, without lights, as quickly as we could until daylight. The convoys were divided according to the size of yacht and the speed it could handle. The plan was well-organized, fed by material gathered by cruisers from the previous year. We would sail at least 30 miles off the coast of Yemen, far enough to avoid small Yemeni fishing crafts, and just outside the dangerous commercial shipping lanes.

The Gulf of Aden was a narrow stretch of water about 600 miles long and 150 miles wide, dividing lawless Yemen to the north, and poor and lawless Somalia to the south. At the western end of the gulf was crime-ridden Djibouti, a French territory. In the centre of the gulf was an extremely busy shipping channel, handling container ships and bulk carriers, both mammoth ships passing through at incredible speeds in order to avoid the pirates. No place for pleasure yachts, especially at night.

Most of the previous attacks by pirates had been carried out by Arab fishing boats, illegally transporting Somalis to Yemen and happening upon one or two sailing yachts by chance. The pirate crew were thought to be armed with AK-47s, machine guns, or other automatic weapons. They would strip the boat of anything valuable and disappear quickly. The war in Iraq was taking place with the invasion of American forces. No one on the sea had an interest in private boats. All of us felt we were on our own to guard our safety. To prepare our boat, Al and I put our valuables in hidden places down below and left out an old wallet containing only American ones and discontinued credit cards. What more could we do?

Solara and 13 other boats left Salalah harbour the next morning. Al felt that we should sail in Oman waters as much as possible during daylight, and reach the rendezvous point just after dark. We were so scared about this passage that it was hard to concentrate. There was no small talk, as we just wanted to get it over with as soon as possible. On our way, the prop of *Solara* got caught on a fishing line. Oh, that was all we needed to make things more interesting. It meant Al had to dive down below our boat and cut away the thin threads, even with his finger still healing.

All the cruising boats in our convoy contacted each other on a secret channel on our marine radios every six hours until sunset, in order to keep updated and form convoys at the special waypoint. It had been decided that our boats should enter the "pirate area" during a weekday when there would be no moonlight. The first night we were in a group of four: *Solara*, *Free Radical*, *Revision II*, and *Klondike*. Two boats, *Destiny* and *Honeymoon*, were ahead and would enter the danger area on the same night. The following day, *Klondike* decided to catch up with the two boats that were ahead. That left the three of us. In spite of the tense situation, we sailed through the most incredible phosphorescence surrounding us in the water. It was a brilliant green colour which painted our whole boat with a florescent hue. It almost made me forget the fear I had. Another day of sailing before we would tackle the "pirates."

Our lights were off and we used our radar to keep our formation as one unit. There would be no sleep that night for either of us as we watched the radar down below as not to show a light in the cockpit. We looked all around us constantly, in case we would see any unknown vessel. The large fishing boats we were trying to avoid would also be moving in the dark without lights. It was like a WWII movie; we were the merchant ship, and the pirates were the submarines and destroyers.

Not long after we had formed our group in the dark, there was a terrifying Mayday call blaring out from our radio speaker. It was *Klondike*, the boat 10 miles ahead, alone. They were being pursued by a large Arab fishing boat.

"Mayday Mayday," called Katie excitedly. "A large fishing boat powered by a diesel is pursuing us. We are trying to evade them, and so far can outmanoeuvre them. They are armed and dangerous and trying to board us."

Al answered the Mayday call, but we were over an hour away. What could he do but continue to keep up the radio communication? Al offered to use our satellite phone to call an antipiracy number in Australia, which relayed to Kuala Lumpur and then to authorities in the gulf like Yemen and the coalition warships. That was a decent suggestion, but how could that help immediately?

In the meantime, *Klondike* had eluded the fishing boat and our hearts – which had sped up considerably – slowed to a normal rhythm. But later that night we heard the Mayday call from *Klondike* again. Their boat was being pursued by the fishing boat again, which got so close that the crew almost jumped into their cockpit. The pursuit went on for almost three hours. How terrible if must have been for Katie and Don. Fortunately, they outran the boat and headed toward our small convoy. Were they bringing back the bad guys? I hoped not. Oh, that the passage would be over; it was so stressful, especially with the dark cloud covering the stars, leaving no light, and the water below our boat flowing black and menacing.

There were five boats now in our group after *Klondike* and *Black Wattle* joined us in the dark. We continued on, more stressed than ever, looking around us for the fast fishing boat which had been in pursuit. Would Al get a response from his satellite call? With so many warships and commercial ships in the area, why hadn't any of them come to help our friends? Daylight brought stability and comfort. At least we could see all around us, and we had reached the last waypoint of the "pirate area." I knew that after *Klondike's* experience no one could depend on any support during an attack. A few days later, I heard that a French boat had been boarded and robbed in the same place, one of 10 boats that year.

A loud noise was heard above our boat. We had gathered quietly in the morning, trying to recover from the night's passage. It was a military helicopter. There was a call to our boat on the VHS.

"Are you the boat *Solara* who phoned the piracy centre last night?" spoke one of the crew in the helicopter.

Al answered. "Yes, one of our convoy was pursued by pirates."

"A coalition warship is heading your way and would like to speak to the yacht that was under attack."

Oh goodie, I thought, what good timing. Where were they last night? Not long after that thought, a beautiful, grey metallic ship came alongside our small group of yachts. It approached in all its splendour, with large machine guns and innumerable aerials for communication. Our yachts looked like tiny bathroom toys alongside the immense vessel. It was a Spanish coalition warship, plying the waters during the Iraq War. The ship lowered a large zodiac and a number of young sailors climbed down, visiting each one of us on the convoy and spending a considerable amount of time interviewing *Klondike*. This young crew were a happy lot, and before waving goodbye gave each boat two bottles of very nice Spanish wine, and assurances that they would watch out for us on our way to Aden. What a wonderful surprise! After all the excitement was over, the helicopter flew over once more to get all of our particulars. Al asked the crew on the helicopter if they had a number that could be called in case we ran in to trouble again. Believe or not, they gave him his own satellite number. Hopefully, we wouldn't have to call that one.

PART 8

North From Yemen

CHAPTER 33

The Red Sea

WE WERE GOING to make it! We reached Bab-el-Mandeb on time; that is, before the end of February. It was important to travel up the Red Sea before the strong northerly winds kicked in. A few of our cruiser friends decided to explore Yemen for a few days, while *Solara* and *Black Wattle* from Australia continued on.

The southern entrance to the Red Sea posed a number of problems. The Bab-el-Mandeb Strait was divided by a small island. Historically, it was an important passage between Asia and Africa, and was considered to be the first passage by early man from Africa. Our two boats decided to take the eastern channel, which was only 2 miles across, while the western channel was much wider and used by large vessels.

I'd heard all kinds of stories about the difficulty of the strait. It wasn't called the "Gate of Grief" for nothing. The waters around could be very dangerous. Three forces drove the currents in those waters: the winds, the southerly flow from the Red Sea, and the narrowness of the channel. Unfortunately, the strait couldn't be circumvented. But our two boats decided to go at night when the winds were lighter. We had reefed the sails just in case of higher winds, but we passed through without any problems, followed up the eastern side past Al Mukha, Yemen, and when the sun came up were able to pass west through the shipping lanes without incident, which was a blessing. Private yachts from non-Muslim countries weren't allowed in Saudi Arabian waters, and we had to make our way to the western coast of the Red Sea which happened to be our preferred route. Entering the Red Sea was only the beginning of that formidable passage to the Suez Canal.

In the morning, the seas began to churn in scary waves as the wind kicked in to 25 to 30 knots and the sky filled with dark clouds. After such a long passage from Salalah, through the "pirate alley" and into the strait, the tension stayed throughout my body. The strain of sailing was too much to handle, and the anchorage where we had planned to stop was difficult to see in the swirling mist of the water. Al decided that we couldn't go near such a scary approach amongst reefs and sand spits. I couldn't agree more despite how tired I was. We continued north, and with the good winds changing direction from the south the sailing was more relaxing with no ships or fishing boats nearby. The land was barren and brown, with little habitation, but beautiful in a rugged, haunting way. We were later told that the Eritrean and Sudanese governments had severely restricted or banned fishing boat activities for military reasons. I wasn't sure where *Black Wattle* had gone, but they were probably close by. Our direction to Massawa, Eritrea, was straight ahead, but too far away.

"Let's stop here," I said to my husband, after looking up our pilot guide and seeing a small bay not far ahead. It was called Anfile Bay, and as we approached there was a sheltered cove amongst low-lying sand dunes and scrub bushes. How quiet it was; just a beautiful and peaceful place. Maybe I could talk Al into staying two nights for the rest we needed. *Black Wattle* had called our boat from three hours away and decided to join us in the anchorage. They, too, were exhausted.

Unfortunately, I couldn't convince my husband to rest an extra day. I should have remembered that he always thought onward and ahead to our next destination.

It was an anxious moment before arriving in Massawa. Eritrea had just resolved a 35-year war between Ethiopia and their independence movement. Although Eritrea gained recognition in 1993, there was a border dispute between 1998 and 2001, again with Ethiopia. Before 1962, Italians had had their roots in Eritrea as a province of Italian East Africa for almost 50 years. With all that background, our visit to the conflicted country would be most interesting.

As we entered the harbour in Massawa, the ruins of the war were evident. Massawa was a bombed out city, but the Eritreans worshipped their freedom fighters, young teenagers who sauntered around the streets carrying machine guns slung across their breasts as badges of honour. The open sandals they wore were a mark of privilege. The young fighters had defended the Eritrean people and sent the Ethiopian Soviet-made tanks back to Ethiopia with their Molotov cocktails. Unfortunately, the government was turning the country into a Marxist police state and human rights had worsened.

Massawa was the only shipping port in Eritrea. There were many large vessels inside and outside the harbour. Al called the port authority and was told to enter and tie up at a very high, concrete dock. It looked formidable, with immense black tires hanging down on the concrete, probably to protect the sides of larger ships.

"This looks bad," I said to my husband. "The side of our boat will be ruined by the hot tires." I could just see our almost-white, sparkling boat covered in sticky black rubber. Just then, Ted called over to us from *Black Wattle* which stood against the pier.

"Come along side of our boat. We're much higher than you, and it'll be easier to climb up to the pier from here."

It was nice of them to solve the problem. After climbing off *Black Wattle*'s deck onto the pier, Al took all our necessary papers to the various authorities and, within a very short time and at very little cost, *Solara* and crew were legally entered into Eritrea.

We were told to anchor some distance away from the busy port to a large holding area full of derelict boats, rusted iron-hulled vessels, fishing boats that seemed to have gone to their final resting place, and old industrial ships with overhanging contraptions. Where would we anchor in that dirty inner harbour and unpredictable holding in what was probably deep mud? It turned out that there was plenty of room for us and for the yachts that would arrive later. I felt that we were being treated like second-class visitors with *Solara* surrounded by a multitude of derelicts.

But that was soon forgotten once we met Mike, short for Weldemicael Habtezion, who was given the job of seeing to our needs. This wonderful man – dressed in a traditional white robe, Arab-style, contrasting sharply against his dark skin, with his wide open smile and friendly manner – helped us purchase fuel and water, as well as the means to bring it to our boat. We hadn't stopped in a harbour since Salalah, and our needs were plenty.

Massawa was a tired and war-torn city. Its ancient Turkish and Italian buildings were now mostly ruined hulks of crumbling mortar, rising out of muddy streets. You could still see the damage, and border conflicts had yet to be settled. The rebel heroes were idolized in posters pasted to walls still standing. A large bronze statue of the sandals worn by the young fighters stood in a square in Asmara, the capital.

We felt welcome there, nevertheless. I wandered around the ancient streets with my husband with no sense of trepidation. The local people seemed to be living in the lower levels of bombed out buildings. Their smiling faces and enjoyment of life, as it was, surprised me, and I wondered how they managed amongst the ruins. The cafes, such as they were, had white plastic chairs spread in front of a doorway and opened to a small kitchen inside. We tried the food, which was a mixture of Turkish and Arab flavours. I enjoyed the spicy stew, which could be meat or vegetable based, and was eaten with pieces of delicious bread used as a utensil. I tried to ignore the multitude of scrawny cats wandering around, trying to jump onto our table. Eating among the ruins in the strange city of Massawa made it possible for both of us to be overcome with food poisoning or diarrhoea, but we were lucky. Unfortunately, many of our cruising friends became very sick. We often took chances eating local food.

The highlight of visiting Massawa was the invitation from Mike to participate in a coffee ceremony put on by his wife. The coffee ceremony was similar to the tea ceremony they have in Japan. Four of us went to Mike's home in downtown Massawa. He lived in the lower half of a large former Turkish-style home with large cavernous rooms, high ceilings, and wooden carved pillars. His family were basically "camped" in the building, only taking up a small portion of the immense structure. Mike's wife was settled in a smaller inner room serving as a kitchen. We were invited to watch her ceremony in the kitchen area. First she roasted raw beans – only raw beans were sold in the stores – on a primitive charcoal stove. Next, she hand-ground them with a mortar and pestle made of stoneware. The ground coffee was then spooned into a special clay pot with very hot water and put on the charcoal stove. The next step took a very long time as she swirled the coffee and water over the stove but didn't let it boil. She then picked up the clay pot, with its handle and especially fine spout, and placed some of the cooked coffee in another pot to cool, and later returned that cooled coffee back into the clay pot. The procedure of moving the cooked coffee to cool and back again to cook was done several times. The smell was tantalizing, and I was beginning to get impatient with the delay. Finally, she gestured for us to return to the sitting area since she was ready to serve the coffee in small ceramic cups. Wow! I'd never had coffee that tasted so good. I had brought some home-baked goodies to accompany the coffee, and all of us had a wonderful evening. Going to someone's house was always a highlight in our travels. I treasured the moments.

Before leaving Eritrea, a few of us took a tourist van to Asmara, situated over 7,000 feet in the central and mountainous area of Eritrea. On the way, the road passed beautiful mountain valleys with bare, stony, dry creek beds. We were there in the dry season, and the land around us was a rusty, reddish brown colour. Tiny shrubs of eucalyptus and aloe and cacti dominated the landscape. The road climbed round and round, higher and higher, and looking down from the van window I wished it was wider and that we were not so close to the edge where there was no barrier. As I looked around me, I saw small stone huts packed against the hillside in clusters of small villages. The villagers walked on the same road in their colourful robes, often behind their donkeys or camels. I saw a small stand containing a Christian cross and a statue of a saint. Perhaps an accident had happened at that spot. Life went on as though war had not touched this mountainous region. As we rose, I saw in the distance a small, green, old-fashioned train sitting in all its splendour and looking like a child's toy on the narrow track. I was told that there was sporadic service, but that it didn't go all the way from Massawa to Asmara as planned.

Driving into Asmara was like going from devastation to a well-kept modern city. The Italian influence from years of domination before WWII still lingered in the city. The colonial Italian architecture with its art deco features was like a breath of fresh air after Massawa. The streets were palm lined, and a variety of cafes, bars, and shops were available. The only white people I saw were UN workers who were observers during the conflict. There couldn't be much to observe in this beautiful city, protected, it seemed, during the latest war.

"I must have a pizza," I said. Where else could one find the best Italian food for miles around? Not only that, but I found a shop where I could buy Parmesan cheese, salami, and other precious goodies we had not seen since Australia. The "yachties" stood out in bold contrast to the local Eritreans, but apart from us and the UN personnel I saw no tourists. I felt welcome and accepted as we strolled around in the cool and clean air of the high-altitude capital of Eritrea. We planned to spend three days enjoying the atmosphere.

Asmara was where Al could get our visas for Egypt. Far from the main street, we found the small office of the Egyptian consulate. Apart from the cost, the procedure was very simple.

It was March 8, International Women's Day throughout the world. It was exciting to view the large parade of beautifully dressed women in their long, multi-coloured gowns and heads covered in scarves. There were also military women, young schoolgirls, nuns, and nurses, all in their various uniforms. Music played, singing was heard, and their marching feet moved with the rhythm of the drums. I watched all this from our large window in the Ambassador Hotel on the main street. Did our women at home celebrate in such a manner? Of course most of us were much luckier than these women, who had suffered greatly from the war. I should have gone down and marched with them, I thought afterwards. At least, it seemed that their men were in full support of the day.

After a week in Eritrea, it was time to leave for Sudan. Another trip to the large cement pier, but soon all the papers were filled out and *Solara* was given the go-ahead to depart. I said goodbye to the shell of Haile Selassie's palace, looking over the Red Sea, destroyed by the war. He had been Ethiopia's regent from 1916 to 1930 and emperor from 1930 to 1975. He had been revered as the returned messiah of the Bible by followers of the Rastafarian movement, very popular in Jamaica. How beautiful the palace looked even in its derelict splendour.

There was only one direction to sail: north. It sounded easy but was far from it. There were the northwest winds to stop our progress; there was the anxiety of finding the best places to anchor; there were the hazards we had to avoid when anchoring, such as reefs, which were plenty, and shifting sand in the shallow inlets; there was the unwelcoming presence of the Sudanese; and there were only a few stops where we could leave our boat and walk around due to landmines embedded in the sand. In spite of all the problems ahead of us, off we went with trepidation, eager to have the passage over. I spent time looking at our charts for the best possible anchorages, and listening to a Red Sea radio net each morning, organized by a few cruisers to keep in touch with each other. The yachts travelling through at that time relied on each other and no one else. Weather was unpredictable, and the Red Sea net tried to give the best information available. We hopped from anchorage to anchorage, sometimes beating through the waves and other times by motor. I hoped Al felt my concern about travelling at night in the dark when it was possible to get too close to the immense ships passing through the shipping lanes.

Our first day away from Eritrea was a weather window; that is, light winds from the south. We sailed near dusty, dry land dabbled grey on our port side. The air was filled with salty red sand, which coated our rigging, sails, and the rest of the boat for the next three weeks. We made our first stop between Sheikh el Abu Island and Harat where we found a very comfortable anchorage for the night.

The next day we stopped at Difnein Island, a very small island with little protection from the high winds which started to appear. Our wind generator sparkled with delight as its speed increased dramatically, giving us more necessary power. This would be our last offshore anchorage, as we planned to enter a popular *marsa* (bay) called Kor Narawat, which was on the South Sudan coast. All the *marsas* that we anchored in were beautiful, lonely, but stunning with their sandy, deserted shores and stunted vegetation, where we could see for miles in all direction. Once anchored in Kor Narawat, we saw a number of cruising boats, but none of us were socializing as it seemed that we had one goal in mind, and that was to reach Suakin, Sudan, as soon as possible. Suakin had a wonderful protected harbour and we would get a chance to do some limited sightseeing and perhaps find some vegetables, fruit, and bread.

It was impossible to plan our passages. We were subject to wind and weather and stopped when the winds became intolerable. We ended up anchoring at Talla Talla Saquir, an outer island about 15 miles off shore, even though we hadn't planned to. The winds were increasing right from the north, which was not good. There were some Sudanese fishing boats of many sizes anchored around the island. That was the first time we had seen any sign of life, except for other cruisers. Fortunately, they weren't interested in us and left us alone.

How slow our progress continued. We measured it in miles, feet, and chipped away the inches as the passage seemed to go nowhere. We struggled against the wind. We powered. We tacked. We slowly sailed. Would the struggle never end?

Our next anchorage was at Long Island, at the entrance to the Shubuk Channel, notorious and supposedly difficult to navigate. We could take shelter from the 20- to 25-knot winds before tackling the channel. Eight other boats were waiting for calmer weather.

"I'm going to try to motor through," said Al the next day. "These wimps sitting here are just are waiting to see how it goes."

I wasn't interested in arguing, but felt that many of the cruisers probably knew more about the hazards of the channel than he did. So off we went. It wasn't long before we returned. The wind and waves had slowed us down to 2 knots using our motor. It wasn't worth the trouble. Two days later, we tried again as the winds had lightened. We crawled along this time, watching out for the numerous reefs and markers which denoted the deeper depths.

"Turn 5 degrees to starboard," I would shout from the bow. "Now straighten out and go ahead." This continued until the next hazard. The channel was no friend to a husband and wife's relationship.

When I looked back beyond our stern, there were three boats following us. My God, did they really wait for us to be out in front? Were they ready to help if we ran into trouble? We finally reached the end of the channel and headed 15 miles to the entrance to Suakin, motoring straight into the wind, not our kind of passage-making, but eager to reach the shelter of Suakin harbour. The three boats behind stopped at a *marsa* just beyond, probably to wait for better weather.

We passed armoured vehicles sitting on sand dunes and fortified soldiers guarding the port as we entered the harbour. Sudan, since independence, had been in political turmoil, economic chaos, and civil war, as well as disputing the border to the north with Egypt. The result was widespread famine and a chronic refugee crisis. We passed old Suakin sitting on an island just before the anchorage. It was a crumbled ruin of formerly beautiful coral buildings, destroyed by the force of nature over many years. It had been a slave trading post since the 10th century, and was supposed to be the last known open auction slave trading post in Africa, operating until just after the Second World War. Before the construction of the Suez Canal, Suakin was one of the richest and busiest ports in the Red Sea. Now, camels, donkeys, goats, and chickens wandered through the dust. Although Sudan seemed like the last place we wanted to go, the Red Sea was driving us crazy. We needed to stop and rest.

Mohammed, the agent, appeared on shore once we were settled on our anchor. He stood there in his flowing white "gown," like a saviour coming to our rescue. He had a friendly face, and hopefully we would have no trouble with our paperwork to enter his country. Al lowered our dinghy, which hadn't felt the water since we left Salalah, picked up Mohammed, and then came back to our boat for entry procedures. Mohammed kept our passports until it was time to clear out. As with most of the agents we encountered, Mohammed arranged diesel and helped with provisioning, if we needed it.

I looked around this wonderful, protected harbour and felt the importance of its position years ago as one of the safest stops on that side of the Red Sea. Now, all I could see was desolation, dry, sandy roads into nowhere, and a pathetic, impoverished town. It was like going into the past. Donkey carts and camels were the means of transportation for carrying goods and travelling. We walked to a market of sorts where I bought round, tasty loaves of bread that looked like flat pancakes and a few scrawny carrots that folded over in a U-shape, but no fruit. Following a dirt "street" of sorts, we came across a market that sold trinkets and handicrafts for the few tourists who visited. The women sitting in front of their wares were covered from head to toe in black *chadors*, with piercing eyes looking out at me from a mesh-covered slit. I stopped and showed interest in a display of beautiful wood carvings. The bargaining began in earnest. It was all done by finger counting. The woman with the carvings had her hands completely covered in tattoos, and her nails were painted black from tip to bottom. I was getting nervous as a crowd from the market began surrounding me – men, children, and other women. Where was my husband? Apparently, he didn't want to have anything to do with this display. The price stayed too high for my liking, and I wanted to take a diplomatic retreat. The crowd looked angry and disappointed, but fortunately let me wander off. It was frustrating not being able to communicate in their language and at least tell the woman how much I admired the wood carvings.

Tourists were few, and I began looking for Al, who had wandered toward the anchorage. I passed a camel "parking lot" with many camels resting, probably from a hard ride through the desert. With my camera ready, I tried to sneak a picture or two, but stopped quickly when looks from the men nearby left me nervous and frightened. I was clearly not welcome there.

Mohammad was able to arrange a bus ride for Al and me into Port Sudan, a popular center for scuba diving and probably more welcoming to tourists. Al wanted to find an internet café to check our banking information since our account had been jeopardized too often. The bus left Suakin in the morning. It was a rundown, antiquated vehicle, showing how much the sand and desert conditions wore it down. As Al and I climbed onto the bus and sat down, I looked around me. We were the only Western faces on the almost-full bus.

"I hope that this paper Mohammad gave us instead of our passports will be accepted by the police," I said to Al when our bus was stopped by armed Sudanese soldiers in their casual brown uniforms, soon after we sat down. The men climbed onto the bus and deliberately headed towards our seats, not taking notice of the other passengers. Al gave them our paper which they scrutinized for some time. Oh well, I thought, we don't really need to go to Port Sudan. Finally, we got the paper back, saw the police depart, and the bus continued on its way. After a bumpy, arid drive on the highway, we were in Port Sudan.

We stayed only long enough to visit the hard to find internet café and have a meal at the only hotel that looked dependable. There were a few scuba diving outfits. Port Sudan was well known for its nearness to clear waters full of brilliant underwater life. The town was also the jumping off point for Muslim pilgrims making their way to Mecca via the ferry, crossing the Red Sea to the nearest port in Saudi Arabia. Neither activity was on our agenda, nor were we wanting to stay any longer, but anxious to get the bus back to Suakin.

Before leaving Suakin, Al looked around our small anchorage and saw a small "restaurant" across the water.

"Let's try it. Maybe we can discover what the food is like in Sudan."

The tiny building that enclosed the kitchen was surrounded by a few tables and chairs on packed dirt "floor," covered by a plastic roof of sorts that kept out the sun and rain. We tied up our dinghy nearby and walked over to the restaurant.

"What should we order?" I asked my husband. "There doesn't seem to be a menu."

He looked around at the other clientele and what was on their tables. "Let's have what looks most popular, what those men are eating."

After ordering by pointing towards the adjoining table, a man plopped down a bowl of what looked like beans in a tomato sauce.

"This tastes good," I said, after taking a piece of bread and scooping out a mouthful of beans. In spite of the dirt and shooing away a number of chickens who were trying to fly up to our table, we managed to finish our meal. That was a dinner to remember.

Mohammad completed our paperwork for departure from Sudan. We were hoping to do some overnights and get our Red Sea passage finished. The weather was cooperating for once, and Al decided we could head out further from shore and take advantage of the northerly wind by tacking back and forth until we reached the Egyptian border.

We were making good progress for two nights, but the weather suddenly became a nightmare. We were motor-sailing across the Red Sea towards Saudi Arabia on a long tack, with a view to coming back on the opposite tack to an anchorage, well up the western side of the Red Sea in Egypt. About halfway across – where we shouldn't have been, into the shipping lanes – the wind began to strengthen. The waves grew from 3 to 10 feet in a few minutes. The visibility was down from being able to see clearly to only being able to see a few feet. Our speed dropped from 7 knots to 1, and our boat was covered with a blinding spray coming from the turbulent seas. Huge monster vessels rumbled past us in each direction, oblivious to our existence as we struggled to get out of their way. I was terrified by the size of the ships and their closeness, which we saw only when they came towards us. They would have run us down with no trouble and wouldn't have stopped. I knew my husband was also terrified, but never showed panic in front of me. He quickly turned our boat to a downwind tack back toward the west and a safe anchorage.

It was midnight and very dark when we finally reached the coast. Despite all our efforts to make headway, we were back 30 miles south of where we started. That experience summed up our frustrations on the Red Sea passage. But we were safe, thank goodness. Al put the boat in a heave-to position in the lee of a small island, as we couldn't enter the Foul Bay anchorage in the dark. In the morning, I contacted two boats who were sheltered in the bay. One gave us its waypoints, and for two hours we made our way to a place called "Dangerous Reef" and dropped our anchor.

It was wonderful to get some sleep after the experience we had in the middle of the Red Sea. I looked around in the morning and saw only flat water in all directions. The only shelter we had from the high winds was a small reef at our bow. Thank goodness for waypoints and the other boat already in the anchorage, or we wouldn't have found the place. .

But suddenly after feeling very settled, the wind shifted south/southwest. Of course, that shift was typical of the winds there. Both of our boats were getting too close to the reef, and we had to leave quickly. It wasn't called "Dangerous Reef" for nothing.

White Rock anchorage was our next stop. It was extremely beautiful. The quiet water around us seemed to go on forever. We were alone, except for a large rock jutting out of the water. Many fish swam around the reefs which surrounded the anchorage, keeping the turbulent waves away from our boat. We sat there waiting for better weather.

"I could stay here forever, or at least until I can relax," I said. The last few days had taken a toll on my patience. I wasn't prepared to tackle any more problems, and my anxiety was at its peak.

"We've been through the worst of this passage," replied Al. "It won't be long before we settle in Abu Tig Marina in Egypt for a few weeks." I could hardly wait.

Once the light was good and the weather calmed, we motored to Ras Banas and anchored that night behind a sandy, lonely outpost. There were Egyptian soldiers keeping guard, likely due to the border dispute between Sudan and Egypt. They looked at us from afar, but had no other interest in our presence.

Calm weather prompted us to continue the next day and night. There was supposed to be a new marina at Ghalib on the way to Abu Tig, our planned destination, but it was dark and too late to enter. We moved along instead. I went on watch about 21:00 when the winds suddenly went from 10 knots to 25 knots in 30 minutes. That was too much wind for me.

"I don't want to get caught out in this wind," I shouted through the noise. "Safaga is close and maybe we can slip in there and anchor."

Safaga was not only close but only 33 miles south of Hurghada, where we would officially enter Egypt. Nevertheless, it took us until 02:00 to put down our anchor in Safaga harbour, having almost been hit by a ferry coming out of the harbour as we were entering.

"That was too close," Al said in a voice that was close to panic. "It almost hit us and wouldn't really care, since we were trespassing in his lane."

Finally, we found a quiet spot with the best depth for our boat and dropped the anchor, making sure it was holding, and finally went to bed. That night was one I wanted to forget.

The next morning on our way to Hurghada, we passed many new resorts and their numerous dive boats. Safaga was a main tourist town for divers. The daylight navigation surpassed anything we had at night. Being able to see around us was 100 percent better than trying to find our way in the dark. We were able to sail most of the passage because of favourable winds, and entered Hurghada harbour sooner than expected.

"Look! There's *Sliver*," I said to Al. The yacht belonged to a French/Canadian/Australian couple, who had been in many anchorages with us. *Sliver* was anchored nearby which gave us the best location for depth as most of the harbour was 60 feet or more – too much for our winch.

First, we had to go to the dock and contact the agent from Fantasea to process our entry. He never appeared, and Al was getting anxious, as usual, and decided to try to process the papers himself, without the agent, using the local police at the port. His decision was probably a first for the agent, who wanted the payment for himself. Nevertheless, when the agent finally appeared he demanded the US$125 payment, although not having done the paperwork. We were learning about Egypt firsthand.

Abu Tig was definitely a holiday resort. Sitting amongst all the grubby, sand-covered boats were beautiful and sleek motor yachts, which we snobbish cruisers referred to as "gas guzzlers." There were many wealthy Egyptians who used this marina. They had little to do with our group, but the marina welcomed us with open arms, perhaps knowing how difficult our passage had been. On top of that, we only had to pay $100 for our berth for the month. I was introduced to "Med mooring" as we approached our appointed place. That meant manoeuvring our boat stern to the dock. With our monitor wind vane at the stern, Al worried about the difficulty backing in and being able to disembark once we were tied up. Thankfully, the marina crew was right there to give us a hand.

We needed the month to clean off the reddish brown, gritty, salty sand permeating our boat. Poor *Solara*! Everything on her topside had to be cleaned. All her lines came down and went into buckets of warm water. The metal pieces that had moving parts needed to be washed thoroughly. The sails were dirty and grey, as well as our boat cushions and bedding.

"The Red Sea passage was the toughest sail we've had so far," my husband said once we were settled in Abu Tig. I couldn't have agreed more.

Some cruisers who had easy access to their dinghies shared the experience with others, moving from boat to boat once at anchor, sometimes eating together or walking on the sand dunes surrounding the *marsa*. They had seen flamingos, turtles, nesting eagles, and a few wandering camels and goats looking for water. I missed the companionship and support from the other cruisers battling the Red Sea. Why did we end up by ourselves? I feel it was partly my husband who wanted to quickly finish sailing the Red Sea and didn't want to take the time to socialize. At least the worst was over.

The most impressive sight I saw on our travels north was a huge flock of migrating birds, which passed over us as we were sailing on one of our good days. The birds darkened the sky completely. Their large bodies filled the spaces around them, and I heard the soft rustle of their wings pushing through the hot air. I suspected they were storks heading towards Europe for nesting time. How I would have liked to join them in their travels and leave the waters of the Red Sea.

It was time to do some sightseeing. After all this was Egypt, home of the pharaohs, Valley of the Kings, and the pyramids. Our friends Ed and Julie on *Free Radical* wanted to pursue an economic tour of the sights. We were happy to go along. A few days later, we travelled on a local bus to Luxor, driving through the dry, yellow desert filled with wandering camels, donkeys pulling carts, and families of nomads living in tents until we reached the Nile Valley where the irrigated landscape suddenly became green and lush. The local farmers grew sugarcane, wheat, and date palms in the rich, black soil.

On reaching Luxor we stayed in Nefertiti, a budget hotel costing only $10 per night; but it was clean, and included an ensuite as well. That first night, we were entertained with wild Egyptian music and calls to prayer blasting into our windows, while the men in the alley below drank mint tea and puffed on their "hubbly bubbly," as our friend Ed liked to call it. Our only expense was the price of our guide, Gabriel, who, with a car, showed us around the Valley of the Kings and the Karnak Temple.

Gabriel also took care of the necessary *baksheesh*. He even found a small store selling beer. What a luxury in the hot, dry atmosphere, and in a predominantly Muslim country! The first night in Luxor, Gabriel walked us around and stopped at a hole in the wall, a small store selling liquor. It was offering Stella beer for US$1.50 and bottles of "liquor" with strange names like Gordoon's Gin and James's Scotch. We read in the *Lonely Planet* that these imitation bottles were "poison." We sat on plastic chairs and gulped our beer as though they were the last bottles on earth.

Our first morning in Luxor started with breakfast compliments of the hotel. The four of us sat on the roof terrace of the hotel for toast, boiled egg, cornflakes, and strong coffee. Looking down from the roof gave me a wonderful panoramic view of Luxor, low flat-roofed buildings spreading out in all directions and the slow-moving Nile flowing in the distance. We saw colourful, striped balloons floating above Karnak to the north, giving Luxor a festive air.

Our heads were full of the wonders surrounding Luxor. Here was history and culture that was 4,000 years old, well before the beginnings of Christianity and Western culture as we knew it. It was difficult to take it all in – the tombs and the awesome hieroglyphics, colourfully painted and carved. We walked around in the hot, penetrating air surrounded by thousands of tourists, guarded by soldiers on camels. Security was everywhere since there had been an attack on tourists a few years before.

One of the highlights of the day was having lunch at Gabriel's sister's home outside Luxor. After a long ride to her farm, we escaped from the hustle and bustle of the tourist flocks and the constant demand by vendors to buy this and that. Gabriel proudly showed off his sister's menagerie: one water buffalo and various feathered flocks of chickens, turkeys, and ducks. They even had a plot of papyrus – maybe they were going to make their own paper? The black-robed women of the household brought a delicious lunch to the table of fresh bread, omelettes, salad, and home-made cheese. The quiet atmosphere of the farm was a welcome reprieve before we set out again to visit Karnak Temple full of stone carvings, huge pillars, and buildings scattered over hundreds of acres. We wound our way among hundreds of tourists and left completely worn out from the heat and crowds. A delicious dinner in Luxor completed our second day.

Gabriel had managed to arrange tickets for the Cairo-bound train the next morning. The slow train ride was very pleasant and comfortable even in second class. It was an amazing view overlooking the farmland of the

Nile River. Since it was daytime, we could see the population doing their daily chores just like their ancestors had hundreds of years ago. Tired-looking donkeys were still being used to pull carts, farmers laboured by hand in the fields – ploughing and sowing, and the river was full of people washing their clothes, transporting themselves and goods, and using the river for irrigation. I was glad that we had decided to travel to Cairo during the day.

Ali, our new guide arranged by Gabriel, met us at the Cairo train station. Apparently, the train was two hours late but Ali had the patience to wait. But then he hurried us through the busy streets of chaotic Cairo to find a taxi to our hotel. Ali was a tall man with long, flowing white robes whose pace was well beyond my capability of keeping up. I felt that we were like the rats in "The Pied Piper of Hamelin," following the call of his music as we scurried behind him as fast as we were able to.

Oh, the pyramids we saw the next day were more than I expected. The immense blocks of stone layer upon layer rose majestically high above our heads. Inside were the tombs deeply planted where few people would go because of the claustrophobic effect of their location. It was just enough to stand at their base and wonder how the workers, slaves or not, had moved the heavy blocks and placed them higher and higher. All around us were guards on their camels keeping the tourists from harm. I passed by the Great Sphinx which was being restored. If it wasn't for the hot, dry air, I doubted that any ancient Egyptian sites could have lasted. Robbery and looting had taken place over the years, but the enormous structures remained, along with their beautiful carvings and colourful paintings. I felt very lucky to have seen what I did.

We finished the day with a visit to the museum in Cairo. It was very old and held most of the precious items from the Valley of the Kings that hadn't been stolen. The building was dark and antiquated and items were displayed in small cases. A new museum was being planned and would be built within a few years.

It was finally time to leave the next morning by bus to Hurghada on the Red Sea. As we followed the shoreline, I was reminded that our boat had to make its way to Port Suez and the canal. Back to reality.

After a wait for calm weather, we left our marina shelter on April 18 for the 180 miles north to the canal. It would be difficult to sail during the night due to numerous oil wells just off the shipping lanes, plus the large ships constantly moving north and south. Consequently, we had to day-hop our way north. After three such stops with no problems, the fourth day brought high winds right on our bow, and only 10 miles from our goal. How frustrating! On went our motor which helped doing hard tacks against the wind and high choppy waves.

The Felix Maritime Agency, which we had called beforehand, incorrectly directed us to the mooring balls by way of a line-up for the canal, where we had to fit our boat between two large ships. What a fuss! The pilot boat nearby thought we were joining the big fleet and yelled indescribable words at us. Not long after, they realized that we were veering off and heading for the mooring balls, provided by a rundown yacht club for small vessels waiting for their turn to go through the canal.

CHAPTER 34

Suez Canal

THE RED SEA, before the Suez, was like Grand Central Station with so many boats wanting to go through. I can't imagine what it was like when conflicts closed it down. In 1869, when the Suez Canal opened, the British supported it 75 percent and kept military control until 1953. The Egyptian government nationalized the canal in 1956, prompting the Suez Crisis that closed the canal for almost a year. Then, in 1967, it was closed for nearly eight years because of the Arab-Israeli conflict, resulting in an oil shortage in Europe. No wonder that the canal was thoroughly guarded, as it was a vital source of revenue for Egypt and could easily be sabotaged.

As with the Panama Canal, we had to have a pilot on board while we went through the Suez. This one, fortunately, didn't give us much trouble, and quietly took control of our helm and steered us to Ismailia, the halfway point, where we would spend the night. I would describe the passage as going though one large ditch, three lakes, and, sometimes, a more canal-like narrower section. The security surrounding both banks was tight. All along the sides I could see soldiers, evenly spaced, with their weapons ready. As well, there were many sentry stations giving more security. I was surprised to see ferries going across the canal, pontoon bridges swinging back and forth, and one large new toll bridge which had only a few vehicles.

Once at Ismailia, we sent our first pilot back by taxi. He asked for more money to pay for the taxi, but we expected that it was covered by the fee we had paid. Always more *baksheesh*, but at least he didn't ask for cigarettes, as was usual. The second pilot, Mohammad, was an older, surly man who didn't seemed pleased with anything. He asked for cigarettes and matches, and didn't like my chilli lunch – he actually threw it over-board. That was the first time someone didn't like my chilli. Later, when it was time to get rid of this pilot, Al said, "You can have more cigarettes if the pilot boat that picks you up doesn't ram into our boat." It was well-known that this could happen. What a relief when he was gone. It was my opinion that all canal pilots, Panama or Suez, thought they were the most important people in the world who deserved as much as they could get.

How wonderful it was to have finally finished our Red Sea passage. There were good times and scary times, frustrating passages and boring passages, but extremely interesting people and places. Once it was over, I was glad that we had had the experience of seeing life in that part of the world, but I'd never sail that passage again. Europe was only a few days away. We would have almost two years to explore and savour the food and beauty of life around the Mediterranean Sea. Turkey was our next destination, 315 miles away and three days sailing from Port Said.

PART 9

The Mediterranean

CHAPTER 35

Turkey

It was now April, 2004, and we were finally out of the Red Sea. I was never so glad to see the Mediterranean waters. It would be another three days sailing to reach our first stop: Finike, Turkey, on the south coast. The weather wasn't the best. We had winds over 20 knots, and 10- to 13-foot seas. Not the kind of seas for a relaxing passage. As we neared Finike, Al put the motor on to boost our speed, along with our sails so as to reach the marina in the daylight. Just as we approached the entrance, a severe thunderstorm suddenly came up and visibility became nil. Thank goodness our GPS and chart plotter were working or I don't think we would have found the opening into the sheltered bay.

Immediately, Al called the marina office because arrangements had been made beforehand to have someone come to the entrance and show us in, but no one seemed to appear, and now it was dark, and the lights around the marina were confusing. Eventually, a sleepy person rowed over in a dinghy, and directed us to a dock for the night. This was a poor showing, I thought, and hoped that we had picked the right marina. All was explained the next day. Apparently, there was another boat in the marina called *Solarea* which got all the attention that should have come to *Solara*. In spite of the poor beginning, the marina was one of the best we were in throughout the Med, especially its sparkling clean marble washrooms constantly scrubbed by a diligent employee.

We were going to take a needed break and fly home to Canada for a visit. Over the next few days, we made preparations to leave *Solara* in the capable hands of the marina. The dreaded varnishing would be done by someone else, and the dinghy would be repaired while we were away.

I cleaned up the inside and emptied the fridge. Finding a flight home was difficult as Al wanted to go through Richmond, Virginia, to see his mother who was 97. That meant making many stops: Antalya, Istanbul, Paris, Atlanta, Richmond, Cincinnati, and, finally, Toronto. We would arrive in Canada on May 4.

Our visit home was important. Al's mother was much weaker than the last time we had seen her, almost four years ago. Also, our daughter, Carolyn, was now a single parent and needed our help. More importantly, Al had not yet seen our grandson, born three years earlier. We visited many friends, spent time with our children, and voted in the federal election. Our condo in Collingwood was in good shape, but the junk mail had piled up in feet, not inches.

Al was beginning to get restless soon after we arrived. His focus had been interrupted, and he didn't know what to do with himself. Basically, he had left Canada for the voyage and didn't want to get too settled living in Collingwood, even for a short time. Our condo was larger than our boat, but we seemed to be in each other's way. To top it all off, both of us came down with severe colds as well as trying to acclimatize to the much colder weather, despite it being May. Finally, in June, we caught a flight back to Turkey.

The security in the airports gave us a lot of hassle. Arriving in Canada in May, we were thoroughly searched, probably because our passports were completely full and we had been in the Middle East. Leaving the US from Atlanta, we were once again tagged for a search, maybe this time because we now had new passports, had only one-way tickets to Istanbul, and President Bush was heading to Turkey at the same time. After 9/11, we were experiencing tighter security for the first time. I didn't think we looked like terrorists.

We finally arrived in Antalya after many hours of flying. I begged Al to recuperate there for a few days. Our trip home wasn't the most relaxed, and Antalya was a wonderful place to rest. It had great beaches, Ottoman culture, and historic sites. Its cuisine drove me mad with delight with its spicy Middle Eastern flavours. I was well-rested after two days, so we took a crowded *dolmus* (public bus) back to Finike and *Solara*.

Our boat looked good and well-rested. Apart from one couple we had met in the Red Sea, we were surrounded by European cruisers who used the Med for their summer playground. Their boats didn't have all the special equipment for long-distance passages like we had on *Solara*, which was equipped on top with a wind generator, a monitor steering apparatus, and a life raft. Dirty diesel tanks were tied to the stanchions holding our life lines, and I was sure our vessel looked like it had gone through many storms. It was a tired looking sailboat in spite of its new, shiny varnishing and glistening chrome.

For the next two weeks in Finike, I had a great time shopping in the market for really fresh produce, such as large juicy apples, oranges, and figs, and buying just-baked bread from a nearby bakery. I would wait with a crowd of men just outside the large stone oven for the baker to pull out the loaves. I swam in the cool, clear waters of the Mediterranean just off some rocks where a platform and ladder had been built.

We were able to rent a cheap car owned by one of the marina workers and travel inland. Our first stop was in Konya, a strict Muslim city, home of the whirling dervishes. After a long day's drive, we were both thirsty for a cold beer. Al asked the hotel concierge where we could find one.

"Liquor is not served in Konya," explained the very proper woman. "But if you want to try down this street there is one place that might have beer." She pointed to a street not far from our hotel.

After unpacking our few belongings, we scurried down the hot, dusty street to what looked like a small bar, our throats dry and parched. But, as we walked into the place, all I could see were weird, old men smoking their bubblies, and drinking some kind of concoction in the dark interior, dusty with age. No women.

"Let's get out of here," I said quietly. "This is no place for me." We had to do with canned coke, better than nothing anyway.

Cappadocia was a unique area of 7,700 square miles formed by wind and water erosion after a volcano had erupted and cast out special lava that was porous and vulnerable. As we approached the area by road, I could see large pillars rising up to the sky. They looked like large toadstools topped by small, protective caps. I thought they also looked like huge phallic symbols. But what was underneath the ground was more important.

Historically, Cappadocia was important for thousands of years as home to varieties of people such as the Hittites, the Phrygians, the Medes, the Persians under Alexander the Great in the sixth century BC, the Romans, and Christians hiding from persecution. The underground cities were a place of shelter from enemies and secret places of worship. In times of peace, people would live and farm above ground; but when threatened, they could live underground – in nine levels – for up to six months.

We stayed in Goreme a couple of nights in a cave suite sculpted out in one of the soft lava pillars. The unique cave experience was magical and romantic, but modern in every way. From Goreme, I took a tour of the underground cities. Fortunately, I was short and flexible, making it easier to move around the tunnel-like ant colonies. All matters of living were taken care of: air vents for easier breathing, wine-making, cooking, stables for animals, and deep water wells. There were also churches down below with their frescoes still intact. Booby traps were set up with large boulders that could close off a passage if necessary. Tens of thousands of people could live in this way. My visit was a phenomenal experience.

Because we were driving, I felt we were experiencing the real Turkish countryside. Large golden wheat fields were on both sides of the road, and people farming nearby made me feel like I was at my grandfather's farm in Ontario. Coming back to the shores of the Mediterranean, we took a back road through the Taurus Mountains. That was a mistake. Pavement turned to gravel. We climbed and climbed. I found it extremely scary looking down 5,000 feet below with no side rails. Erosion had taken away some of the road. We were the only ones there except for some frisky sheep that constantly wanted to block our way. The day was slowly giving way to evening. We had to get off and find a place to stay. We passed a village where I saw women carrying bundles of grass to dry on the roofs of their simple stone cottages. There would be no hotels there. After the exhausting day, we finally came to a larger town, Ermenek, which gave way to a much better highway.

"We have to find a hotel here," I said to my husband. "We can't go any further today."

"Well, I don't see this town in our *Lonely Planet*, nor do I see any hotels."

Ermenek was built on a vertical slope of the mountain, and not close to Antalya, our final destination. That was when I took over.

"I'm going to the local police station. We passed it on our way in."

I knew Al wouldn't be bothered to do this, but I was desperate to find a place to rest. The two young policemen were very friendly as I tried to tell them that we were looking for a hotel, although they couldn't speak English. They motioned that we should follow them in their police car. In the meantime, Al was talking to a young girl who was trying to explain where the one hotel was located.

Down we drove behind the police car to a lower level, and found ourselves in front of a vast new hotel overlooking a beautiful valley, and a large swimming pool. We were the only tourists, paid US$50, and were given a room that hadn't been occupied before. We concluded that the hotel was built with government money for conventions, since the only people we saw were businessmen. No one spoke English. Nevertheless, it was a treat and I would have taken anything for a good sleep. The view was spectacular from our room as it overlooked the valley below.

Our drive down to the coast the next morning was slow through the winding roads, but we ultimately arrived at the tourist-packed town of Antalya once again. As it was summer, the beauty of the Med was spoiled by hordes of skimpily clad, often obese English people. Perhaps it was holiday time in Europe. The historic sites, bars, restaurants, and hotels were filled with tourists. We passed quickly through the city to get back to Finike before dark and plan the next part of our cruise.

We had prepared out boat for cruising the Mediterranean. Our steering wind vane came off, was stored, and a passerelle (a small gangway) installed, giving us a way to get off our boat from the stern. Often in the Med, we would be required to approach a dock stern first, and squeeze in between two other yachts.

The summer months were very busy in the Mediterranean, with summer cruisers and many others chartering boats for a week or two. Our cruise along the southern Turkish coast was wonderful. For almost a month, we moved from small ports to quiet coves. We passed a sunken Byzantine city still sprouting old walls, and steps up to the steep slope of its original location. We saw an old castle just before entering a protected anchorage. We met many other cruisers passing through, and could call restaurants by VHF near anchorages and reserve dinner for the night. The owner would come out to our boat and take us to the restaurant. We met many *gulets* which had been hired by tourists. I was usually glad to see them disappear for the night and go elsewhere. Many of them were filled with noisy people, jumping overboard and playing loud music. The *gulets* allowed tourists the marvellous experience we were having, cruising the south coast of Turkey, but with no worries or the need to cook meals.

We anchored at or passed several towns such as Fethiye, Gocek, and Ekincik. Anchorages were pretty and well-protected. We were often surrounded by other boats: German, British, and Italian cruisers who were having a great holiday vacation.

"Look at those Germans trying to anchor," I remarked to my husband in one anchorage. We were sitting in our cockpit having a late cup of coffee. I was watching a chartered boat loaded with at least six German men who were just dropping their anchor, not checking to see if it would hold. It also appeared that they had had a few drinks beforehand which was typical of Germans on vacation.

"Their boat could drag into ours, it's so close," Al answered, looking at it with concern. This wasn't the only time we had had a problem with holiday cruisers who couldn't care less about their chartered boats. This time, luckily, the anchor held.

We became tourists one day. There was a riverboat company near Ekincik offering a visit to the ancient city of Caunos. Although expensive, it was a beautiful four-hour trip up a quiet river that had once been silted up when the Mediterranean Sea had retreated hundreds of years ago. Caunos, founded around the ninth century BC, had once been surrounded by the Mediterranean. It was an important Carian city, and especially worthwhile to see the tombs high on the hill built in the Lycia style. That is, hundreds of tombs were cut into the cliffs in the style of house faces, carved doors, beam ends, pitched roofs, and prominent lintels, which would normally have been constructed in wood. As the sea receded and silting commenced, so did the influx of mosquitoes with malaria, causing the end of the inhabitants. Caunos slowly faded away.

It was interesting to visit the city and walk around what was left of the ruins, all built at different times. I saw a small theatre from the second century, a later church, a temple to Apollo, a Roman bath, city walls, and a medieval fort on top of the steepest hill overlooking the whole valley. I wandered around the ruins imagining how people lived there so long ago. On the way back to our boat, we passed the beautiful sandy beach of Iztuzu, world famous for its loggerhead turtle nesting site, now a protected area.

Marmaris was our next destination after Caunos. After a good sail west, we arrived just before lunch. How well planned! This time, we berthed in the local marina, where boat work could be done. Our main sail had to be repaired. Again! We had to buy a new dinghy and motor, which took a good amount of our budget, but hopefully would last until our crossing of the Atlantic. And the usual boat clean-up and polishing. This was work that I usually left for Al while I made my trips home, but this time I was there to help.

Marmaris was a very popular city, full of tourists, charter boat companies, and expensive stores. I tried to grocery shop, but anything imported from Europe was too expensive. I priced a small bottle of Canadian maple syrup. It was going for 31 million Turkish lira, about $31 Canadian. I just couldn't imagine the price! No pancakes for now. We found a cheap restaurant away from the waterfront, offering Turkish food, where we took most of our meals away from the boat. Their steam table usually held prepared food of hot meat and vegetables. I often ordered kebabs or their version of pizza, covered with fried onions and minced meat. Everything was delicious. There was always fish available as well since we were on the Med.

We had to watch our costs as most of the tourists used euros or pounds, but we had to convert our Canadian dollars which had less value. Even so, the place hopped at night since it was high season. One night, two nine-story cruise ships came in and tied up just behind us. The ships spilled out their oily fumes and 2,000 passengers, as well as blocking our breeze. I couldn't wait until we could leave Marmaris and anchor again, but we were still waiting for our new dinghy.

Finally, in the first week of August, we left for Kusadasi. Our plan was to move southwest along the barren Datca Peninsula, once supporting sizable towns and now dotted with ancient and medieval ruins. The passage would take about a week or more up the west coast of Turkey, since the Meltemi winds from the west were now at their highest and could keep us anchored in place. Several restaurants dotted the shoreline, which gave us a chance to eat away from our boat and take shelter from the winds. At one stop – a holiday village called Kuruca Buku, filled with Turkish families – we were relaxing on our boat after a quiet supper and who should come by but *Klondike* from our Red Sea adventure with the pirates. We had a good visit, but unfortunately our boats were going separate ways the next day. But that was the way of cruising: short pleasant visits, exchanges of information, helpful hints, and then goodbyes.

The city of Knidos, our next stop, was famous for the first naked statue of a woman sculpted in the fourth century BC. It was a statue of Aphrodite. Its beauty brought many visitors to Knidos, but it was also thought to bring good fortune to seafarers stopping there for protection. We were fortunate to find a spot to anchor in the small harbour full of *gulets* and yachts. The winds were light so our holding was good, with little swinging around the anchor. Knidos also attracted visitors to see the solitary ruins scattered about but only partially excavated. There were two theatres, temples, and the city walls and gates. More interesting to me was the fact that a famous astronomer and mathematician, Eudoxos, built an observatory at Knidos. How intelligent those Romans were!

Once we had rounded the Datca Peninsula and were heading toward Bodrum, we were in the Aegean Sea between Greece and Turkey. The Bodrum Peninsula appeared to be suffering from overdevelopment, and an abundance of *gulets* and chartering yachts. There were ugly, highly stacked apartment buildings and hotels covering the coastline which looked like piles of Lego blocks. We sailed straight north to a small town called Altinkum instead of heading inland towards Bodrum. What a mistake that was! I couldn't see the beautiful sandy beach for the multitude of people sunning themselves. It was wall to wall people, as well as heads bobbing in the water in front of the beach. We motored in our new dinghy to shore, manoeuvring between the bodies, and tied it up with the numerous fishing boats.

Altinkum appeared to cater to English tourists on the cheap. We saw one restaurant offering "full English breakfast" and the time for the next important football match. The local market, though, offered fresh fruit. We enjoyed a typical Turkish meal, and then headed back to our boat to sail away from the inevitable noisy bar music expected that night.

A couple of anchorages more, and then we headed for Kusadasi, which brought us abruptly to a terrible scene on the Strait of Samos between Greece and Turkey. We had started early that morning. The winds were light, and the day beautiful for our sail to Kusadasi. After a couple of hours, we came across a large, open wooden boat filled with black men waving their arms trying anxiously to get our attention. The boat had no motor or sail, and was floating on the calm waters. Obviously these were Africans trying to reach Greece, an EU country where they would scatter and be lost among the population or be rescued as immigrants.

"I can't get too close to them," said Al. "They might try to climb on our boat and then what would we do?"

I agreed, but felt really sorry for them nevertheless, as they looked tired and hopeless sitting there. How far had they come to get there? How much money did it cost? All these questions filled my mind as I desperately wanted these men to reach Greece, or be rescued from their boat.

Soon, our decision was made for us as a Greek coast guard vessel came between our boat and theirs. They told us in no uncertain terms to move on. Information later gave us more understanding of the situation. Apparently Turkish freighters, for a fee, dropped refugees on a Greek island, or as we saw just left them to find their way to Greece. The Africans could have come up through Syria or across from northern Africa. Refugees tried constantly to come to Europe to find a better life. The Greek coast guard would probably send them back to Africa.

We made one more anchorage in a historic harbour called Port St. Paul, where Paul, the disciple, was supposed to have anchored on his way up the Anatolian coast. We dug in against the high gusts that twirled us around all night and looked forward to reaching Kusadasi. In the morning, we had the most spectacular sunrise peeking through the high mountains to our right. This short passage, I felt, was just going to be a beauty. The Greek island of Samos was protecting us from the strong winds in the Aegean, and to top it off we had a large school of dolphins following our progress for half an hour. I stood on the pulpit as far forward as I could and looked down at their antics. They seemed to be observing me as well, as they jumped around *Solara*. They looked so happy and seemed to be enjoying the morning with me. That was the first time I had seen dolphins in the Mediterranean.

Finally we entered Kusadasi marina before noon and tied up to the dock for the next three weeks. It was our plan to do some inland sightseeing. I didn't like Kusadasi as it was on the cruise boat circuit, and therefore the town was full of aggressive shopkeepers, expensive restaurants, and money-seeking entrepreneurs. On the plus side, we had a friendly staff in the marina, a swimming pool, and were in walking distance to the town and nearby supermarket. The town also had a lovely waterfront walk, which was a beautiful setting for the daily spectacular sunsets.

With a rental car we began exploring the ancient ruins on the Aegean coast. One of the greatest ruined cities in the Western World was Ephesus, built in 1000 BC. It later became the chief port on the Aegean under Roman rule. I marvelled at the surviving structures, and could go back again as there was so much to see. We saw more sites on our travels such as Pergamum, Troy, and Aphrodisias, a cultural and artistic hub known for its exquisite marble sculptures, plus a few other piles of rock, such as large theatres, temple ruins, and gateways – always spectacular, always intriguing.

Heading north towards the Dardanelles and Gallipoli peninsula, our sightseeing took a different turn. There we saw the various monuments commemorating the WWI battle between the Allied forces and the Turks. It was one of the worst campaigns of 1915-16, lasting nine months. More than 500,000 Allied and Turkish soldiers were wounded or died; thousands in one day. Finally, the Allied troops withdrew with no chance of controlling the Dardanelles Strait. It was a solemn visit. On Anzac Day, April 25, Australians and New Zealanders commemorated the death of their soldiers.

On our way back to Kusadasi, we stopped in the crazy travertine terraces of Pamukkal ("Cotton Castle"). There, thousands of tourists walked barefoot up to the top and over pools of warm water coming from the calcium-rich mineral springs flowing down the white steps of limestone. To me, it was a beautiful sight, the stark white terraces shining with sparkling rivulets of water cascading downward. I was tempted to place my feet in the streams but, unfortunately, for protection the terraces were off limits to tourists at the time of our visit. During Roman times, a large spa city above the pools was built, called Hierapolis. I could visualize

white-clad Romans stepping among the terraces, chatting with each other and warming their feet in the water.

CHAPTER 36

❧

Greece

IT WAS TIME to leave Turkey. It was the end of August, and our plan was to get our boat to Italy for the winter. That meant we had about two months to sail through Greece and around the toe of Italy to Rome.

Our first stop was Pythagorio on Samos Island, the closest island to Turkey. We anchored next to the main harbour and easily motored to shore with our dinghy. Right away, I noticed the cleanliness of the town and its glistening white buildings with bright azure trim. Right then I knew I must be in Greece. We walked around the narrow streets and soaked up the atmosphere: sun-baked squares, small tavernas, and crowded tourist shops.

It was there that we faced the formalities of entering the EU. There was a costly entry fee for Greece, allowing us to cruise in their waters for six months, which would be included in the 18 months of EU tax-free period for our boat. By now, Al took the formalities in stride, and once completed we could sail away to the west toward Athens.

It was there, in Greek waters, that we met the Meltemi, the notorious northwestern winds especially strong in August. Once out from the shelter of Samos harbour, we were caught up in 7- to 10-foot waves and 25 knots of wind right on our bow. So much for the gentle Mediterranean cruising I had been hoping for. Consequently, we looked for the next shelter which was at Marathokampos, near the southwest end of Samos, a small fishing village with a few tourist hotels. I could see that our six months in Greece would be taken up with avoiding the Meltemi winds.

We were outside the main harbour but sheltered by breakwaters on all sides. The wind gusted down from the high mountains nearby as our boat circled around its anchor. A short trip into town gave me the opportunity to buy bread, fruit, and vegetables. There was also the local beer,

Stelle. That was always welcome in the heat of Greece. After two days, we'd had enough of Marathokampos, and since the wind appeared quiet enough in the anchorage, it was time to try to sail to another island – Furni, 20 miles away. We would be island hopping our way across the Aegean Sea. Then a terrible thing happened.

On our way to Furni, the winds picked up again in the open water. The seas heaped up and foam streaked across the tops of the waves. *Solara* bumped and heaved from the relentless gale. I saw 33 knots at one time (force 7 on the Beaufort scale), but before we arrived I looked back at the stern and saw only a dangling rope where our new dinghy should have been.

"Oh God, Al. We have lost our new dinghy," I shouted against the blowing gale. We thought that pulling our dinghy, as we often did, would be much easier than deflating it and putting it on our deck every time we made a passage. That would get us to our next stop much faster.

With sunken hearts, we dropped our anchor in the deep quiet bay of Furni, just before dark. We had just bought the expensive Avon dinghy on our arrival in Greece. Thank goodness the motor hadn't been attached. To lose a dinghy was a disaster since it was our lifeline to the shore. Without it, we were sunk … at least not literally.

We left the anchorage at 04:00. It was very dark, but the seas were quiet at that time. We were sailing to Mykonos, the most visited and expensive of all Greek islands, passing under the island of Ikaria. I loved the mythological origin of the island which came from the legend of Daedalus and Icarus, whose wax melted from his wings, causing him to fall in the sea. Too bad he didn't have our float-away dinghy to save him from drowning. I was still reeling from the loss of our dinghy. It was like losing an arm or a leg. We would have to buy a new one as soon as possible. Oh, what luck for the person who came across the brand new inflatable, bouncing across the Aegean Sea toward Turkey.

Mykonos was crowded but we found room to drop our anchor.

"Oh, there's *Klondike*!" I shouted to Al. "I bet they'll take us into shore for provisions."

I was very glad to see them as I knew they would help us. On many occasions, we had helped each other – in the Indian Ocean when Katie used her nursing talents to take out Al's stitches, and in the Gulf of Aden with the pirates. After radioing *Klondike*, Katie and Don came over with their dinghy and, after reaching a public dock, we went to buy some provisions and try a nearby restaurant to test the Greek cuisine.

The town of Mykonos was a famous tourist town, attractive but completely covered by glistening white clusters of cubes around a crescent harbour. It attracted the cruisers, the jet set, backpackers, artists, nudists, and gays. Even in our anchorage, the bare hills were slowly being covered by expensive looking homes, jutting out from the rocks.

Since we had no dinghy, we had to find a harbour where we could tie up and purchase another one as soon as possible. Our destination was the island of Siros. It was a very comfortable sail, thank goodness, with much calmer seas. I guessed the Meltemi was taking a rest that day. We entered the port of Finikas, a very calm and protected harbour on the southwest coast of the island. We could pick up a mooring on the new pier, and connect to electricity for only 5 euros per day. It was possible that we would be there for a while as bad weather was predicted to arrive.

So there we were for the first week of September, buying a dinghy and waiting for weather took all that time. It was a 30-minute bus ride into Ermoupolis on the other side of the island, where we passed farm fields and orchards, rather than the barren perimeter of the island. I was glad that the island was fresh and inviting, but not overly taken by tourists.

I loved Ermoupolis, the capital of the Cyclades. It was paved with marble, and its 18th century main square was surrounded by impressive public buildings, such as an opera house and a large city hall. We climbed 800-plus marble steps to two churches above the city. One was Catholic and one Greek Orthodox, each set on a mountaintop adjacent to each other. The city had once been the commercial, naval, and cultural centre of Greece, and its grandeur still remained. I saw Italian-designed neoclassical mansions which showed wealth, still evident in the population. Just walking on marble gave me a feeling of splendour.

Unfortunately, it was there that my digital camera was stolen from an internet café. The room was very dark and the black cover on the camera was lost in the dim light. When I went back to retrieve it, the owner claimed no responsibility. I would only have my memories of that beautiful city.

It was a week before the gale force winds lessened. As we sat in our cockpit in the small harbour, sand was continuing to blow around our boat and into the cabin below, which reminded me of the Red Sea not so long ago.

Finally, the weather reports predicted lighter winds; we were anxious to leave. Our destination was a short sail to Kythnos, but once out of Finikas harbour we encountered 20- to 29-knot winds and 6-foot seas. I wasn't surprised, but was frustrated that we had to fight the Meltemi again. *Solara* bounced playfully over the waves, while the two of us caught the backlash of cold, salty water in the cockpit. It was a wet ride, but we arrived in Kythnos after rounding the south point of the island, heading for a quiet anchorage on the west side called Apokruisis. It was a beautiful quiet bay, and well-protected from the Meltemi. I could have stayed there for a few days, but that was not to be.

As usual, Al was anxious to leave the next day, and I agreed reluctantly that it would be much better to get out of the Aegean and into sheltered waters, even though we would leave our quiet and beautiful bay. So it was that we left Apokruisis at 05:30 for the 50-mile journey to the Saronic Gulf, which was the entryway to the Corinth Canal and out of the Aegean Sea. If we proceeded on a northerly course, we would be close to Athens, but if we stayed south we would be closer to the canal. The Olympics was taking place that summer, and the waters surrounding Athens, we felt, would be very busy.

There was a very narrow channel between the island of Poros and the mainland of Peloponnese. We motored through the channel and passed colourful tiered houses piled high on the hillsides of the island, behind a very crowded yacht marina. Just beyond was a small anchorage called Russian Bay where we could spend the night and have a cool dip. I was extremely glad to be out of the Aegean and the Meltemi. Although Greece was an interesting country with beautiful islands to visit, our time trying to make a westerly course was more of a nightmare than a comfortable Mediterranean passage.

Beyond Russian Bay was the Corinth Canal. This canal had a fascinating history, and gave us a quick passage to the Ionian Sea beyond. We would save 150 miles by taking the canal; otherwise, we would have had to sail south and around Peloponnese. The method used until the 13th century had been to drag small ships on rollers across a paved slipway. Many leaders in the past considered a canal, but it was Nero who actually began digging in 67 AD and left it for 6,000 Jewish prisoners to do the hard work. That was stopped by wars, but the work began again in the 19th century, using a French engineering company that completed the canal in 1893.

The Corinth Canal cut through limestone and sandstone for 4 miles and a width of 75 feet. It was a small canal in comparison to the Panama, but used by smaller vessels like our cruising yachts. Al sped up, and we were able to reach the entrance of the canal on the eastern side before it closed for the day. He contacted the authorities on our VHF, hurried in to pay our fee, and fill out the paperwork. A large tour boat called *Tourist Canal* was taking a group through, and Al was told that if he hurried we could follow behind the tour boat. That would be fun, I thought. We could shout back and forth with the happy, waving passengers as we motored through the historic canal.

There were no locks, and passing through took just a short hour. I looked around me at the high limestone walls on each side and wondered how the canal had been cut out from such solid rock. One cliff rose to 250 feet. There were two bridges crossing the canal that were raised when we passed through. I could see lines of cars waiting for the bridges to be lowered again. There was also a high rail trestle bridge that we passed under that looked very scary.

Soon our passage was all over, and I waved goodbye to the tourist boat that was just going to turn around and return the same way. We were now in the Gulf of Corinth and could find anchorages more protected from the north Meltemi winds. After one night in such a place, we headed for Galaxidi, which would be a good spot for visiting Delphi.

Galaxidi was a pretty resort town that had a few places at the town dock for boats to slip into. "Slip into" was not as easy as it sounded. Al had to drop our bow anchor first some feet away from the dock, and I had to back our large yacht into a small space that appeared much smaller than the width of our boat. That was the first time we had to back in to a dock, and I was feeling really nervous. But with some instructions from other boaters nearby to let the wind help turn us in, I must say the job was perfect. People on the quay took our lines, which was very helpful, and then gave me the thumbs up. That made my day.

The scenery around the Gulf of Corinth was very beautiful with its mountainous terrain on the north coast and Galaxidi's location deep in the bay, surrounded by high hills. Although once a prosperous port before the construction of the main road, it was now a well-preserved ghost town with charming, sparkling white houses with painted ceilings of many colours, as well as impressive views of the sea and the mountains reflected in the water. It reminded me of a picture puzzle.

The next day, I did my usual shopping in town, and later we took a morning bus to Delphi. The public bus wound its way up on the road to the high mountains of Parnassos. The view from the top where the ruins of Delphi sat in splendour made it a most spectacular site. It was regarded as the centre of the ancient world, and sat amidst ravines, rocky bluffs, and sheer cliffs. The Delphic oracle was famous throughout Greece, and many important decisions were made, although influenced by corruption and ruthless power plays. When we returned to our boat later that day, I could see Mount Parnassus from the harbour through the clouds, and wondered how the people in the past could have built such a monument to superstition, magic, and serious prophesying.

CHAPTER 37

❧

Italy

I WAS TIRED of Greece. Perhaps if I had been a spoiled tourist who had been transported here and there by ferry, with all accommodation planned, I would have like the country better. But we had to make our way west during the most threatening Meltemi season. I was glad to finish the passage.

Now it was the middle of September, and our plan to keep the boat in Italy for the winter loomed closer and closer. The best plan to leave Greece was from the town of Patras, where we could check out and then go straight across the Ionian Sea to the toe of Italy. It would mean a passage of at least three days, but the weather was predicted to be good, and what was a three-day passage after all we'd been through.

In Patras, there was a yacht harbour of sorts. For 40 euros, we didn't get much service. I had trouble finding the showers and toilets, but finally I saw they were almost hidden in a small corner off a large stage and amphitheatre that didn't looked used. At least there was hot water. Nearby, I found one small store within walking distance, and I could provision for a few days. My preparations were finished for our passage – newly cleaned clothes, a shower, and some fresh provisions. Al looked over our boat and filled it with fresh water and diesel fuel. We were ready.

The Messina Channel between Italy and Sicily was approximately 400 miles away. Al calculated that it would take 80 hours at 5 nautical miles per hour to reach the channel. Fortunately, the Ionian Sea was quiet and pleasant – no winds. I loved the change of pace, but unfortunately we had to motor most of the way. The light breezes were refreshing and I could read in the cockpit to my heart's content instead of working on sail changes, etc. The weather was about to change though, so instead of going directly to Messina on the northeast tip of Sicily, we decided to stop off at a new unfinished marina near the town of Roccella Ionica. We had heard through our cruising communication system that Italy had built several marinas that were free. The only reason they were free was that they weren't quite finished. Italy and other countries in the EU were given monetary support to enhance their economy. Thus, a few marinas had been started but payment wasn't due until they were finished. Hence, a free marina. We slipped around the growing sand spit at the entrance of Roccella Ionica harbour and saw a number of boats on the dock from many European countries: Swiss, German, Portuguese, and Italian. After finding a vacant slip and tying up to its hardware, I saw a restaurant up a small hill adjacent to the marina.

"Oh, good," I said to my husband. "I'd love to have my first pizza in Italy."

So, once our boat was settled, we ambled up to the open-air restaurant. There were only a few people sitting around as it looked like it was ready to close. They were mostly fishermen relaxing after their meal and smoking cigarettes. A waitress came to our table and asked what we would like to order.

"Could I have a pizza?" I asked.

"A metre or half a metre?" she answered. *Did she really mean that?*

"A half-metre, please," I said, not knowing what else to say and wondering if I could share it with my husband.

"I'd like what those fishermen are eating at the next table," Al told the waitress.

"Do you know what that is?" I asked, perplexed at him ordering something sight unseen.

"Well, I don't like pizza that much and I should try the local food."

Not long after that, our order came out. My pizza looked delicious. I hadn't had a chance to eat pizza for a long time. When Al's dish arrived, it came with a silver-coloured dome covering his plate. The waitress took off the cover with a flourish as though we were eating in an expensive New

York restaurant, and there were 10 fish heads looking at him in all their glory, eyes staring as though he was the main show on stage. I looked at my husband's face which changed quickly from anticipation to a sickly hue. I had trouble keeping from laughing, but I knew that would not be welcome.

"You can share my pizza now if you wish." And that is what he did.

We went to bed early, after not sleeping well on our last passage, and woke up hearing the neighbouring yacht crew busy working on their boat and preparing to leave that day. There were agitated shouts of Italian, scurrying feet darting here and there, and one man on the deck looking over the equipment. The crew consisted of four Sicilian men who had had a sailing holiday and were hurrying to get back to their jobs. They were very friendly, telling us about their trip and their lives back in Syracuse. They were very anxious to leave. Al, having received the weather on our ham radio, suggested that they should wait at least another day since a storm was heading our way.

In the meantime, we walked into town. It was about 2-mile walk away and the hike was pleasant along the beach, which also had a path designed for bicycles. There were a number of produce markets, meat stores, bakeries, and delis to satisfy my needs. Al tried to check into Italy but any official-looking uniforms couldn't have cared less about our arrival. I guess once we were in the EU it didn't matter. The calm weather changed to heavy thunder showers, and the high winds kept us in the marina for several days. The four Sicilians made an effort to go south and around the toe of Italy, but soon we saw them heading back to the marina as the high waves were too much for them. They looked bedraggled, wet, and tired. I'm glad we hadn't decided to leave at the same time.

Finally we left Roccella Ionica, after a stay of many rain-soaked days. Thankfully, the seas were calm with a light breeze just off the bow, which meant we could sail close-hauled for steady sailing. We left in the afternoon, planned to sail overnight and reach the Messina Channel in the daylight. As we headed for the southeast tip of Italy, called Capo

Spartivento – *vento* meant "wind" in Italian, so we should have foreseen a change – we experienced strong gusts of wind coming from the mountainous mainland on our starboard side.

"Sail change, sail change," shouted Al. I got up from my comfortable position in the cockpit and began to do my job as crew, making sure *Solara* was steady and capable of handling the strong gusts around the cape where I saw a historic lighthouse built in the 19th century and giving us a landmark in the diminishing light of day.

It got dark early as we motor-sailed up the channel. There were so many fishing boats in the water that we almost hit one that wasn't lit. Al quickly stopped the motor, and made a 90-degree turn away from the scared and bewildered man. The passage was scary throughout the night. Our eyes were constantly watching out for small boats, and later, as we approached the Messina Strait, we had to watch for the large boat traffic which plied back and forth from Sicily to the mainland of Italy. The most confusing and numerous were the ferries which, though brightly lit, seemed to be crossing constantly across the channel. All boats had to get out of the ferries' way.

As we neared the narrow tip of the strait, the ferries increased in number. Al and I looked around us in confusion and apprehension. Should we wait for one ferry to leave or go ahead? Another ferry was coming across from the other direction. With interminable slowness, we finally reached the narrowest end of the strait (only 1.5 miles across). Warnings given in the *Italian Waters Pilot* book made us wary about the tidal streams and whirlpools, plus high squalls blowing off the mountains on both sides.

In *The Odyssey*, Ulysses encountered two perils, Scylla and Charybdis, in the Messina Strait. Obviously, in antiquity small boats were often in peril, being subject to the tides and whirlpools they couldn't control. With all this in mind, we started into the last 8 miles of the strait with no problems, no winds, and only once was the boat violently shoved by the water off our course, quickly corrected since we were motoring. With no trouble at all we conquered Scylla, the 12-foot monster with six long necks and horrible heads, and Charybdis, the giant whirlpool.

Our plan was to motor or sail up the Tyrrhenian Sea, following the west coast of Calabria, coming around Cape Vaticano and into the Golfo di Santa Eufemia to a small marina at Tropea. There we would find another half-finished marina costing us very little. I looked up at the high mountains on the starboard side, astounded by their beauty. The small towns teetering on their tops seemed to hang over the edge. I also saw many small beaches with Italian tourists basking in the bright sunlight with their colourful umbrellas and lounge chairs. Even in the middle of September, the weather seemed to bring summer temperatures.

Entering the marina at Tropea was easy, and a well-built breakwater kept the water calm inside. I saw some boaters that we had met in Roccella Ionica, plus a number of Germans, Americans, and others who planned to keep their boats in Tropea for the winter. The marina wasn't quite finished as we had expected. We did have intermittent power and water, but the restrooms were hard to find and not quite finished. We were told that the marina had been taken over by the mafia but I wasn't quite sure, although the restaurant that had been owned by a local man had closed suddenly.

To visit the delightful town on the cliffs above our marina meant walking up 200 steps. We made the climb every day, and sometimes twice. That had to be good for my sea legs. We enjoyed Tropea and its historic character. There were remnants of old grand palaces, old town walls, and many churches. The restaurants offered local dishes of spicy foods, my favourite, and the pizzas didn't come by the metre. It didn't take long to walk the streets, and from the cliff end we got a magnificent view of the Mediterranean – sparkling blue water scattered by white waves blown by the wind. We remained at the marina longer than usual due to a nasty storm with high waves that fortunately were kept back by the breakwater, but flew high over its wall to our side.

The storm gave us a chance to take a trip to Mount Etna in Sicily, Europe's most active volcano. Arrangements were made at the tourist office in Tropea to go by train, across the Messina Strait to Catania. I couldn't believe it when the train was split into three parts and put on a ferry – one of those we had avoided on our way through the Messina Strait – which crossed over to the other side to the town of Messina. From there, the train went to Catania, where we met a backpacker in the train station who suggested we should go to a small town called Nicolosi, halfway up the mountain, and see Mount Etna the next day by local bus.

The local bus was late, and while we stood in the town square of Nicolosi waiting, many tour buses passed us coming up from Catania. I wondered why we took the backpacker's advice. Finally the bus arrived. There was a well-paved road winding up the mountain to a spot where we could board a cable car part way up, nearer to the active volcano. I looked around at the grey, dusty mountain sides and up to the top where at 11,000 feet I saw swirling plumes of smoke directed by the winds.

After a short ride, we could take a guided walk on a trail that would take us to various active places, still hot from the eruption the year before. In 2001, an eruption damaged a hotel and the cable car. I began to wonder if our excursion to Etna would be interrupted by another vast explosion. The worst one we were told was in 1669 and killed 20,000 people, destroying Catania far below. Nevertheless, the walk was fascinating. It felt like I was on a different planet, perhaps Mars. The ash emissions covered everything. Molten lava that had run down the mountain sides had cooled somewhat, but was still too hot to touch. We examined nearby stones and when told to pick one up I dropped it quickly from the heat. I could imagine the last eruption filling the sky with a red glow, bolts of lightning, and steam and ash rising hundreds of feet. In spite of the danger of living near Etna, farmers continued to work because the falling ash fertilized the earth.

After our tour, we were once again in the main square to catch the local bus back to Catania for the night. I was beginning to shiver and shake from the cold that had suddenly swept the mountain. Rain came down and turned to snow. We weren't dressed for the weather. The tour buses arrived for their passengers and quickly took them away. I tried to get a ride and offered to pay, but the driver wouldn't take us. We had to wait four hours for the local bus, and the one restaurant had closed for the day. It wasn't a good part of our trip, and a tour bus from Catania would have been the best way to see Etna.

Finally we got to our hotel where I took a hot shower, had a quick supper nearby, and headed for bed. The storm continued that night with sharps bolts of lightning, heavy rain, and claps of thunder. Was Etna telling us to move on?

In the morning, the weather had calmed somewhat and we could take a walk around Catania. I was struck by the lava rock used for many of the roadways, sidewalks, and squares. The grey-coloured city had been covered by lava and destroyed centuries ago, so why not use it for rebuilding? We took a train back to Tropea and sailed north again.

We found ourselves close to Salerno which was a good place to make a visit to Pompeii. There were two marinas in Salerno, but because they were finished would cost much more than we wanted to pay. As we were looking around trying to find our way, a man on a nearby dock at Porto Nuova called us over to take a spot he had available. We slipped in with help as it was a tight squeeze and made the boat secure.

Then I asked, "How much are you charging?" Probably a question we should have asked before securing the boat.

"Sixty euros for each night, and I have only two nights available," he answered with no hesitation.

"Too much," I said. "I think we'd better leave."

In the meantime, my husband was enjoying the exchange, and had stopped his work to listen. Reluctantly, the dock master gave in and let us have the slip for 50 euros, which wasn't that much cheaper but we really wanted to see the famous ruins of Pompeii.

It was possible to visit Pompeii from the nearby town of Salerno, historically known for when the Allies landed there in 1943 during WWII. Salerno was described as a mini Naples, but we gave the town a once-over, looking for the bus terminal and the trip to Pompeii. I had read Thomas Harris' book *Pompeii* and was most interested in how Romans lived in 79 AD. During the time of the tragedy, the town had a population of about 20,000 people. Why didn't they move? It was as though life just stopped while they were doing their daily chores. Apparently, the eruption of Vesuvius was so intense and deadly that those who remained behind had no time to leave because of the extreme hot ash raining down from above. Pompeii buried in ash was lost for 1,500 years when it was finally discovered, but not excavated until 1748. I marvelled at the site. The streets were laid out just as they had been built. The foundations of homes, wall mosaics, tiled floors, fountains, remains of temples, and bathhouses still stood. They had been well-preserved by the ash. Indentations from the bodies that had crumbled in the ruins were filled with plaster which gave the visitor an idea of what the people were doing just before they died. We left for our boat in a sober mood after spending the day among the ruins of Pompeii.

It was the beginning of October and we were continuing our sail north to Rome. As we were about to leave, Al couldn't find the dock master to pay him for our slip. He looked all over but no man.

"Let's just head off," he said. "Maybe the man will show up."

So off we went, and sure enough a fast motorboat left the marina in pursuit of us. Hey, this is fun, I thought. I felt like James Bond being pursued by international thugs. It wasn't long before the dock master caught up with *Solara.*

"What do you think you are doing?" he yelled in his strong Italian accent that we could barely understand.

"I couldn't find you when we needed to leave but here's your money."

The man took it in disgust, probably thinking that we were trying not to pay. There was no chance we would be staying at his marina again.

Capri was considered to be the most famous of the small islands off the coast of Italy. I wanted to take a visit and see how the rich and famous lived. The marina would cost at least 150 euros per night, but we found a spot where we could drop our anchor just outside the expensive marina, and as the weather was calm we sat comfortably for two nights along with large powerboats and daily cruisers.

I was sure we weren't legitimately anchored, but there was no one there to tell us to leave. The only problem was that, when we motored into shore, we had to watch out for the constant ferries, also arriving. They were huge beasts with churning waves 6 feet high. We almost got overturned by two ferries leaving at the same time. Our dinghy rocked back and forth, leaving us scrambling to keep it steady. But once we were securely tied to the dock, Capri lived up to its reputation.

There was a long stairway climbing round and round and ending at the top. At each twisted turn, I could peek into gated villas, surrounded by fragrant and colourful flowers. The precipitous island was once occupied by Greeks and Romans, and now by famous residents. Even though short, my visit to Capri left me with beautiful memories.

Our sail north to Rome gave us a chance to island hop. Since it was October, the groups of tourists had reduced in size, thank goodness. We could enjoy the quiet beauty of the islands we were visiting. First there was Procida, part of the Phlegraean Islands in the Gulf of Naples and close to the mainland. A staircase took us up to town and across to the north side of the island where there was a marina and tour boats from Naples. It seemed that we were always climbing up to towns since we had left the Messina Strait.

Next there was Ventotene, 29 miles away. We arrived there after leaving Procida in the early morning. Ventotene was part of another chain of islands called the Pontine Islands, which were crater islands. Historically, Ventotene and Ponza, further away, were used as exiled islands for undesirables such as Julia, daughter of Augustus Caesar; Octavia, wife of Nero; and Flavia, granddaughter of Domitian (hey, those were all women). The tiny harbour called Porto-Vecchio was an old Roman galley port excavated from the volcanic tufa. The sheds behind were carved out of the rock, showing a marvel in Roman engineering. There was no room for manoeuvring so we decided to drop our anchor in the modern outer harbour. Ventotene was used as a penal colony during Mussolini's time, while across the Tyrrhenian Sea was the small island of Santo Stefano, which held a prison, now closed. We enjoyed the solitude and beauty of this tiny island. From our dinghy tied up at the dock we were able to zigzag up the steep stairs to a large piazza. The inhabitants numbered few, and the houses built of tufa blocks sat quietly above the high and ragged coastline. It took no time to walk around and a small restaurant we discovered had freshly caught fish for a tasty meal.

The next day we motored to Ponza, the last island we visited before Rome. The weather remained calm, but stormier weather was predicted for the weekend. I liked Ponza. The town was layered up the hill from our anchorage. Its picturesque beauty was obvious immediately. The rock formations around Ponza were spectacular, making the island a very popular stop for tourists. Continuing north we passed Anzio, famous for when the Allies attempted to beat the Germans on their way to Rome during WWII, finally taking the city six months later in 1944. Now it was our turn to settle near Rome, leave our boat in the nearby marina outside Ostia, and go home for the winter, to our first Christmas in Canada since 1999.

Why was the marina making our arrival so difficult? The entrance to the marina was remarkably a test of Al's sailing ability. The entrance was poorly planned. High breaking waves due to strong winds met us as we approached. Because we had a strong motor, we managed to avoid the rocks on both sides as we rode the waves into shelter.

We were in Turistico di Roma for a few weeks as *Solara* had to be prepared for storage during our time in Canada. A short train ride would take us into Rome. We made several trips to see the wonderful sights and take in the flavours of the many restaurants. In fact, one day we met friends of ours from home who were visiting Italy. We had arranged to meet them right in front of the Trevi Fountain. How fun it was to get news from Collingwood.

The marina, on the other hand, was a showplace for the women of Rome. On weekends, they would come to parade up and down the very long dock in their fine clothes and very high heels, adding to the festive atmosphere around the marina, which took away from the importance of preparing *Solara* for the winter. I couldn't get used to trivial visits made by the Italian tourists. There was no barrier to the outsiders as was usually the case in most marinas.

Nevertheless, our boat got stripped of its sails and the boom was taken off to be replaced. All the canvas would be stored and repaired, we hoped. Finally the food was gone and my packing completed. I would fly home before my husband, who would follow 10 days later. He would have the job of finishing the rest of winterizing the boat and getting it on to storage blocks while staying in the town of Ostia.

We were both ready to see our family, but not sure how we could handle the colder weather after so long. We would be back in May to pick up *Solara* and make our way west toward the Atlantic.

PART 10

Spanish Waters

CHAPTER 38

❦

The Balearic Islands

AFTER A PRECIOUS visit with our family, it was with trepidation that we arrived in Ostia, Italy. Had the boat been well looked after, the sails mended, the batteries working, the canvas in good shape?

The lift manager told Al the next morning, "We are going to put your boat in the water *oggi*."

"You mean tomorrow?" Al replied.

"Yes," said the manager.

Actually, *oggi* meant today which I soon found out when the crew arrived to put our boat on the lift. Al had left *Solara* wide open in order to air out the dampness, and expected a day free. Suddenly the boat was on a trolley and moved to the lift. I was beginning to dislike the Italians and their work habits. They would promise to come at a specific time, but arrive one or two hours later, and we'd perhaps wait a week to have something done despite being told it would be done soon.

Once in the water, the boat was pulled to a side dock as the motor wouldn't start, and the rudder, which had been broken by the work crew, disabled the steering. A mechanic came to repair the steering and replace our starting battery. All costs went back to our bill! As I was beginning to feel that we shouldn't have gone home, there were further complications. The four large boat batteries, which powered all the instruments, etc., hadn't been charged and had to be replaced at a high cost, even though Al had been in touch with the marina each month during our time away to remind the manager to charge the batteries. We found out later that replacing the batteries incorrectly caused a surge to the marine radio transceiver. Until we had better servicemen, we had no transmission for email, weather fax, and connection to other cruisers. We would have to wait until we got to Spain to have the radio fixed.

And that wasn't all. The rigging which was supposed to be completed before Al left hadn't been done. The canvas which surrounded our cockpit had been "stored." The plastic windows on the dodger (looking out toward the bow) were scratched and difficult to see through. All the canvas looked like it had been thrown in a heap, walked over, and neglected. What more had gone wrong? Well, a new zipper holding a side window didn't fit and was useless, and a repair had been made in one window with no explanation as to how it had been torn. I was ready to leave that so-called boat repair shop. The wonderful times we had had with our children were erased by such a disastrous beginning.

Nevertheless, I wouldn't leave Italy without seeing more of the country. The summer before we had been in Calabria, and the islands off the Amalfi Coast in the Tyrrhenian Sea. It was important for me to see Tuscany, and especially Venice. I had been in Venice many years earlier, but Al had never set foot in that charming and most unusual city. A car rental had been arranged while back in Canada, and we visited areas in Tuscany and Umbria, including Siena, Florence, and Assisi. There were too many tourists to my liking, but the country was beautiful in the spring as we wound around the small roads and villages. Many flowers were in bloom and the trees covered in bright green leaves. The fragrance of the flowers was overpowering.

We found a small family hotel outside Venice in Mestre, which was only a bus ride to the Grand Canal. We delightfully got lost in many of the side streets in Venice which curved here and there between the old stately buildings. It was like a second honeymoon, just like our first in Paris, wandering the streets with little care in the world and soaking in the atmosphere. How like Italy to wrap us in its romantic blanket!

Once back to our boat a week later, there were final arrangements to be made. Near the end of May, we were ready. Our first hurdle was to get out of the marina. The wind outside had caused a surge of high breaking waves at the entrance, and a huge yacht was blocking the way. We headed for the breakwater, our engine at full power after the opening was clear. *Solara* bounced over the 10-foot waves and seemed to be tossed into the sea beyond. What a way to start our new venture!

Quickly the seas calmed, and we were again sailing our boat as if we hadn't been away. I soon readjusted to boating life with new rigging, new boom, and hopefully a working engine. All came together as we headed to the north coast of Sardinia. Fortunately, it was an overnight sail with favourable winds. Just south of Porto Cervo was a small anchorage near the town of Cala Volpe, a lovely quiet bay with several boats anchored away from its open mouth, where a strong wind was coming from the east. Being early summer, the water was very cold and not welcoming for swimming.

"Oh, look," I pointed to a swimming body. "Someone doesn't mind the cold water." Sure enough, it was a German cruiser. I was never surprised at what the Germans were doing. They could be found swimming in all kinds of conditions. That night on watch, I had trouble keeping warm. It was a very cold May that year.

Porto Cervo was famous as a retreat for the wealthy. The Aga Khan built a marina and luxurious getaway many years ago, but it was too expensive for us. This one was finished, and held all manner of luxurious yachts. We had sailed the short distance from our last stop, dropped our anchor feet away from the marina, and admired the beautiful setting at no cost to ourselves.

We motored to shore with our dinghy and explored the town. Beautiful homes were surrounded by flowering bushes and fragrant blossoms, and overlooked the azure blue of the Mediterranean. I could pretend for a while that I was part of the scene amongst the expensively dressed. We stopped for a beer on one of the patio restaurants. The cost was 14 euros. Oh well, we did have a good view, and the ambience was high class.

The winds were high and the choppy waves soaked me with cold, salty water as we came back to our boat in the dinghy. Thank goodness I wasn't dressed like the rich and famous. We expected to be there for a few days waiting for calmer weather.

Our next stop was Porto Palma, on the Isola di Caprera, part of the Maddalena chain of islands between Sardinia and Corsica. What beautiful scenery! The sparkling blue waters flowing through barren rocky shores surrounded us on our travels. The winds were light, my favourite kind. The bay at Porto Palma was wide and well-protected from the northwest and northeast winds. There were two sailing schools taking up much of the area, but we could anchor out in sand at 4.5 miles. There I could wash clothes and have an indoor shower. What bliss as the diesel tanks were gone from our beautiful shower. The weather was cooperating, warm and sunny, drying out our clothes and myself. I was delighted to watch all the young people learning to tack and jibe in the bay. I remembered the wonderful time my husband and I had in the BVIs, taking a sailing course and learning those manoeuvres which were most important to our learning to sail.

Our destination was Corsica, the only French stop we would have in the Med. I was looking forward to the cuisine, especially croissants in the mornings. We made one more stop at the island of Sargi. Once anchored off Spargi at Cala d'Alga, I felt like staying forever; it was so beautiful. The round-shaped rocks scattered here and there along the shoreline looked like large pebbles, thrown long ago by a gigantic monster. There was a small sand beach a dinghy ride away which we took to explore the deserted island, now a nature park. An anchored powerboat which we passed had two nude people sunbathing on deck. Anything went around there.

Al climbed the rocks to take a picture of *Solara* from above, and I sat amongst the interesting, round-shaped granite stones eroded over many centuries by wind and waves. We loved the quiet atmosphere and cool nights, and chose to stay another day. I got out our portable video player and watched movies under the stars just like in an outdoor movie theatre, while the boat swivelled around on its anchor with the current.

Twelve miles to Corsica, specifically the historic port city of Bonifacio, the most protected in the Med. We tied up in the small marina at the base of a large and prominently high cliff. The small town ran along the shoreline and climbed up to a large citadel sitting high on the cliffs, protecting the harbour in all directions. The shops below on the harbour were filled with woven baskets and coral jewellery. We walked to the old town up very steep steps to the winding streets above, where many of the population dwelled in sturdy, well-built apartments. We had lunch there, although expensive, reminding me that French food was still the best: delicious soup, tasty sandwiches, and melt in the mouth French fries that only the French could make. I tried to retain the wonderful taste in my mouth, but unfortunately it soon got swallowed up by my mediocre boat larder.

I walked to the nearby hospital to get my shot of B12, which our family doctor had recommended during our trip home. My arms were losing feeling and he determined that I was lacking in B12 which affected the nerves. I flew back to our boat with a bottle of B12 and an order to get a shot every month. Al said he would do it for me, but I had qualms about that. So I found myself in the hands of a flamboyant, French, earring-laden male nurse, and got a shot of B12 for 2.80 euros – not bad. Each month I would have to find a hospital wherever we landed.

It was June when we left Bonifacio. We made our way to Stintino, Sardinia, which would be our last Italian stop. There was another free marina that never got finished. This time there was no water or electricity, but it was protected from the high waves outside. Stintino was a small fishing town developed only after the government moved people from a nearby island to make a prison. We found a restaurant in a nearby hotel which served tasty pastas – maybe my last pasta for a while.

The winds beyond were beginning to whip through the harbour. It was a wet ride back to the boat, but we sat in the cockpit taking a needed rest as the wind generator happily whirled around and hopefully gave us our needed electricity. The next day we would head for the Balearics, which Al estimated to be a two-day and one-night passage.

Our destination was the town of Mahon, Menorca, with a possible arrival in the dark, always making me anxious. The winds were right for a passage west, just on the beam. Somewhat rough at first, then calming down once we were away from Sardinia. We had to motor through the Fornelli

Passage, a shallow link between Sardinia and Isla Asinara. I had to watch carefully at the bow as the passage was just deep enough for our boat and not much more than 6 feet in places. The atmosphere was tense but the current was going our way, and soon we finished the mile-long trip. From there, the sailing was just right until 23:00, and then no wind. There was nothing worse than hearing our boat motor when I'd rather be enjoying the rush of wind pushing us along.

A dove landed on our boat early in the morning. It sat on the boom, rocking back and forth, trying to keep from falling off. It was still there in the afternoon but had changed its perch from the boom to the bow, seeming very content to rest there. I prayed it would stay with us until we approached the island of Menorca. That wasn't the first time we had had birds on our boat, but they either flew away or died, depending on how far we were away from land. That passage included an overnight which we hadn't done for some time. We decided on watches of two and a half hours since it was cold and very dark, no stars or moon showing. We had to motor most of the time, unfortunately. The bird must have flown away. When I checked in the morning, it was gone.

It was noon when we arrived at Cala Taulera, the large anchorage some distance from the port of Mahon. It was a long dinghy ride to the main port, but the beauty of the anchorage made up for the inconvenience. I would probably get wet riding to town, but at least the anchorage was free, and nearby was a large fortress called La Mola which took 25 years to build and, when finished, became obsolete due to out-dated artillery.

We took the day to visit the fortress with a knowledgeable guide to show us around. I was impressed by the strength of its walls made of large stone blocks. The immenseness of the structure and its impenetrable architecture should have protected the harbour. Recently it had been used by young Spaniards doing their two-year military service, and during the Civil War Menorcan Republicans had been imprisoned there and executed by Franco's forces. .

The next day, we took the long dinghy ride into town. Al got a haircut and I found a supermarket. It was all very mundane and seemingly unimportant, except that it had been too long since we had had the opportunity to indulge ourselves. A very wet dinghy ride got us back to our boat. We waited two days for good weather for our trip to Mallorca which would have to be an overnight as Al was anxious to get the necessary boat work done, especially the marine radio.

We left Mahon, Menorca, in the afternoon, motoring most of the way. After one quiet stop, it was time to get to Palma and settle into a berth at Club Rial de Palma. Not that I liked a marina, but that was where all the competent people were to fix what had been broken in Italy. Sunday was a nothing day – no stores, no museums, no life – so we arranged a trip on an open sightseeing bus to see Mallorca. We sat among the tourists gazing at the Gothic structures, beautiful buildings from long ago, the Italian-style houses with their stone facades of the 15th and 16th centuries, and the Gothic cathedral, the major architectural landmark of Palma. Its walls of limestone, according to the guide, changed colour depending on the time of day – ochre, golden, or pink. The bus drove some distance away from Palma, giving us a view of the rocky coastline, sandy beaches, and palm trees everywhere.

Our main concern was getting the radio fixed, and many calls on our cell phone to suggested names became a chore. The dodger's window had been replaced, thank goodness. Now I could see where we were going. An American expat sail-maker was very efficient, picked up our canvas one night and replaced it the next day. Our water-maker was repaired which would be necessary for the Atlantic crossing. And finally, a man came about the radio and said he would fix it in a few days. When all work was finished, we planned to take a three-week anchoring trip around Mallorca and Menorca. It would be a restful holiday once the headache of sailing a broken yacht was over.

Kenneth, a Norwegian radio man, came back. He was conscientious and trying very hard to repair the radio, but finally said he needed input from his boss. Eventually, without the radio company's help, which turned out to be more of a hindrance, it was finally discovered to be a connection near the battery that had been disconnected when new batteries had been installed.

I finally said, "When the Italian guy put in the new batteries in Rome, Al asked him if he had disconnected the radio, because the radio stopped working after that. He told us that he hadn't disconnected the radio and although it didn't work it was nothing he had done."

Oh, those Italians! I wanted to put them out of my mind and start thinking of our next move. Thank goodness our radio was back in working order.

Finally, on a Sunday in the middle of June, we left Palma and sailed to Ensanada de Rapito, an anchorage we had enjoyed on our way to Mallorca some time ago. The beautiful clear blue water beckoned me in. It was wonderful to feel the coolness of the water as I swam around the boat. When in a marina, I didn't have the chance to jump off the boat into the water, and now I really felt that we were having our due holiday. There were many recreational boats and toys all around us, but by suppertime we were almost alone. From this anchorage, it was a matter of jumping from one nice anchorage to another along the east coast of Mallorca. Most of the beaches there were filled with holidayers with their charter and paddleboats, and on the shore multitudes of bars and hotels. I was beginning to feel the heat and decided it was time for swimsuits and frequent dips in the water. Our final stop in Mallorca was Cala Magraner, just 10 miles or so from Porto Colom. It was surrounded by high cliffs and full of nesting cormorants and gulls. I welcomed this noise over screaming tourists. The water beneath us sparkled from the bright sun. This was what sailing in the Med was all about.

For the next two days, we got some boat work accomplished – cleaning, changing oil on the motor – and had radio communications with our family, with Al receiving two late Father's Day messages from our children. On top of it all, a full red moon was rising in the eastern horizon.

"I could stay here for a few more days," I said to my husband. "Everything is so beautiful." The weather was great, the anchorage was quiet, and our radio was working. But it was time to sail back to Menorca.

It was a four-hour sail from Cala Molto, on the northeast point of Mallorca, to Cala de Son Saura in Menorca. The winds were just right for the sail across but our destination on the Menorca coast was full of charterers and crowded beaches. Many boats seemed to be chartered by German men, perhaps getting away from their wives. The beach was full of young Spanish nudists enjoying the hot sun. We didn't want to stay long in that anchorage, despite the nudist beach, as the waves rolled in from the southeast winds.

In the morning, seeing no other bay for anchoring, we headed for Mahon. We spent a week there in the large anchorage and motored into the town each day. Our usual haunts were the internet café, the supermarket, and some of our favourite restaurants. It was time for my monthly B12 shot. I made an embarrassing mistake, going into a five-star hotel with a large *H* and mistaking it for the hospital; the concierge directed me to a private clinic. Al had been waiting for me at the hospital which I hadn't found. At the clinic, there was an incompetent male nurse who suggested I have the shot on my hip, although no one before him had suggested that. I gave him my arm instead, and he seemed to take forever to inject the serum. I probably should have let my husband use his expertise.

The following Sunday, the weather calmed down and it was time to head to the north part of Menorca. After getting fuel, we finally got away, passing a multitude of weekend boats enjoying the day, and sailed up the beautiful eastern coastline. This passage was one of our most memorable ones, as the winds were just right at our beam, the sun shone brightly, and the waves ran with the wind to keep us moving along at a good speed.

Our final stop was Cala de Addaya, a long narrow bay, very sheltered and pretty with a small marina full of small motorboats. A fairly new built-up area surrounding the hillside held many small homes with sparkling white stucco exterior and red roofs. We discovered that most of the homes were owned by English people. The houses were surrounded by beautiful flowering bushes and trees. I guessed that the English lived away from home during the cold, wintery months. We climbed stairs to the top of the development and saw the spectacular view of the Med well beyond the bay where our boat sat. There were also a few restaurants and a supermarket. Unfortunately, the restaurants catered to the English with specials of fish and chips or other indecent English fare.

There was only one American boat in the anchorage to celebrate Independence Day on July 4, so no firecrackers. We should have invited them over for drinks, but the Americans were nowhere to be seen. There was some excitement that evening as the winds came up from the south with a reading on our instrument panel at 29 knots. Nearby boats, turning around in a different direction due to the wind, got too close to each other. We had learned not to get close to any boat in an anchorage because the winds could change. Again, experience proved a worthwhile teacher. Nevertheless, a French boat was too close to us when the wind changed again to northerlies, and after a few chosen words the French boat reanchored. Even though we knew how to anchor, other boats didn't and often caused problems.

Our next passage was to Barcelona, where we had reservations. But we were waiting for better weather and no cold northerlies. We rented a car for the day to visit Ciutadella which was the capital of Menorca during the Middle Ages. Little remained of the walls that surrounded the city, sacked by Turkish pirates in the 16th century. There were remnants of the old quarter with a town hall and a palace. But, best of all, there were quayside cafés and restaurants which bustled with life. We could sit by the harbour and enjoy the sun and breezes from the sea.

Back to our boat and more boring work like laundry and changing the oil, which we had to do often. Al swam off our boat but found that the bay was full of small, stinging jellyfish. It didn't take him long to scramble back and shower off. Our time there was dragging and I was restless. For excitement, the Irish pub up the hill made good hamburgers and showed rugby on their large TV. I went to the book exchange in the timeshare office and read several books, but the choices were very English – love stories – and not too interesting. By then, I was ready for Barcelona and the excitement it had to offer. I would have liked some female company, some partying, and some visiting with other cruisers in that small bay, but we didn't see anyone we knew and other European cruisers seemed to have each other. That would change soon since our daughter Carolyn and our grandson were coming to visit us in Barcelona at the end of July.

CHAPTER 39

❧

Barcelona and the Costa Del Sol

IT WAS 150 miles to the downtown marina in Barcelona. That would be an overnight, but it was favourable sailing with a good weather high. Unfortunately, we had to do more motoring than sailing. On our way, we saw very little boat traffic, but then a very spectacular sight crossed our passage.

"What's that smell?" I asked Al.

We looked ahead, and there was a huge whale. It smelled like rotten fish as it opened its mouth. Its large grey body splashed violently as it soared in the air several times in front of us before disappearing into the sea. It was probably a minke or fin whale, which we had seen before in our travels, but I could never get enough of seeing whales. The rest of the night we sailed under a beautiful crescent moon which partially lit up the sky around us. How beautiful the night sky that enhanced our passages so many times.

I loved Barcelona, and had been there a few times before, but not with a boat and not tied up in Port Vell, the downtown marina. Before our family arrived, we explored the narrow windy streets, walked up Las Ramblas, the busy wide boulevard with its many shops and sidewalk hawkers, visited as many Gaudi buildings as we could, and went to the Joan Miro gallery. We learned many bus routes that would help us get around that vast, interesting city, tried many good restaurants, and went to two concerts. The one I liked best was a flamenco group performing late at night – everything was late including restaurant dinners – at the most gorgeous building called Palau de la Musica Catalana, built between 1905 and 1908 and decorated at the entrance with lavish mosaic pictures in colourful ceramic. The audience was completely Spanish, as far as I could tell, and their excitement and thrill during the performance was contagious.

I finally met two American women cruisers in the marina who were planning to cross the Atlantic that year like we were. The three of us went sightseeing to places that wouldn't have interested our husbands. It was fun to be with other women for a change. When the six of us got together, husbands included, there was much reminiscing.

"I told my husband I was getting much too old for cruising," one woman told me.

"How old are you?" She didn't look that old to me.

"I'll be 57 this year."

I wondered if I should tell her my age, which by then was over 70. "I'm older than that, but it's how you feel about the experience that is important. Just remember how much you learned, and that nothing you experienced can be taken away from you."

We now knew Barcelona enough to show it to our daughter, Carolyn, and TJ who was 4. He was so excited by our boat and got used to it quickly. We ate out every night, a treat for me as well. Al took TJ to Tibidabo Amusement Park, high above the city centre. A small cog railway took them up to the park where children had the thrill of many rides and amusements. At the same time, Carolyn and I took a train to the Dali Theatre-Museum in Figueres, about 60 miles north of Barcelona. What a crazy artist. The museum was full of his works, and Dali had called the structure a gigantic surrealist object. It took most of the day to see everything. My guidebook stated: "Dali expresses his personal world through bland forms loaded with sensuality and sexual connotations." There was no doubt that sexuality was in its glory.

Al wanted to give our daughter and grandson some sailing experience. We took a passage to Ibiza overnight; once there, they would be able to take a ferry back to Barcelona and catch their flight to Toronto. It was a lovely night, although we had to motor all the way. The stars were brilliant in the dark sky. Carolyn took one watch and very professionally avoided an oncoming ferry. The waters were very busy with freighters that took a more specific course, closer to the mainland of Spain. TJ slept right through the passage and seemed to take the movement of the boat well.

Our first stop in Ibiza was Cala Portinatx on the north shore. It had a busy beach with lots of tourists enjoying the water. It was TJ's first ocean beach and of course he had to bring all his many trucks and cars. The next day, we crossed the large bay to Cala Bassa, a pretty bay but full of beach activity as well as tour boats bringing more people. Being August, everyone in Europe was on holiday. It was another beach play for our grandson, and some swimming right off our boat, which was better than the beach. There were many fish feeding around *Solara*, and then we discovered that TJ had found some bread to throw down. He was taking to the boat just like a pro.

We had to anchor in Port San Antonio the next day so our family could catch the ferry. It was a busy port, noisy with young English holidayers who didn't sleep until the middle of the night. I was anxious to leave for quieter waters.

In the morning, I waved goodbye with my eyes glued to the ferry as it pulled away until I only saw two small figures up high on the ferry's bridge. It was a sad goodbye, but an enjoyable visit. We wouldn't see our daughter and grandson again until we had sailed across the Atlantic, and how that would go was as of yet unpredictable.

It was almost 19:00 hours. The cost of laundry and email came to 13 euros plus the cost of groceries. Ibiza was a very expensive island. Unfortunately, the diesel wasn't available that night, which meant another night in that most unfavourable place. Up early the next morning would get us underway, we thought, but there were so many boats manoeuvring around the dock and waiting for fuel to come by truck that Al determined we would never get away from there. We then set sail without refuelling for Formentera, about 20 miles south of Ibiza, and a good stepping stone for the mainland of Spain to the west. I was glad to leave the hedonistic town full of bare-topped men who drank on the streets or sat in the bars all day long. The English liked to party on their holidays.

The wind was right on our nose and, though it increased, it was faster to motor than to tack back and forth forever. In spite of the crowd of boats, we anchored in front of a long beach. Along the beach were the "mud baths." Occasionally I would see a group of mud-covered bodies walking along after their holistic romp in the mud. The baths were supposed to provide herbal remedies for all kinds of conditions. I was tempted, but instead was happy frolicking in the water by the sandy beach. Although Formentera wasn't in the tourist area, two tourist boats crowded with people pulled up on the beach for the day. So much for August in the Med!

We had one more anchorage in Formentera near the small town of La Savina. After getting our needed fuel at the port dock, we found a place to anchor just west of the town, and some shelter from expected high winds. The holding for our anchor was bad, and we only set our anchor after many tries. The number of boats in that anchorage increased until a family house type powerboat anchored very close to *Solara*. The boat was full of people with two dinghies tied to the back. As it became dark, the southwest winds came up and we settled down for the night. Before that, I looked out from our boat at the monstrosity next to us and wondered if their anchor was set. We were lying in the V-berth and ready to sleep when suddenly I felt a hard bump at the bow. Al jumped out of the berth, ran up the companionway, and headed for the bow of our boat. The powerboat had dragged when the wind increased and one of their dinghy motor propellers had hooked on to our anchor chain. The men on the powerboat looked perplexed, but one of them dived into the water to unhook the propeller. Another man on the powerboat started the motor to drive the boat away. Then the unfortunate man in the water got his hand caught between our chain and the propeller. After hearing a painful cry, I thought "Oh! He's lost his hand," but he brought up his hand from the water to show us he had all his fingers. After that incident we didn't get much sleep. I was looking forward to getting away from this busy part of the Med.

We had our last day for swimming and relaxing before moving onto the Spanish coast near Cartagena. There was a sheltered spot at Ensenada de Mazarron just behind a point of land. The bay was quiet and clean, with a sandy bottom where we could dig in our anchor. We continued to work our way south toward Gibraltar, our last stop in the Med. Unfortunately, in Garrucha harbour we were kept awake all night by fiesta celebrations nearby, as it was August 15, a national Spanish holiday. The music, fireworks, and noise kept going until five in the morning.

I was nervous about our next move which would be around Cabo de Gato, the division between Costa Blanca and Costa del Sol. The German weather forecast was giving force 6 to 8 (about 20 to 30 knots), and 6-foot seas. We hadn't had those winds since the Red Sea. Would we be able to handle our boat? I shouldn't have worried since Al started with a full sail, then a reef, and finally we used our stay sail, which was a small sail near the bow. The winds were moving up to 37 knots but we expected they would die down once we had rounded the cape. But no such luck.

We had trouble anchoring into 25-knot winds, but experience proved that it could be done. A few boats tried to anchor but just gave up and returned to port. Once stable, I felt I could relax and enjoy the quiet night once the winds died down. I always enjoyed the time when the work of sailing was finished for the day. It was year five, and I felt more like a sailor than I had ever felt before.

After Cabo de Gato, we were heading west toward Gibraltar. The next stop was Almerimar where we could take on diesel and stay a few days in their harbour. Almerimar was somewhat secure, but our dock had no gate from local traffic, and theft was an issue. The bathrooms had no toilet paper, and the showers had intermittent taps that had to be pressed continually – nothing like the marina in Turkey. On the plus side, we had a reasonably priced internet, a self-service laundry, a small shop that bought our used navigational books, and a good supermarket. There were various restaurants, and a small condo development for tourists, but many were unsold and empty.

It was there that we rented a car to visit a few places in Andalucia. We locked the boat tightly, and left nothing that looked tempting on board; I had stopped worrying about thieves. In Granada, we visited the famous Alhambra gardens, and the old Islamic quarter called Albayzin. There was a wonderful view of the city from the top of the Alcazaba, the fortress of Alhambra. After walking up and down the streets of Granada for hours in the intense August heat, I was overcome with heat exhaustion. Unfortunately, I felt too sick for dinner, and hoped that I could enjoy the rest of our inland trip.

The next day we drove through miles and miles of olive groves, and dry and dusty landscape. The olive trees cut a symmetrical pattern across the bright blue sky as the road followed an up and down landscape. The town we wanted to visit was Cordoba, situated on the Rio Guadalquivir. Its main attraction was the Mezquita, formerly a mosque and now a cathedral. The beauty of the mosque, with its arches open to the light and air, had been filled by many small chapels that darkened the interior. After visiting the mosque, Al continued exploring Cordoba while I returned to our hotel to recuperate from the day before. The next day, we drove back to our boat with a short visit to Malaga on the way. Spain had always been a favourite country for us. We had been there in the '60s when it was almost primitive with no development on the eastern shore. What a change after 50 years! Every seashore property seemed to be overloaded with developments, filled mostly with tourists from the UK.

We left early in the morning in the dark to go to Estepona, where we could get our propane tanks illegally filled with butane for our propane stove. It had been impossible to buy propane in Europe, but butane worked, although not as well.

CHAPTER 40

❦

Gibraltar

ESTEPONA WASN'T FAR from Gibraltar but it seemed to take forever to reach the base of the high rocky peninsula. Our sails were down, and our motor did most of the work as we made our way toward the Queensway marina where we were reluctantly given a berth, for there were very few available. It was a very old marina with considerable history, having been there for centuries. There was a new addition to the marina being made further out toward the sea.

My first impression of Gibraltar was from the water where I looked up at the towering "Rock" looming over the small city, one of the last remaining outposts of the old British Empire. Although English in tradition and language, I heard mostly Spanish or English mixed with Spanish spoken by the Gibraltarians. There was a community of Sephardic Jews that were very conservative in their long robes and uncut locks of hair. There were also Muslims in traditional dress, and a large mosque was situated high above Europa Point. Basically, Gibraltar had a very eclectic population of Brits, Jews, Genoese, North Africans, Portuguese, Spanish, Maltese, and Indians.

The Spanish border was on the other side of the local air strip. If one wanted to visit Spain, it was just a matter of walking across. Franco closed the border from 1969 to 1985, virtually stopping all land travel. The Gibraltarians had always been united in their wish to be independent and apart from their neighbour Spain. The border closure had been difficult for those living in Gibraltar, whose only access to other countries was by water.

Of course, Gibraltar – called "Gib" locally – was famous for its Barbary apes, which occupied the "Rock" above, living freely, swinging from place to place, and bothering the tourists who were unaware of the apes' antics until some of their possessions went missing. There was a cable car that took people to the top of the "Rock" to view the magnificent vista beyond. On a clear day, it was possible to see the mountains of Morocco across the strait.

Our purpose in Gibraltar was to repair my stove – again! – and fit ourselves out for the next passage to the Canaries. We wandered around the town each day, up and down the small streets and numerous hidden passages. The people were very social, but close-knit in their own ethnic groups. At least that was what it felt like to me. I received polite replies to my questions and helpful hints when I went looking for a place to get my monthly B12 shot.

"You could ask the druggist up the street to get an injection," said a woman from the clinic where I had gone first.

"I don't give injections now," I was told at the pharmacist's. "But there is a woman down the street who is a nurse and now owns a store for infants. I'm sure she would help you." And that is where I went.

The street names were sweetly English. Some of them were descriptive, such as Library Street, where the old Garrison Library was located. There were also many military names, such as Horse Barrack Lane, stemming back to the time when Gibraltar was a fortress. Many shops were British-based like Marks & Spencer, one of my favourites, no longer available in Canada. An English flavour permeated the city: police with their bobby hats and bright red phone booths and post boxes.

We were there long enough to take a bus trip to Seville for a couple of days. The bus trip gave me a wonderful view of the southern coast of Spain. At the time, the winds were high and the coastal waves very strong. The bus was filled with young surfers and their boards, who disembarked at a popular spot called Tarifa Point on the coast. Along the highway, I saw fields of wind generators wildly spinning.

I loved Seville. We stayed in the old quarter, walked everywhere, and enjoyed the Spanish cuisine. But too soon it was back to the boat, waiting for the right weather to take us through the strait.

It was an easterly wind we were looking for on our weather reports coming in online or from the US Navy buoy weather report at the internet cafe. Al decided that September 15 would give us a relatively strong east wind to take us against any adverse tidal stream and eastbound current. Before that, Gibraltar celebrated their anniversary: Gibraltar Day. Everyone who knew about the celebration was wearing red. When I walked down Main Street, I felt out of place in my grubby, well-worn garments, but was game to take in the celebrations. There were bands in the large square near the airport and a flypast by the British Royal Air Force coming from England – it probably didn't take them long to reach Gibraltar from there. I felt it was a wonderful way to remember Gibraltar before leaving on our next passage.

CHAPTER 41

❧

The Canary Islands

THERE WAS SO much to think about for the next passage. We had to contend with the eastbound current and tidal stream rushing into the Med. As well, the shipping lanes back and forth were extremely busy. We needed the winds from the east to help us buck any adverse, unexpected problem and to get us on our way past Spain and Portugal to our north. With that in mind, we left at noon and motored our way through the shoreline current to the middle of the Gibraltar Strait. As we passed Tarifa Point, the winds were very high, and the seas very turbulent, but after that the move west became easier. Some of our cruising friends planned to sail to Morocco just across the strait, but that didn't appeal to my husband, who wanted to make land again in a week's time.

Unfortunately, the easterly winds didn't behave and we soon encountered south and southwest winds. Nature never understood our needs. Once we changed direction to the south, we were bashing through high waves on a close reach for the next 24 hours. With our reduced sail, *Solara* drove through the cauldron of waves solidly while Al and I just got tossed around in the worst weather we had experienced for some time. Cooking wasn't an option, and we survived on cold sandwiches. Finally, on the third day, the seas calmed down and we had three lovely days of sailing, enjoying the brilliant full moon each night. We were in the Atlantic Ocean for the first time!

By our sixth day, we were 50 miles from Este rock, the northern point of Lanzarote in the Canaries. After deciding to spend one night at anchor, we found a good anchorage beside La Grasiosa, a small island just west of Lanzarote. We were finally in the Canaries. I didn't realize how tired I was and bedded down as soon as we knew the anchor was holding.

The next day, it seemed like a slog to make our way down the east coast of Lanzarote to our final destination of Puerto Calero. One moment we would be at full sail, and then a few moments later at reduced sail and hand-steering. There were, we had heard, acceleration zones on the southern coasts of the Canaries and especially strong currents between the different islands. While jibing the boat, a school of high jumping dolphins passed us. That was the first time on that passage that we had seen dolphins. I had missed them terribly. They had been such fun to watch in the Pacific. Unfortunately, I didn't get a good look at them as jibing took all my concentration in the cockpit.

Lanzarote had been designated a biosphere reserve due to its black landscape punctuated by oases of vegetation and crops. The black soil and contrasting colours of the vegetation was a beautiful landscape to behold. For many centuries, Lanzarote was a base for expeditions to other islands, and prey to marauding slavers, but in 1730 the eruption of the main mountain range, lasting six years, changed the texture and appearance of the island to what we saw on our arrival. Lava fields and thick black ash and pebbles surrounded more than 100 craters. The fires from the volcanoes still burned and bubbled. It was like a visit to the moon, if it had been turned black.

We entered the pristine port of Calero for a month's stay. I was flying home for a visit while Al worked on the varnishing of the boat. I loved leaving when varnishing had to be done. It was a lovely but expensive marina, and very secure. Al would rent a car for necessary errands to Arrecife, the largest town nearby. We needed supplies for the boat and my fridge was acting up. Once disconnected from shore power, it stopped working and started to defrost. I had no working fridge on arriving in Puerto Calero.

While I was home, Al diligently varnished our teak with six coats of varnish sanding in between each coat. I was aware of the tedious work involved, having helped him with the job in Malaysia. When I returned we did a bit of sightseeing into the interior to view the black lava covered island. It was said that meat could be roasted over fumaroles where the temperature 20 feet down was 1400 degrees Fahrenheit. Volcanic rock was used for buildings and walls, creating a bleak vista. We tried the special wine produced in the black sandy soil. It tasted like smoke.

In our marina, we saw few tourists. There were a number of good restaurants and a small supermarket. We met a few cruisers but most of the cruisers we knew had anchored in Gracioso or Arrecife. We visited a nearby marine museum in Puerto Calero which gave me a better understanding of whales and dolphins. It would have been much better if I had known more when encountering those beautiful creatures during our travels. While staying in Calero, the participants of the Mini Transat race arrived from La Rochelle, France. There were about 75 young people who had single-handed their small boats to Puerto Calero, taking about eight days with little sleep. After a rest of two weeks, they would be racing to Brazil. It was exciting to see them. How insignificant I felt when two of us had taken a week to reach the Canaries in our large yacht.

Our plan was to sail south to Gran Canaria by the end of the week. It was now near the end of October. How time flies! Our new roller furling drum had to be installed, and a new fan was put in the fridge which seemed to solve the problem. Before leaving, we had a nice dinner with Martha and Richard on *Transit* who were crossing the Atlantic at the same time as us.

In the morning, we left Puerto Calero for an overnight to Gran Canaria. We reduced the sail when rounding the south coasts of Lanzarote and Fuerteventura, but then had to motor the rest of the way to our final destination. The glow from Las Palmas on the north coast of Gran Canaria was seen for miles, and at night could be mistaken for a sunset. We would stay in the south end of Gran Canaria until it was time to cross the Atlantic. On arrival in Puerto de Mogan, we were given a berth on the concrete wharf with an unsteady metal ladder to climb from our boat. The tide was at least 3 feet so we had to adjust our lines every time the tide changed. Al added chains to our lines at the stern since they would have worn through the concrete in a couple of days. The bathrooms were public, not far from the wharf. I didn't like that arrangement.

It was an interesting spot to watch the tourists who strolled constantly past our boat. At the end of the wharf, the ferries, which moved from island to island, dropped off or picked up mainly German tourists. There were many restaurants that fronted the marina, mostly serving German meals and with German staff. Where were the Spaniards? Since I had lived in Germany many years ago, I enjoyed the variety of dishes, mostly comprising meat and potatoes, a change from the Spanish fare.

One day, I had a dramatic accident on the high metal ladder. My foot slipped off, and I was about to plunge into the dirty harbour water. I was hanging by one arm. Luckily, one of the tourists on the dock saw me and quickly saved me from falling. My husband was working at the bow and hadn't seen me fall. Thank goodness for the help. The bruises on my body lasted for some time, but I believe the accident helped us get a better location on a proper dock.

We were on the far side of the marina, but the walk to town was very interesting. I could see all the various European boats preparing to cross the Atlantic. Some of the yachts were huge – over 100 feet long – with a multitude of crew busily preparing the boat. I saw only one American yacht, but the Mini Transat boats were there plus a number of curious ocean rowboats. Apparently, some robust men and women were preparing to row across the Atlantic to the Caribbean. I also saw many colourful fishing boats, and a busy yard where boats on stands were getting new bottom paint or other repairs.

Two large supermarkets were available for supplies, the internet was cheap, and a small DVD rental store kept us entertained most evenings. The island of Gran Canaria was a good place to rest and relax before the arduous Atlantic crossing. On Fridays, there was an outdoor market strung along the pier above us selling cheap goods and hand-crafted items from Africa. Tourists came in droves either from the ferry or buses, usually from the busy hotels further away from our marina. There was never a dull moment.

I wasn't looking forward to the long journey, but I was anxious to get back to North America. Our daughter Vicky arrived to help us on our crossing. She was familiar with *Solara* and a very accomplished sailor. We rented a car and drove to Palma, the large city at the north end of the island, to do some last-minute shopping: a lifejacket for vicky, boat parts, and provisions. Then we had to wait for the best weather to leave. Al spent most of his time looking for the next weather window. It appeared to be very calm the following week. A French captain who was also looking at weather on the internet told Al he felt it was time to go, and after gathering his crew set sail the next day. But after a few days, the French captain came back to the marina. Their boat had drifted for days without any wind. There was nothing like being becalmed with nothing you could do to get the boat moving.

Finally, it was time to go. My nerves always took over when a long passage was ahead. Having our daughter there eased the tension, but I knew we had at least a few weeks sailing before we reached the Caribbean. To add to the tension, the forecast stated that two hurricanes would be in the Atlantic. The large hurricane, Katrina, had devastated New Orleans and was followed by other storms. The usual alphabet of names from A to Z was now into the Greek alphabet. To avoid the storms, we would have to sail south to Cape Verde near the African coast. Our time on the Atlantic wouldn't be short.

PART 11

Coming Home

CHAPTER 42

❧

Crossing the Atlantic

FOR THE FIRST few days, the winds were light. We could relax and enjoy our usual routine: reading, cocktail hour, meals, and of course sailing the boat. There was one problem: our old main sail had become thin and worn from the salt air and water. All of a sudden, a rip appeared from the edge toward the middle of the sail. Fortunately, we had special equipment: needles, sail tape, extra material, and coarse waxed thread. With the motor going, Al got to work and diligently sewed up the tear. I had helped him repair a tear on our sail once before and knew that the work was tedious and that it probably wouldn't last. It really needed a professional repair, but we soldiered on.

The winds came up at last which meant higher waves and a less comfortable sail. During the night, when Vicky was on duty, a large wave, usually the seventh, knocked the boat so hard both Al and I woke suddenly, but soon were back to sleep again. Then calm – usually before a storm – greeted us the next morning. The ocean was always beautiful and eerie on days like that. Quiet ripples and large rollers could be seen for miles. Dolphins played around the boat, jumping in front of the bow and seeming to race us, always winning. At night, we experienced the magical phosphorescence which I had seen in the Pacific. The water seemed to glow greenish blue in patterns. It was though the living organisms in the water were dancing to their own tune. I could never get tired of the display.

Finally, we had better winds from the north/northwest which gave us a speedier sail to the Cape Verde islands, which soon appeared in the horizon. There, we could buy diesel and some provisions before starting on our way again. These volcanic islands, 400 miles off the African coast, were once controlled by Portugal. Now, they were independent but very poor, with little vegetation. We made it to the Mindelo harbour in the dark. Mindelo was a small village in one of the northern islands of the large archipelago. We were greeted by a man who rowed out to our boat in his dinghy just after we had anchored.

"I'm one of the local boat guys," he said. "My name is Arlindo, and I can take you to shore in the morning."

Arlindo was a thin, raggedly dressed man with a winning smile. Though his rowboat appeared unpredictable, Al was happy to leave our deflated dinghy on the deck and agreed to the arrangement. But it was another man, Orlando, who came the next morning. I chose to stay on the boat and rest while Al and Vicky went to shore to check into this new country and get our passports stamped.

Vicky described Mindelo on her return as a pretty town with architecture similar to what she had seen in the Caribbean. There were Regency and Georgian buildings, bright colours and wrought iron railings. I was sorry not to have taken the trip. Since the local market wasn't open that day, there was no chance to buy local produce, but some provisions were available in a nearby shop. It was time to get diesel fuel, but that was a problem, with a long wait for other boats buying and a small fuel dock. It was once again dark when we could at last leave the Cape Verde islands and get on our way. With the small archipelago behind us, we were greeted by spotted dolphins having fun around *Solara*. Dolphins were always fun to watch and I imagined that they were playing with us as they practised jumping and deep dives in the ocean. Usually the pods of dolphins were herding schools of fish for their next meal.

Again, we had the calm before the storm. With no wind, *Solara* bucked and lurched with the large rollers coming in from two directions. We took down the sails and floated with the current, heading westerly towards our goal. It was a good time for a careful swim, a bath, and a few chores. But I saw ominous dark clouds in the horizon, and I knew that our quiet time would soon be over. Up came the sails again, and unfortunately too much sail. Vicky and I looked at each other and wondered why Al would put up the large main without a reef, plus the large genoa at the bow. Consequently, another rip appeared in the main sail from the leech up to the third reef. It was too large to tackle with needle and thread, so Al had to reef the sail to that point. That meant sailing with a small main and the forward stay sail. When the winds became consistent from the northeast, we made more time even with such a reduced sail. Of course with the wind came the rain, and less time to relax. We were told by Herb, our ham radio weather guru from Ontario, that the stormy weather was the remnants from Hurricane Epsilon, which later hit the Canaries. Consequently, our transit went without incident for the next two weeks.

Herb, with his ham radio weather reports, had been helping sailors in the Caribbean and Atlantic for many years. He had saved many lives in that time by veering sailors away from storms. The only stipulation he had made to me, as the weather crew, was to be available on the ham radio at the same time every day. If I were to miss a day, he wouldn't be there the following day. Of course, I was most consistent in radioing him every day at 16:00 with our direction, speed, and position. He was very helpful to our navigation as we neared the Caribbean.

We decided to land in Antigua instead of our first choice, Guadeloupe, which had recently experienced some serious robberies. Al had finally heard from Jolly Harbour in Antigua, letting us know they had a berth available, which also contributed to this decision. Nearing the Caribbean, there was another rough day with high winds and stormy seas. I could see dark shadows in the mist. Could that be land? Our boat became a busy place as we started to prepare for landfall. Old or unwanted food was thrown overboard and the little fresh food we had left we ate, no matter which meal. The weather wasn't sunny and warm, unfortunately. The rain met us as we approached Antigua. It was a matter of outrunning the next storm coming from afar.

The island of Antigua was a beautiful sight, with green vegetation and rolling hills and various sailboats in the water having fun for the day.

Our GPS electronic chart on board clearly showed the entrance to Jolly Harbour. Once in, we could leave the rough waves outside and slowly motor to our berth. We were finally in the Caribbean and our crossing of the Atlantic was over after more than three weeks. More importantly, Al and I had arrived back in the Caribbean where we had started. We had successfully circumnavigated the world in a sailboat! There was no celebration at that moment as our flight to Toronto the next day would get us home just in time for Christmas.

After a couple of months at home, we were back in Antigua and our final journey to the Bahamas would begin. It would also be the final goodbye to our wonderful and beautiful *Solara*.

CHAPTER 43

❦

Through the Caribbean

ON OUR RETURN to Antigua, there was *Solara* sitting nicely in her spot in Jolly Harbour. I had missed her. She had kept us safe and warm in all weather. It was because of her that we were able to make the difficult voyages we had taken, and it would be hard to let her go.

We were surrounded by other Atlantic-crossing yachts and had the chance to exchange our varied experiences, as well as help the boats just starting out their passages west from Europe.

There was much to do before our son, John, and his family arrived from Vancouver to visit us and experience the boat for the first time. We had to buy a new sail, which meant ordering it through customs and picking it up at English Harbour, the larger marina on the other side of the island. New varnish and metal polishing was arranged with Peter, a dock "boy." We were pressed for time and didn't try to do this hard work ourselves. We also had to buy a new dinghy since our old one wouldn't stay afloat. Of course, all these preparations were made with the idea we had to sell the boat in good shape. Our wonderful Yanmar motor which had been so reliable for five years was checked out and a few parts replaced. All these jobs kept us busy until our family arrived.

John, Aki, Jaki, and Jake arrived a week after our arrival. It was a long trip and a shock for them, since they had never been to the Caribbean. We kept the two grandchildren, Jaki and Jake, 12 and 8, with us while the parents stayed at a hotel near St. John, a town nearby. I hadn't seen our grandchildren for some time and the week went fast as we tried to have as much quality time with them as we could.

The beach near the marina was the main attraction, but the waves coming in were fierce and high. Nevertheless, a couple of days later Al decided to take the group outside for a sail and to do some snorkelling on a reef. The winds had died down a little, but were good for sailing, so we thought. Once out of the quiet harbour with the sails let out, I noticed a problem with our family. First one and then another were looking pale and sick. I hadn't noticed the rough water since I was used to it, but it seemed that all our Vancouver family weren't taking the sail very well. So it was back into the harbour with a quick stop at an anchorage for a swim.

The rest of the week went quickly. There was so much to see and do, and then it was time for them to fly back to Vancouver. It was a great visit for reconnecting and for them to see our boat. After they left, we had lots to do to get on our way again.

It was an overnight sail with a clear night and a full moon. I couldn't have asked for our first night back in the Caribbean to be any better. The winds were good for sailing all the way. During our first year of sailing, we had island hopped in short bursts, but now an overnight sail seemed just right. Five years of passage-making made all the difference to our confidence and sailing ability. The high winds and waves didn't scare me so much, and now I knew *Solara* as a friend who wouldn't let me down. It felt strange going in the opposite direction and passing the islands we had visited before: Nevis and St. Kitts.

The bridge opened into the large anchorage at St. Martin at 09:30. We had just arrived and were able to anchor in Simpson Bay Lagoon. Our dear friends Ed and Julie on *Free Radical* had been there for a year after crossing the Atlantic. Julie had set up a sail repair business to keep them in money until their next move.

What a great reunion: dinners together and future plans discussed. We made many toasts to finishing our circumnavigation, or as sailors say "tying the knot." Near *Free Radical*'s anchorage was a remnant of a steel contraption. We were told it was what was left of a rowboat that had crossed the Atlantic the year before. *So that is what happens to those rowboats*. The crew of two had a falling out after arriving and just left the derelict in the harbour.

It was sad to say goodbye to our friends, but we had many miles to go. We left with a new dinghy bought in St. Maarten – the one we had ordered in Antigua had been lost by FedEx – another battery, and new port and starboard sheets (lines). Before leaving, my husband bought me a ring with a beautiful Caribbean topaz gem, sparkling with the blue and green colours of the waters around us. It was a wonderful memento of the Caribbean. I talked Al into sailing to the US Spanish Virgin Islands instead of St. Croix, as I thought it would be better for reaching Puerto Rico.

Our first stop was St. John's harbour to check in to the US and get permission to cruise. There were too many boats all cramped together, very few amenities, and the town surrounding the harbour reeked of commercialization. After telling us that to check out we had to enter that disgusting harbour again, I was really put out. In order to avoid coming back again, we stayed the night and decided not to cruise that island as we were told that there were very few mooring balls available.

After settling down for the night on a mooring ball, our neighbour told us we'd have to move if the wind shifted or we'd collide with them. We moved to a new spot just west of the jetty for ferries and anchored. That was a mistake! Again, we started to settle down, but about 21:00 there was a loud blast from a ferry. Our boat had turned around and was in the path of the ferry. I had noticed a noisy rumbling before, but Al was sleeping and I didn't want to wake him. We had to move again. Now we were extremely tired and anxious to get out of that mess. After anchoring once more, much too close to other boats that were moored, a man in his dinghy came up and offered to find us a better place. He led us to a daytime dive ball, just outside the congested harbour, that we could use just for the night. From there, in the morning, we could check out as planned and leave for Culebra. I never wanted to come to St. John's again; it was such a terrible experience.

"I'm sorry I talked you into coming here," I said contritely. "We should have followed your original plan."

On our approach to Culebra, in the Spanish Virgin Islands, we had good winds and 5- to 6-foot seas. The lovely sheltered bay, Ensenada Honda, was near the town of Dewey. It was so pretty and quiet we stayed for several days. There, we enjoyed restaurants, did some needed shopping, and, best of all, found other cruisers. We saw *Pamaceta*, who had been in the Canaries, anchored there. Al had met Neil and his wife who fed him often while I was home. They were also sailing through the Bahamas at the same time as us. We also met a Canadian boat owned by a Polish couple from Toronto who wanted all kinds of information about our experiences around the world. Especially fun was an evening with another Canadian couple on their catamaran, including many guests who had been active in the World Cruising Club in Toronto, where I had learned about cruising life. Now I could provision a boat with few mistakes, keep cockroaches off, communicate on our marine radio, and crew the boat as well as any sailor. Of course, we were bombarded with questions, but no one planned to attempt the difficult journey away from the comforts of the Caribbean.

Our next destination was Puerto Del Rey off the east coast of Puerto Rico. I remembered our last visit there six years earlier on Mother's Day. Would I get the same impression of the island? We approached from the east where there were many reefs and rocks. That problem would have been handled easily, but black rainclouds were coming our way, and we found it difficult to see below the boat for the dangerous reefs which could only be distinguished by their shade and colour. Although the navigation through the reefs took longer than usual, we finally found the entrance to a very large harbour enclosed by a high concrete breakwater, which kept most of the large waves from coming in. I had never seen such a large marina. We were given a berth in the far outer spine, close to the entrance and any swells that might come in. I figured we were classified as second-class cruisers at the best. The marina was so large we had to take a small golf cart to get around and outside to the road.

Al rented a car while we were there since we wanted to visit Fajardo, a town which he thought would be good for provisioning. But some boat parts weren't available in Fajardo, which meant a further trip to San Juan, the capital. I loved old San Juan which was meant for walking with its tiny maze of blue cobblestone streets, colonial architecture, and historic fortresses and plazas. We spent the night in Cape Verde, close to the city but right on the ocean. We also visited the famous Bacardi factory and tasting outlet. We left with a few bottles for the boat and a T-shirt for me with "Bacardi" in glowing letters.

It was into April and time to head toward the Bahamas. I needed to be back in Canada before May as my brother-in-law was ill and my sister needed my help. We planned a four-day passage across the top of Puerto Rico and the Dominican Republic in order to reach the Turks and Caicos, a few hundred miles north. I tried to reach Herb to help us with the weather before leaving. He wasn't in radio contact so we relied on traditional forecasting.

For four days, we had a mixture of strong winds, rough seas, and rainsqualls, especially just north of the Mona Passage, noted for its difficult conditions. The waters were very busy with cargo ships, cruise ships, and small vessels, which meant constant attention in the cockpit when on watch. I had to get used to the two-hour watches again and trying to get enough sleep. How glad I was when that passage was over and the islands in the Turks and Caicos could be seen in the distance.

CHAPTER 44

❧

Turks and Caicos and the Bahamas

OUR FIRST STOP in the Turks and Caicos, just south of the Bahamas, was Sandy Cay, a quiet, sheltered, and tiny island where we were protected from the northeast swells. It was a great spot to rest. The water surrounding our boat was clear with beautiful colours from the reefs and rocks below. A large barracuda swam around our boat, probably looking for scraps of food. Since we hadn't entered legally, we had to reach a place where Al could pay the entrance fee and have all our papers documented. Consequently, we sailed a short way to South Caicos, but a dense downpour kept us from entering the harbour which was surrounded by reefs and rocks where good visibility was needed. When the weather finally cleared, we entered Seaview Marina, which wasn't a real marina but a person who could arrange fuel and help us check in.

Arriving in the Turks and Caicos was like arriving in a primitive country, such as we had experienced in the Pacific. Al was directed to the government dock, which had to be approached carefully due to very shallow water. With help, we tied up *Solara* on the very dilapidated concrete "dock" that was so high that I had to stay on the boat for the duration of our stay. An official finally arrived in the afternoon and charged us US$30 to enter the waters. We checked out, as our plan was to leave the next day. While there, I noticed a disabled boat just down from our spot on the dock.

"What happened to your boat?" Al asked a young man who seemed to be taking care of the boat.

"My friend was sailing alone from Miami when she was rammed by a freighter."

Apparently, she was a young girl who was allowed to take her father's boat across the treacherous Gulf Stream running south to north. The South Caicos "dock" would have been the last place she would get help. There was a great deal of damage to her sailboat. When we left, I hoped her father would come to her rescue.

For a couple of days, we sailed *Solara* around the north of Turks and Caicos in stormy weather, beating against the wind and waves. We were back in the Atlantic, and not protected from the northeast winds. During the night, a loud crack was heard from the deck. It was only in daylight that Al found that the shackle holding the main sheet to the traveller had broken in two. That meant we wouldn't be able to control the boom when we had to change direction. My enterprising husband quickly jury-rigged the boom so it stayed secure until we could anchor the boat in the Bahamas.

Although we should have formally entered the Bahamas on arriving, it was Easter and no one was about. Instead, we anchored in Start Bay, some distance from the harbour of Rum Cay, in beautiful clear water at 35 feet, some distance from shore. On our way to Rum Cay the next day, we happened to talk on the VHF radio to a skipper on a Canadian boat called *Bohemian II*, who then quickly took off and left us behind. I didn't think we were that slow, but at 17:00 we saw the same boat again. It seemed to be drifting and floundering and definitely not moving. As we approached, we heard them calling us on the VHF radio. Their transmission had given out and they couldn't motor. There was no wind and they were drifting toward a reef. Their situation wasn't good at all. They needed a tow, and we were glad to help since no one was around in that remote area of the outer islands of the Bahamas. Around 21:00, we left them at the entrance to Acklins Island and Atwood Harbour, where they were able to briefly use their motor to find an anchorage. They radioed that they were OK before we motored away to Rum Cay.

Well, Rum Cay was definitely a remote section of the Bahamas. At noon, after arriving, we used guided markers to find our way to the Sumner Point Marina. I wouldn't call it a marina as such, but there was a cold front expected and we needed protection from the winds. For four days, we stayed in that strange but friendly place. The slips were wooden boards on large poles with a long, slatted dock. At low tide, I couldn't step off our boat, and the surrounding sand was filled with no-see-ums: biting insects that mysteriously found their way into our boat. There was a restaurant bar nearby called Green Flash, maybe after some TV character, but I never saw anyone eat there. The bar was good, though I ordered a hamburger there which didn't sit well in my stomach. .

There were a few boats there as well, probably getting out of the weather. The anchored boats in the bay nearby were having a tough time with the surge and high winds. For those of us staying in the marina, the cost was very high with little amenities. Laundry was $15 to do yourself, $0.50 a gallon for water, $1.50 a foot for berthing each night, and $3.85 per gallon of fuel. The total cost for the three days we stayed in that "beautiful spot" totalled $444. Because we were so far from the civilization of touristy Bahamas, Rum Cay depended on a delivery boat each week to bring supplies. There had been no supply boat for two weeks, and therefore no groceries to be found.

I met a lost soul here. It was a German woman who had arrived across the Atlantic with her husband at the beginning of their cruising, full of hope and enthusiasm. They were an older couple, who had just retired like us. One morning, they had anchored outside the marina and were preparing to leave. When he was pulling up the anchor, he fell on the deck and broke his back. After some time, he was able to wake his wife but not able to move. When we talked to her, she had been in the marina for a number of days while her husband had been airlifted to Nassau. The helicopter wouldn't take him to Nassau and the hospital for treatment without a credit card payment of $10,000. The poor woman was spending all her time trying to find help from other German cruisers, as the couple had used most of their resources for this once in a lifetime trip. Unfortunately, I never did find out what happened to her.

We had used much of our fuel to tow the Canadian boat a few days before, so we had to buy the expensive fuel in the marina. We were heading for Conception Island, only 25 miles away. It was a beautiful day as we motor-sailed northwest toward this tiny island, tucked between Rum Cay and Cat Island further north. Conception Island had a beautiful anchorage with clean and clear water fully protected from the east. And no bugs!

Although I wanted to stay another day, at least, Al said we had to leave early in the morning in order to reach Smith Bay and finally check into this remarkable archipelago of the Bahamas. It was dark at 04:00 when we left, but by morning light we could see to navigate in the gusty winds that had come up suddenly, until we rounded the south end of Cat Island. Trying to pull our boat into the dock was a problem with the wind, but two sturdy men came to help with the lines. I offered them a beer. One said he didn't drink, but the other took the two beers with a gleeful grin.

After paying the Bahamian officials US$300, we were free to move on and go ashore. On our way again, to Little San Salvador Island with full sail and a beautiful passage all the way with 15 to 20 knots of wind. Oh! How I loved the times when I could sit back and let the sails do their work. West Bay on the island was now owned by Holland America cruise lines. We were allowed to anchor there as long as we didn't interfere with their guests. When the cruise boats were anchored outside, the guests would be motored into the bay on zodiacs where they could rump and play all day on the beach. As it was, we were alone that day along with two other sailboats, one being another Cabo Rico, whose owner motored over to say hello. He was alone as his wife didn't want to cruise.

"I guess you're glad I came with you," I remarked to Al as he left. "That would be you wishing for company."

"Since we're up," said Al very early the next morning, "we might as well leave for Eleuthera."

With reluctance on my part, we set out in the dark. It was easy leaving the bay and not far to Rock Harbour in the southeast corner of that long island. Now that we were in the Bahamas, it was important to watch the depth as we moved. At times, the depth gauge showed that we were scraping the bottom, and we probably did.

Rock Harbour in Eleuthera resembled an "out island" harbour, similar to the small towns on the North Channel of Georgian Bay. After a long, hot walk into town, I found only cans of food, some produce, but no bread. The tide had gone out when we got back to our dinghy. After loading up the tender with groceries and me, Al had to wade out, pushing the dinghy until it was deep enough to put down the motor. So much for provision shopping! I was ready to get back to my own grocery store, where I could load up my car and drive home.

Our next stop before Marsh Harbour in the Abaco Islands was Hatchet Bay. After sailing for five hours, I saw a narrow channel ahead of us that would take us into the bay. On both sides of the channel the waves were churning and flying high in the air. There was little room between the many rocks on both sides.

"Are we really going through this mess?" I shouted. "What if our boat hits the sides?" That would be the end of *Solara*. I saw my husband, with grim determination, ready to gun the motor and head for the turmoil where all I could see were rocks and foam. Our sails were down, and we had no recourse but to go through. Right behind us, a ferry was waiting. If the weather hadn't been so unsettled, I'd rather have gone somewhere else instead of braving the unknown.

Just after we had anchored and settled down for a relaxing drink, I saw an ominous black cloud coming our way. Sharp lightning bolts appeared amongst the clouds and thunder was heard soon after. We were going to get a fierce storm sitting there in the bay not knowing if our anchor would hold us in one place. Al donned his raingear and turned on the engine to prepare for the worst. I went down the companionway to find my raincoat and help him if I could. I hated storms and the possibility of our mast being hit by lightning even though it was grounded. Suddenly, the winds came and our boat started circling around its anchor and placing us in much shallower water, from 23 feet to 5 feet. Fortunately, the anchor held, but for how long? A neighbour on the next boat offered to help us tie up to a mooring ball which was nearby. We took up the offer, and I sighed with relief knowing that the mooring ball would keep us secure.

We decided to stay there for a few days as the ocean outside that cosy bay was turbulent due to a storm from the north. I was thankful that my husband agreed to skip fighting the waves and wind. While there, I got domestic and made focaccia bread from the recipe given to me back in Panama. It turned out just fine, thank goodness. I also started sorting out my belongings in anticipation of leaving *Solara*. What to throw out?

What to keep? What to give away? My old cruising clothes – shorts, sandals, hat – were worn and faded, not worth keeping. Canned fruit and packaged meals I wouldn't need at home. Al would probably give away charts and maps, not useful without a boat. Our 70 flags, one from every country we had visited, would go in a bag and be taken home. Pots and dishes, except for a few, would stay with the boat. The list was long.

The storm continued for the next few days. Winds from the north brought colder temperatures. We were experiencing what Americans from the Eastern Seaboard called northeasterlies, which could last some time. But, my husband said, the waves were getting smaller; they were only 14 feet now. I didn't need 14-foot waves out there, but Al was getting restless again.

We were on our way to Royal Island but watching our time in order to enter the anchorage at slack tide when we wouldn't have to fight the tidal waves. It was mid-afternoon when we entered the bay. There were lots of boats there but we found plenty of room. We were all waiting for better weather before heading north.

Royal Island was once owned by a wealthy American who built a beautiful plantation there in the 1930s. We got out our dinghy and motored to a derelict concrete wharf partially underwater. The island once had large stone buildings, now left in pieces but showing intricate tile work. It was sad to see very little left. But Jamaican workers were cutting down bushes that had overgrown the roads throughout the island, and I was told there were plans for a hotel complex which would include the sheltered beach, protected by a large reef from the Atlantic Ocean.

After Royal Island, it was just an overnight trip to the Abaco Islands, my last trip on *Solara*. I didn't feel sad at the time, but knew it would come to me once I left the Bahamas. My husband would sail the boat to Chesapeake Bay with his brother and a friend, Ron Kaye. *Solara* would then be up for sale. I needed to help my sister in London and couldn't go with them. In the meantime, we had a few more days at Harbour View Marina in Marsh Harbour. I arranged my passage home and helped clean up the boat. It was now May and if *Solara* wasn't sold within a year, we would have to leave American waters and sail away again. That wasn't such a bad idea!

Between the months of May and October, I had a chance to visit Chesapeake Bay in Maryland. We stayed once on the boat in a small marina without air conditioning in 100-degree Fahrenheit temperatures. It wasn't pleasant except for many visits to Washington, an hour away. Our sales agent had polished the boat so it was ready for sale. It looked very beautiful. I would miss it. It had served us well and given me a view of the world as nothing else could do. I hoped that whoever took her over would love her and take care of her as well as we did. Goodbye *Solara*.

Conclusion

I STARTED AS a reluctant sailor and finished our trip with confidence and surety in the cruising world. It wasn't easy at first. *Solara* was a complicated yacht with complicated equipment. Ocean sailing, with its tremendous rollers and waves, differed greatly from the Great Lakes.

My relationship with my husband took many turns, from hesitation to trust. He was more relaxed in difficult situations while I was still learning. Storms scared me, but storms brought him excitement. We learned to work as a team by necessity. Having a crew at first was a comfort but became a burden. We continued alone with little difficulty after that.

Solara became my home. Its cosy cabin, solid structure, and seaworthiness couldn't be duplicated. On the occasions when I was back in Canada, the connection to our boat was strong and I felt the need to get back to her. Back home meant the reality of retirement and aging. I didn't need that in my life at the time. I could see why my husband wanted to sail. Cruising made us feel young and carefree.

Other cruisers were important. We couldn't have survived without their help and companionship. Cruisers supported and encouraged each other, especially in the Gulf of Aden. No matter where we were, there were other cruisers planning their passages and preparing the way. I couldn't say enough about this special entity of hearty souls sailing around the world.

Sharing the ocean with whales, dolphins, and other large creatures was exciting, and seeing the multitude of stars, moon phases, and constellations as we drove through the waves during night passages was unforgettable. Those experiences couldn't be duplicated in my mind. The people we met in so many countries were friendly and happy to share their food and include us in their festivities. Being white and non-Muslim was not an issue in Muslim countries, where people treated us as welcomed visitors. We never felt threatened unless we had what they wanted, but that was rare.

I was saddened by the dying of the coral wherever we went, and the plastic neglectfully tossed here and there, especially in poorer countries. Fish farms were the norm in the Mediterranean, and fishing was poor in many of the countries we had visited.

The world changed while we travelled. Communication became more sophisticated, bringing the world closer together. The twin towers in New York came down in 2001, the Iraqi War took place in 2004 while we sailed in the Middle East, and the SARS virus was a threat. In the small cocoon of our boat, these threats didn't affect us physically, and we blissfully sailed on unaware that on our return to the Western World our life would be changed forever. Unfortunately, we couldn't see the world like that again. I knew I was too old for the job, but my husband loved the casual life with little clothes on his back and bare feet on deck.

I would go back to the Pacific, if I could. The beauty of the Pacific islands was breathtaking and their people openly welcoming. I also loved New Zealand, overwhelmed by Australia close by as we were with America, which made me feel closer to that small country. Its beauty was incomparable, and varied immensely between north and south islands. We were lucky to have had six months travelling there.

I was glad I went. My reluctance lessened as time went on. My husband and I were close friends and soul mates who relied on each other while sailing *Solara*. The experience couldn't be duplicated and I feel we were better for it. We would always have these wonderful memories in our pockets.

Acknowledgments

THANKS TO KELLY Dignan, my editor, who kept me on the straight and narrow, being most helpful with my choice of words. To Sheila Wilson and Gina Schurmann who spent many hours reading my work and correcting grammatical errors. And my Memoir Group, Mary Brereton, Vanda Kilpen, Mary Skelton and Sheila Whitton who politely listened to my chapters, offered encouragement, and kept me from giving up. To my fellow cruisers: no circumnavigation could be done without them, especially Ed and Julie on *Free Radical,* fellow Canadians, who came to our rescue many times, Dave and Di on Amoenitas who knew so much about boats and others too numerous to name and who played a part in our venture.

Thanks to the Collingwood writers group which meets biweekly. They listened critically and helped keep me focused. And to Ken Haigh who has kept this group together. And especially important are my children who didn't say, ' don't go' and made sure to keep in touch with us. To my daughters, Carolyn and Vicky who set me up with a web site and especially Vicky, a competent sailor, who crossed two oceans with us and helped in so many ways.

Lastly, to my husband who encouraged me all the way and whose memories of our trip were especially helpful when I needed them. We still speak to each other.

56224041R00215

Made in the USA
Middletown, DE
21 July 2019